Vol 1 only
1200/-

Issues in Ethics and Applied Ethics Series

Volume - I

Ethics in Business, Applied and Environment

Issues in Ethics and Applied Ethics Series- Vol. I

Vol. 1 Ethics in Business, Applied and Environment
Vol. 2 Ethics in Feminism

Forthcoming volumes

Vol. 3 Socio-political Ethics
Vol. 4 Bio-Medical Ethics
Vol. 5 Metaethics, (Part I)
Normative Ethics & Virtue Ethics (Part II)
Vol. 6 Ethics in Economics and Educational Thought
Vol. 7 Companion to Bio-Ethics
Vol. 8 Ethics in Charvaka/Lokayat, Morality and Secularism (Part I)
Philosophy and Ethics of the Jainas (Part II)
Philosophy and Ethics of Buddhism (Part III)

About the Editors

Shiva Nath Prasad, after completing his studies, served Bihar Government in several capacities. After retirement he became a full timer in the pursuit of philosophy. He edited a bilingual journal Abhrant later edited two journals separately one in English namely Journal of Bihar Philosophical Research and Darshan Digdarshan in Hindi. He authored one book *Charvak/Lokayata Analytical and Hermeneutics Study,* a very unique book, which is a "singular attempt to reconstruct this almost a vanished system of India." He also published an Anthology namely Phenomenology: Methodological Introduction with Prof. V.T. Sebastian of Punjab University. His Multi Volume Anthology on Ethics and Applied Ethics (22 volumes) are being published by Concept Publishing Company Pvt. Ltd. and some are being processed. Recently, he has publish. This book "Reflections of Charvaka. Lokayata, the Gita & Rajehish," a book of immense value.

Avinash Kumar Srivastava, born, December 1955 (Nalanda District Bihar) completed Master's degree(philosophy) from Patna University, Ph.D. on the topic "A Comparative Study of the Samadhi (yoga) in Early Buddhism and *Bhagavad Gita*" from Magadha University, Bodh Gaya. Presently he is Associate Professor & Head, P.G Deptt. of Philosophy, Magada University, P.G. Centre Darshnik Traimasik (Patna), Nalanda College Biharsharif. He is a prolific writer. He has authored two books *(Living Buddhism and Bhartiya Darshan Ki Mool Samasyayen)* and edited three Anthologies. His about forty research papers have been published in India and abroad. He is a widely known scholar of India. He was *Joint Secretary and Secretary* of *Akhil Bhartiya Darshan Parishad and General Secretary, Bihar Darshan Parishad, Vice President of Indian Society for Buddhist Studies.* And member of editorial board of *'Bauddha Prajna Sindhu, and Ocean of Buddhist Wisdom (Delhi), Journal of Bihar Philosophical Research, Darshan Digdarshan (Patna).*

Issues in Ethics and Applied Ethics Series

Volume-I

Ethics in Business, Applied and Environment

Edited by

Shiva Nath Prasad
Avinash Kumar Srivastava

CONCEPT PUBLISHING COMPANY PVT. LTD.
NEW DELHI-110059

ISBN-13: 978-81-8069-976-4 (Series)
ISBN-13: 978-81-8069-977-1 (Volume-I)

First Published 2015

Published and Printed by

Concept Publishing Company Pvt. Ltd.
A/15-16, Commercial Block, Mohan Garden
New Delhi-110059 (India)
T : 25351460, 25351794, *F* : 091-11-25357109
E: publishing@conceptpub.com, W: www.conceptpub.com
Editorial Office: H-13, Bali Nagar, New Delhi-110 015, India.

Cataloging in Publication Data—*Courtesy:* D.K. Agencies (P) Ltd. <docinfo@dkagencies.com>

Ethics in business, applied and environment / edited by Shiva Nath Prasad, Avinash Kumar Srivastava.
pages cm. — (Issues in ethics and applied ethics series ; volume-I)
Includes bibliographical references and index.
ISBN 9788180699764 (Series)
ISBN 9788180699771 (Volume-1)

1. Business ethics. 2. Applied ethics. 3. Environmental ethics. I. Prasad, Shiva Nath, editor. II. Śrīvāstava, Avināśa, 1955-, editor. III. Series: Issues in ethics and applied ethics series ; volume-I.

DDC 174.4 23

Foreword

Contemporary philosophical temper has been occasionally circumscribed by some major practical concerns which emanate from human condition.

The historical perspective makes it almost true by definition that morality is essentially related to action or conduct. In contrast with predominantly conceptual analysis, present day thinkers have shown greater interest in "praxieal" and pragmatic significance of problems and issues we confront within our lived experience. Philosophical interpretations and examinations have been tied to some specific needs and purposes. Moral discourse does not any more comprise abstract questions and hypothetical answers concerning meanings and definitions of concepts like "good", "bad", "right", "wrong", *et al.*, Areas located within applied ethics were treated as sub-altern discourses within the meta-discourse of grand narrative of philosophical ethics. However, it is notable that there are problems which are commensurate with social and political debates. Hence, practical ethics assimilated and deliberated upon large number of issues like suicide, abortion, euthanasia democracy, justice environmental and biogenetic issues, etc.

What is urgently needed, as some thinkers believe, is the return to the Greek spirit from purely intellectual and rational approach.

The essential feature of Aristotelian thinking is employment of practical wisdom (phronesis) which has been highlighted by moral philosophers like G.E.M. Anscombe, Bernard Williams, John Rawls and many post-modernists. The advocates of applied ethics, following Aristotle, justify the acceptance of goods life as the ultimate ideal within the bounds of deontology and consequentialism.

The present volume, edited by Shiv Nath Prasad, is an interesting and valuable collection of several Chapters written with proper understanding of the subject. The areas of study include culture, environmental ethics, feminist study, religious understanding, ecosophy, business ethics and various professional and scientific/technological areas where moral issues emerge with significant relevance. It is indeed a praiseworthy attempt on the part of Prasad to collect so many Chapters which is a painful, though commendable, project. It will be of great help to scholars working in the area of applied ethics.

S.A. Shaida

Retd. Prof. I.I.T., Kanpur

Preface

The present multi volume series "Ethics and Applied Ethics" is an ambitious enterprise and is intended to bring man to the right rails of morality as the basic end of life, society, as also to wed morality to all departments of knowledge, framed, created, and developed by man. Since all developments are for man, and man always aspires to be at the centre, so to devoid man of morality, would be nothing more than devouring the same man, who, being at the helm of everything, developed all arts, science, crafts, knowledge, by his own hands through rational deliberation. Is this not great malady and a tragedy, indeed!

The present world is ridden with multitudinous crisis, i.e., crisis in the plural and the main anxiety of man in the present scenario of moral destitution, is to end the crisis that has created an impasse or halt in several ways and man now is feeling suffocation of the worst kind. His heart-felt desired need is, naturally, to make all out efforts to resolve the crisis forthwith. But can it be possible? This is a question, which once tackled and solved, the other thing would be normalized naturally and bring a scope for peaceful sailing of life.

In this context, it would be essential to know the meaning and the content of the very word "crisis", which is eating into the vitals of every man, whether the common man on the street, or those who are enriched enough to avail all luxury. Fortunately, the word crisis is a good word and it is not incorrigible too. The word crisis has been defined as a "process of transformation", so to mean, crisis is not close-ended, but on the contrary, it is open-ended. When crisis is not close ended, it would signify that crisis as a process can be reversed in order to amend, if the very process is wrong, thus by reversing the process, one can reach at the right point, rather than remain in the state of flux or helplessness. But who can reverse this process; it is only man who can help himself. Man's omissions and errors can be amended, set right or rectified by man himself.

In this context it is essential to make a distinction between *crisis* and *natural disaster* or *natural calamity*, like earthquake, tsunami, flood, etc. Natural disaster is caused by nature's fury or any supernatural causes, as it commonly understood. But contrary to it, most of the crises are man's own making and what man has done, can be amended by man alone, it is within man's capacity to either control the crisis or remove it altogether, for all time. But the tragedy is that man has become confined by the cobweb which man himself has created, out of his venom, out of his own wilfulness, out of his devilish desire of discrimination, divisiveness, angularities and everything that is evil in him lying dormant, every moment, goading man to behave in wrongful ways. The question then is, can man succeed in destroying the fetter of multitudinous crises like social, political, economic, psychological, and technical and a spate of others. The answer is a positive assertion of "YES", but how?

Earlier, it was believed that God created everything, to top it all, He created man as the crown of His creation and in His image, but having created man, He also made a provision for sin, owing to marl s disobedience, in not eating the forbidden fruit. Thus God also created sin and disobedience too, He himself created His own limitations and constraints. Man was created by God, but man out of his own mental capacities and imaginations, created the image/ photograph/ idol of God and God was fettered in His own creations, he became captive to his own made prisons of limitations. Man also created many things, many arts, artifacts, art crafts, sciences, technologies, society, wealth and thousand of things, thousand types of knowledge, but to the result that he became captive to his own creations and now that he wants to set free from his own cobwebs and cocoons. Man can free himself, provided he wills firmly, resolves firmly. All this involves a process, to develop faith, trust, reliance in himself, to change himself to bring a total regeneration by removing what are evil aspects in him, his needs, his limitations, his envy, jealousy, instincts and impulses, anguish and angularities, his wants, his hankerings which are really captivating him and not giving a way for moral upliftment, to make him see every thing as divine, to take all as equal, brotherly, friendly and humanly. This is really a lack of moral sense, that is causing moral crisis, which is the mother of most of the crises, if not all. So by inculcating moral sense, man can rise to the level of perfection, often attributed to the Divinity. With the advancement of knowledge, there has been enlargement in the domain of ethics and ethics with its lots of theories have enriched its stock. The volumes to come would take up separate department of knowledge/sciences and try to examine how the crisis caused and crept therein, can be rectified by the touch of magic wand of moral ideals, which have now come to lowest ebb, or placed in a state of stupor and now, by ridding which, man can create a new humanity on earth, a spiritual moral globalization, rather than bring about a consumerist culture of material globalization, or global competitiveness, callousness, cold war, terrorism, fundamentalism or global barriers to humanity, dividing man from man. If our efforts succeed even a little bit with the ethical discussion presented in these volumes, we will feel prized beyond all bounds and rewarded amply.

Shiva Nath Prasad
Avinash Kumar Srivastava

Acknowledgements

We wish to record our deep sense of gratitude to all the authors of this first volume, under the Series "Issues in Ethics and Applied Ethics ", out of our multi volume series, for contributing their very scholarly essays. In fact, we have been involved in this work for a longer period and confess that we received numerous enquiries from many of our contributors regarding the fate of their Papers because of inordinate delay in publication. We are extremely sorry and beg their pardon for the delay. We feel remorsement for those contributors who are no more in this world, rather we find ourselves guilty for it.

We express our thankfulness to all the contributors for their perpetual support, confidence and patience shown by them.

We are grateful to all those who have directly or indirectly helped us in our hard and strenuous academic endeavour.

We are thankful to our family members who have cheerfully endured the trial of our work and shared the stress of editing such an anthology.

We express our thankfulness to Shri A. K. Mittal, Proprietor, Concept Publishing Company Pvt. Ltd., New Delhi, for taking personal interest in the publication of this volume and the series.

Bhavatu Sabba Mangalam

Shiva Nath Prasad

Avinash Kumar Srivastava

Contents

Section–I

BUSINESS ETHICS

Section–II

APPLIED ETHICS

Section–III

ENVIRONMENT ETHICS

List of Contributor's

Archana Srivastavam, Associate Professor, Department of Economics, Jwala Devi Girls P. G. College Kanpur

Avinash Kumar Srivastava, Professor&Head, P. G. Dept. of Philosophy, Magadh University P.G. Campus, Nalanda College Biharsharif NALANDA

Begum Bilkis Banu, Professor of philosophy, University of Guahati Assam

D.C. Srivastava, Associate Professor & Head, Department of Philosophy, Christ Church College Kanpur

Debashis Guha, Professor of Philosophy, Allahabad University Allahabad

Kakoli Basak, Associate professor, Dept. of Philosophy, Jamshedpur Women's Jamshedpur, Jharkhand

M.P. Chaurasia, Professor, P. G. Dept. Of Philosophy, J P University Chapara

Mritunjay Kumar, Associate Professor, P.G. Dept. of Philosophy, Tilka Manjhi Bhagalpur University, Bhagalpur BIHAR

Nirbhai Singh, Rtd. Professor of philosophy, Punjab University Patiala PUNJAB

Late Dr.Nityanand Mishra, Rtd. Professor of Philosophy, Puoa House, Bank Colony, Tilka Manjhi Bhagalpur, BIHAR 802001

Protima Ganguli, Rtd. Professor of Philosophy, Prantic Parivar, Block C/604-605, 121/B. R.B. G.T. Road, P. O. Bhadrakali, Dist. Hugli, Pin. Cod-712239

Ramesh Chandra Sinha, Rtd. Professor of philosophy, Patna University Patna, BIHAR

Sanjay Kumar Shukla, Associate Professor of philosophy, Ewing Christ College Allahabad

Sarita Kumari, Head Dept. of philosophy, S.S.Y.S.N. Mahila College Daltongunj, N.P.University, Medaninagar, JHARKHAND

S.A. Shaida, Professor of philosophy, I.I.T. Kanapur

Dr. Shiva Bhanu Singh, Christian Ewing college, Allahabad (U.P.)

Shiva Nath Prasad , Road No.21 Sri krishan Puri, Patna BIHAR

Sucheta Shukla , Associate Professor, Dept. of Philosophy, Dayanand Girls P. G. College Kanpur

Introduction

Coming to the second half of the twentieth century, it appears, that some thing have started going drastically wrong with the course of human events. The wide spread faith, optimism and confidence in science, politics, education and progress in all walks of life started dwindling down, if not shaken from the very root. The socio-political and ethical scenario changed negatively. The precariousness about life, fear for decline of the civilization, political corruption, dishonesty in all spheres created vague uneasiness in life. These have resulted in changed mood, attitude and outlook of the modern man. The velocity of social change accelerated the growth of industrialization. It gave birth to the modern mechanical civilization, wherein the society became interdependent and impersonal. The rise of physical science and revolution in atomic research and technology gave birth to such a society, which is mechanically efficient but appears to be self-destroying. The twentieth century witnessed two world wars and a cold war, as well as, revolution and terrorism that undermined our traditional morality. The demoralizing effect of these on the one hand, dulled the edge of sympathy and confused the moral codes; on the other hand, these taught us to hate, to kill and to applaud the destruction of life, property and natural resources; so long it is not our own. The cumulative effect of these, gave rise to a new socio-political philosophy that challenged the traditional beliefs and *modus operandi* of our way of living. It gave momentum to a new social order in place of the old one. It also attacked the global civilization by a rival civilization with immense resources like rapid growth of mass media of communication which affected our morals and manners adversely. Television, computer, mobile phone and other made inroad in our houses. These have not only influenced the taste, habits, attitude and our mode of thinking, but also served the interest of powerful groups. Once, school, temple and homes were considered as the institutions of socio-moral grooming and reinforcing moral standard and social patterns. Now motion pictures, televisions, internet, radios, newspapers, etc., are performing these functions. Moreover, the people of stake, for money minting, run these business. Their interest lies in publishing the news of catastrophe, rape, riot, etc., because these increase the T.R.P. of any channel and sale of a newspaper. Their interest also consists in escapism, mediocre and perverted type of things, as a large group of the population or the average people liked these.

The modern education system has neglected the field of moral values and aims of human life. Most of the youths complete their education (academic degrees or courses) without devoting their time and attention to matters of morality, ethics and human values, as these are not the part of their syllabi or educational programmes. It has taken away from the heart and mind of the modern man, the meaning of value of life and sense of dignity. These have resulted in moral chaos, unbridled crime, breaking of family system and failure of marriage institution. In the age of globalization, we have brought the world physically closer, but it has lost the bond of unity and man failed to produce understanding, sympathy and unity of cultural aims and shared conviction that is necessary to give meaning and aim in life.

In the west with the industrial revolution and rising business class, there started resentment against antiquated laws, ethical codes, social values and governmental interference, as they demanded *laissez faire* freedom in business money-making and earning. This led to a new individualism, because for them business is business. One must be free to express one's own interest. Today, it has become a global phenomenon. The professionals (doctors, engineers, artisan, advocates, farmers, teachers, businesspersons, etc.) have set their own standard. They demand their own right along with freedom from moral and religious ends. These have also some hazards or dangers as well as some benefits. The reason is simple. The cleavage that separates morality from business or politics, arts from science and education from religion has created a serious defect in our society.

Today we are living in a world where it is not important to pass a moral judgement or make decision, but to seek right or wrong ways to do a thing. There are right or wrong ways for a physician, builder, industrialists, businesspersons, or a driver, in treating the patient, building the bridge, running the industries, company, business or driving an automobile, etc., respectively so far. Now morality lies in living under the existing conditions in a best possible way. For that, we may revise the old moral code of conduct to meet with the need of the modern life, because it is not merely a matter of convention, inheritance, impulse or emotion. It is our duty to apply the moral codes to the facts of life. Our experience and intelligence in that field will be of much help in doing so. For that, we must critically evaluate moral codes and ethical systems of our pristine civilization and of the present in the particular individual context. Thus, the application of values of life and ethical principles, which is ingrained in the human mind as the sense of duty and conscience, shame and remorse, praise and blame or in contentment or dissatisfaction of an individual, may help improve the socio-moral situation. In this background, traditional ethics got entry into the age of applied ethics, as there was an urge to tackle the practical individual and existential, socio-moral and professional problems of the modern world.

Applied ethics is relatively a new development in the field of ethics. Instead of discussing abstract ethical theories, it is a way of doing ethics wherein, it tackles practical ethical issues encountered regularly by environmentalist, doctors, nurses, journalists, businessmen, attorneys, etc. Hence, it cannot be said to be a totally a new departure from the traditional ethics. It emerged as consciously pursued and recognised area of ethical enquiry in the middle of 1960 and took a shape of a surge very shortly. It is another fact, that even earlier there had been substantial and influencing works within the frameworks of applied ethics, such as, '*Professional and Business Ethics*' by Taeusch, Carl F. in 1926, '*Business Ethics; Studies in fair Competition*' by Sharp, Frank

Chapman and Fox in 1937, "*Business and Ethics*' by A. William in 1948, '*The Ethics of Redistribution*' by Jouvenel Bertrand, published by Cambridge University Press London in1952, '*Public Medical Care; Principals and Problems*' by Goldmann, Franz, from Columbia University Press New York in 1945, '*The Second Sex*' by Simone de Beauvoir in 1949 '*The Ethical Basis of Medical Practice*' by Willard L. Sperry in1950, the works of Environmental philosophers like Henry David Thoreau, Albert Schweitzer and others. In addition to that '*Land Ethics* of Aldo Leopold in 1949, '*Historical Roots of Our Ecological Crisis*' by Lynn White Jr. in 1967, '*The Tragedy of the Commons*' by Garrett Hardin in1968, Discrepancies between Environmental attitude behaviour: examples from Europe and China' by Yi-Fu Tuan in1968, and many others. However, though these earlier works were very important but could not form part of a concentrated programme to investigate the applied ethics as a field of philosophical concern. The Feminist and Environmental ethical movement of the West as well as Peter Singer can be said to have played an important role in popularising it. His primary work 'All Animals are Equal' in 1974 and his book *Practical Ethics* generated enormous awareness in this field. But applied philosophy in academic sense of the term made its formal debut in the field of environmental ethics in 1971 at a small conference at the University of Georgia. It published a collection of papers entitled '*Philosophy and Environmental Crisis*'. Thereafter a number of works were published in different journals and anthologies. And thus Applied Ethics became popular in the field of ethics and philosophy

Emergence of *Applied Ethics* was a direct response of a widespread belief that there is an impending disastrous crisis in the world, whether it is of cold war threat of nuclear holocaust, or human unrest due to corruption in all affairs of life, crash in Sensex or clash between management and employer or an environmental crisis. Meanwhile, college course in applied philosophy began to be offered in different centres of academic power and prestige. It percolated in different universities and colleges and became a part of Graduate and post-graduate syllabus. And thus applied philosophy and applied ethics took a form of independent study.

It might have been clear from the discussions of the first volume of this series, that ethics is the normative science of human behaviour in ordinary business of life, comprising the objective tools and principles that evaluate the human conduct on the basis of the parameters of morality. The Meta Ethics deals with the analytical evaluation of the language and structure of moral statements and its abstract theories. On the contrary, Applied Ethics is a discipline of philosophy that attempts to apply the ethical theories to a real life situation. It is a distinctive category, that deals with difficult moral questions and controversial moral issues that people actually face in their actual everyday life. It attempts to use philosophical methods to identify morally correct course of action in various fields. It also examines philosophically, a particular issue of private and public life, consisting of specific and controversial moral issues such as euthanasia, right of non-human entities or future generations, abortion, etc., Any ethical issue in order to be applied one requires to fulfil two criteria, i.e., (a) it must be controversial one and different people must speak for and against it; and (b)The issue must be controversial one and normative principles like personal or social benefit, benevolence, honesty, lawfulness, autonomy, justice, right, etc., must have been used in it. Thus, it is the reason that here we talk of the issue of fair distribution, fair compensation for the harm afflicted to human and non-human, or acknowledge personal right to life, privacy, free expression, duty, information, etc.

The present volume is the first or introductory volume of our ambitious multivolume series on a broad subject "*Issues in Ethics and Applied Ethics*". Hence, it becomes imperative for us to present a blue print before the readers what are we going to discuss in this volume and the series. It is reflected by the title itself that we are concerned with the study of ethics and applied ethics. It entails that here we have to confront with the questions like what is applied ethics, how is it related to normative ethics and how is it different from meta-ethics and traditional ethics as well as its different branches that may enter into the broad head of Applied Ethics. Roughly speaking the relation of ethics and applied ethics is that of theory and practice. In other words, what theory is to practice is ethics to the applied ethics. It, in fact, involves the practical application of normative ethics in any contextual problematic situation. A few scholars are of the opinion that traditional ethics is concerned with three questions; (a) *is it legal* ? (b) *Is it fair (balanced)* ? (c) *How will it make me feel about myself* ? So far as the question of the relation between traditional ethics and applied ethics is concerned, some critiques are of the opinion that "there is no connection between legally right and morally wrong. Ethics has not changed people have". This discussion further leads us to the question regarding the difference between ethics and situational ethics. Some scholars, while explaining this relation, say that in philosophy it has its chief concept, the concept of "good" and its relational concept is "right". "Situational ethics usually refers to the belief. Its basic fact is that ethics is every day affair". It cannot be avoided at any cost. Since the world in which we live in is grappled with multiple problems, which have structured different branches of applied ethics and this is our subject of prime concern. It is evident from the above discussion that the domain of Applied Ethics is too vast. It includes in it, various fields of practical life. Hence, it is difficult to discuss all the issues in one volume. The elaborate discussion of each part will continue in forthcoming several volumes. The present volume comprises three sections, Business Ethics, Applied Ethics, Environmental Ethics, Taken together the number of all the chapters falling in different sections of this volume comes to twenty four.

Business Ethics

Business Ethics is a classification within applied ethics or professional ethics. It evaluates ethical principles and moral problems in a business environment. It is, basically, a part of Philosophy of Business, the branch of philosophy that deals with the philosophical, political and ethical underpinning of business and economics. Business Ethics operates on the premise, that ethics of a private business is possible. Though, it is a new phenomenon in the field of applied philosophy, yet it has made a forceful entry during 1960 and very soon it attracted the attention of moral philosophers. As an academic discipline, Business Ethics emerged during 1970s, since before it, no academic journal for Business Ethics was published or Conferences held. Over time, specialized peer-reviewed journals appeared and more researches were conducted in this field. Coming to 1980, it occupied a very important place, such that a systematic study was needed for the students of management, bankers and business persons for their future prospect, in both the fields, service in corporate sector and in business proper. By the middle of 1980s, about 500 courses in business ethics sprang up all over the world, with about 40,000 students. About twenty text books and ten case books were published in this field. In 1982, Manuel G. Velasquez and Richard D. George authored their books *Business Ethics*: Concept and Cases. After 1987 European Business schools adopted Business Ethics in their Courses. They also started European Business Ethics network. These compelled the business firms to pay attention to the ethical concern in their business activities .They started highlighting their ethical stature. Business ethics gained popularity through corporate scandals in early 2000s, as all the firms tried to distance themselves from the business scandals of the day. By the end of the cold war, it caught the attention of media, business firms and academics. By 2009, about 16 business journals devoted to various issues of business ethics came into existence, among them, The Journal of Business Ethics, *Business Ethics Quarterly* and *International Journal of Business Governance* and *Ethics* are important.. Before discussing its origin, nature and scope, it seems proper to define the term itself. But even before doing so, it is desirable to understand two terms *Business* and *Ethics*. Since we have already discussed the term *ethics* earlier while explaining applied ethics it is not proper to repeat it here.

The term Business has different shades and meanings. It has been used in very many contexts with slight variations in its meaning. Primarily, it implies man's occupation and employment or the labour by which he obtains his maintenance. Now it conveys the idea of attention to a man's affair, his investment of capital or stock by the management of which, in bank, shops or in a factory, he obtains his income. Now business is used to indicate legitimate employment of man's power, his right to act in certain affairs that is normally supposed to be meddling or interference. Broadly speaking, business is a systematic attention to these affairs and duties by which the necessaries and comforts of life are obtained and by which social organizations are supported. In this sense, it becomes co-extensive and practically coincident with the field of economic enquiry, i.e., production, distribution and exchange of wealth. Economics is generally considered as the theory of business. The exposition of principles that determine and regulate making and sharing of wealth, constitute the scientific treatment of the business. Economic principles set forth the fundamental ideas and laws that underlie the business phenomenon and procedure, and protect its basic norm, *premium non noncere, i.e.*, not to harm any one. Since business has been recognized as a subject for scientific treatment, it has taken a practical form by its introduction into public education and university curriculum. A number of schools of business management have sprung up across the globe. The universities have introduced the study of business management as a separate subject in the vocational course. Now business is regarded as offering career, similar to professional and scientific pursuit. Its scientific base has been established; methods are formulated and supposed to be capable of highest efficiency that may cause progress and prosperity. These add dignity and importance to it, as it tends to advance civilization and comfort. Hence, it is expected to apply moral codes on all aspects of the business conduct and right in human purpose, as well as standard and value in life. It deals with general conditions involved in the rightness or goodness of the conduct. Thus, we can say that ethics is the normative science of human conduct in ordinary business of life. It is primarily concerned with the rightness, goodness or wrongness of the conduct, which is decided with reference to some standards external to it. It also sets a goal in human life, mundane or supra mundane, towards which life has to elevate. It is relevant to the conduct of individuals as well as entire organization in order to maintain its purity, prosperity without injuring anyone's ethical and legal interest

Since business involves intricate and complex human actions and motive, it enters into the arena or purview of ethics and business activities become the subject of moral judgements. The positive sciences, like economics or business management, cannot neglect the fact that moral considerations often affect in business life. This relation becomes close and apparent in business application, wherein problem of "distribution of wealth" and "fair wage", demand justice in greater prominence. An objection can be raised here, that business itself is not related to normative science. It may be considered as positive science, like physical nature, which also conditions the business activity. We can think of a businessman, who pursues wealth along the line of least resistance, and is not polluted by ethical course, or any other motive than aversion to labour and desire for enjoyment. Hence, this action is divorced of even those moral factors that admittedly influence human conduct in business life. But this would be a pure fiction and abstraction, divorced of even the tinge of real business life. But, as a matter of fact, no such man exists.

Someone may be of the opinion, that business and morality are conflicting subjects. Business has nothing to do with ethics and ethics has nothing to do with business. Both have different domains. But the consideration of the both will reveal that such sharp division is untenable. No one can remain indifferent, whether one is a capitalist, an economist or a businessman on the issue of immoral practices adopted in the trade for acquiring profit or to protective policies that lead to corruption. If one interferes into it, one enters into the realm of ethics. Solving such problems regularly gave birth to Business Ethics. Regular encountering, these problems makes us think in terms of morality related to business affairs, such as, for the highest welfare, equal distribution of wealth, or slight check on the wealth production for highest good, etc. Although problems related to money, media or banking practices may not present any ethical inconsistency, but labour problems are increasing day by day. It cannot be treated adequately without due consideration of ethical factor. Honesty may not be the best policy for an individual from the stand point of acquisition of wealth. But for the society as a whole, honesty is an economic, as well as moral virtue. It may be possible that a person or a community may gain immediate material wealth by some immoral act. It may also be the case, that the act of moral gain may result in immediate material loss to a society. But in the long run, this conflict will not subsist. At the same time, from the society's stand point, what *economically injurious is likely to be ethically wrong*, while that which is *ethically good is likely to be economically advantageous*. This suggests that, it is quite important for the moralists to give due weight to economic forces, in the same way, economists must recognize the ethical aspect of the social problem. Today business world is suffering the greater neglect of the normative science, *i.e.*, ethics. This has given birth to the need of Business Ethics.

When we cast a glance on the antiquity of the human history relating to business activities and the role of normative principles in it, we find that primarily the need of ethics to regulate the business activities was not considered essential. The business activities were simple in nature and were conducted at a very small scale. The isolated homesteads and cross road villages were largely economically self sufficient. Barter system was prevalent in the name of marketing or trade. Hunting, fishing, raising cattle and cultivation were main source of income and supporting the livelihood. Industrial pursuits were carried on under indigenous domestic and handicraft system. Here the industrialists had the ready access to the raw material. Workers performed their work either in their homes or a nearby shop with their simple tools, which they carried everyday to their workplace. The relationships among the workers and with their owner were personal and intimate. They sold the product of their labour to someone they knew. There came a radical change in the business conditions with the rise of industrial revolution and growth of factory system. The work place was changed. Complicated and expensive heavy machines of factory owners replaced the simple tools of the workers. The number of workers in industry increased tremendously. The mill owners hired skilled and unskilled labourers from different parts of the country and even from foreign lands. Due to *laissez faire* policy, free movement of labour, capital and raw material facilitated the industrialists to set up their industry even in remote places. Now the relationship among the labourers, among themselves and with their employers turned more and more impersonal and of the master and the subject respectively. They produced the articles for their profit and even the distant buyers purchase it.

With the rapid development of banking system and credit facilities, the establishment of limited liability in the joint stock corporations, the separation of ownership and management and concentration of advanced technologies changed the scenario of the business environment. It multiplied the socio-economic and political problems. With it, cropped up some most serious moral problems relating to industry, banking and marketing or in corporate field. An increasing number of persons started raising the question regarding the adequate measures to deal with the problems of the intricate industrial mechanism. The ethics and philosophy of oxcart days became obsolete, as this was inadequate to deal with the problems of automobile, atomic power and aeroplane age. Since our ethical standard and our ways of thinking could not keep pace with it, the demand for a new business ethics was felt, which can eliminate numerous immoral practices in the business world. At the same time there was a need of a new ethical standard in order to tackle with the new emerging problems of the corporate world. In this connection we find two trends or movements in the industrial or corporate world to tackle with the new emerging situations. One movement arose by the sincere efforts of the business and industrial leaders. They tried to control the moral mechanism from within through self regulation. Another movement was from outside of the business world. This was an attack from outside the business world. This was an attack upon the industrial system itself. It took a form of a demand for a completely different type of social system. This attempt was made on the part of the society to regulate the business through external control of government by implementing new policies. They also made a demand to remove some of the functions from the realm of private business. Businessmen started functioning in a positive way by setting their house in order through forming codes of conduct or by setting the standard of correct practices. They visualized that if they do not establish high ethical standard for business, society will set up regulatory measures and take away more and more functions out of their hands. The American Trade Association and The Better Business Bureaus of America are the examples of such efforts. These are the organizations of businessmen or employers that are active in promoting high ethical standard and practices. Their attempt is to elevate and to standardize their practices, form of contract, products and the like. The Trade association as well as other groups of businessmen adopted several moral codes to improve the situation.

The effort from outside was made through two fronts, one by government itself and other by the social organizations. Governmental agencies like Federal Trade Commission were established in order to impose check on the malpractices of the companies. Several rules were also framed by the government and their agencies for the fair and better performance of the business world. From the side of society several services clubs sprang up worldwide, such as, Rotary International, Kiwanis and Lions, etc., to take up the moral cause in corporate society, besides their other social and extra curricular activities. The aim and objective of the Federal Trade Commission is to promote free and fair competition in inter-State commerce in the interest of the public by preventing deceptive practices, unfair methods of competition, discrimination in price fixing, etc. In order to enforce the moral reforms, the commission was empowered to take disciplinary action against the business organization concern. The social clubs also took several measures and issued directions for promoting higher standard in business professional groups. Rotarians were urged by their association to use their influence as members of trade association to secure the adoption of the written code of correct business practices. It appointed a committee on business methods, whose task was to promote the fair dealing in business. And thus, slowly and stealthily, business ethics knocked the door of Applied Ethics as an ethico-philosophical method for business. And thus, we find that the norms of business ethics reflect the norm of each historical period. As the time passed, norms evolved, causing accepted behaviours became objectionable. Business Ethics and resulting behaviours evolved as well. Now we can define Business Ethics as a *form of Applied Ethics that examines the moral principles or ethical problems that arises in a business environment.* It is also known as Corporate Ethics. It applies to all business conduct as well as it is applicable to all the conducts of the individuals and the entire business organization.

The development of the business ethics is not in a straight way, it took multidimensional forms, owing to the multiple issues or problems of business organizations or corporate world and business ethics. An ethical issue in business organization includes right and duties between a company and its employees, supplier, customer and neighbours as well as its fiduciary responsibility to its shareholders. There are very many issues of business ethics, such as relation between different companies. It includes hostile takeover and industrial espionage. Related issues are corporate governance, corporate social entrepreneurship and political contribution. Its legal issues are debates over introducing a crime control of corporate manslaughter and marketing of corporate ethical policies. Besides these larger economic issues are there, such as, immigration, trade policies, globalization, trade union effect, and workplace problem and other ethical dimensions. According to the ethics of trade union, management strategy, sale and marketing ethics, human resource management and other developed under the umbrella of Business Ethics. The present section tries to deal with these issues. It comprises of six chapters.

Prof. Nityanand Mishra, at the very outset of his learned paper *The Necessity of Professional Ethics in a Business Concern of the Present Age,* has tried to compare the situation of earlier business concern with modern one. He points out that today, the business is more conflicting, highly complicated and tough in comparison to the earlier days. The reason is simple. In earlier days one man was capable to perform the entire process of production. The products were sold to someone he knew or to the labourer who was his employee. Thus business transaction was non-competitive and a few person's affair. The profit they charged was simply to support their livelihood in a dignified way. But with the spread of industrial revolution and rise of *laissez faire* economy, trade became complicated. Today rise and fall of prices affect the whole world. The reign of moral values, which once controlled the human greed became ineffective. Now dignified livelihood means nursing the unbridled human greed. It has accelerated the profit making tendency of the businessmen, which has resulted in the increase of the profit margin unreasonably. The time tested ideal of contentment (*santos*) and not hoarding (*aparigrah)* have been replaced by gross consumerism, discontent (*asantos*) and the tendency to accumulate, amassing the wealth (*parigrah*) through right or wrong means. This affected the business world and the common people adversely. Now business does not remain a service to the society, rather it has become a profit making affair and has turned into a centre of corruption. The business professionals have become vulnerable to corruption barring a few exceptions. And thus, business and ethics are seen as two rival fields, because contrary to it business ethics is perceived as benevolence, charity and social responsibility. But it is not the truth. For the author, the holistic meaning of ethics covers the entire gamut of business operations, transparency and principles. Since ethical practices are deeply embedded in business plans and forms the core of business strategy, there is much scope for earning profit there also. He cites the example of Vipro, a leading business firm, which has undertaken high moral values and is also earning profit of it. This firm is rendering near perfect service quality to the entire overseas customers and has paid rich dividend to its share holders. He concludes, "ethics is necessary for a business profession. . . . it is only remedy for all the deteriorating professions. . . . it must be made integral part of the very mode of one's behaviour".

At the very outset of his learned and ethically technical Paper "Profession and Ethics— talk in Profession "Professor Debashis

Guha says, that despite all the hue and cry of the Meta ethicists of A. J. Ayer's legacy against "Applied Ethics", slowly but stealthily, it has fully set its feet in its new found land of ethics with its mushroom growth in several ways, including professional ethics. First of all, Prof. Guha tries to make the concept of the two terms, profession and ethics talk, clear. While explaining profession he takes an oblique turn and distinguishes it with other terms, with which profession is often confused. He says it is not business, though, it is a full time activity. It is not a fixed salaried job, although it implies certain rights and duties as well as certain legal claims. Another type of confusion that arises with this term is of two types, positive and negative. Positively, it indicates one who does his duty selflessly, even sacrificing worldly things for it. Negatively, it refers to a cunning person who, either for earning money or for self-interest can go to any extreme extent of neglecting his duties. For Prof. Guha both the meanings are inappropriate and wrong. He is of the opinion that profession carries with it the sense of "due" and in turn it involves right or legal claims to what they owe. It also changes upon time, energy and rightful expectations to receive back what they should. Hence, it involves extrinsic and intrinsic limits to earning, dues and rights as well. It is neither mere occupation nor a business, it is something more. It requires accurate or near accurate dynamic knowledge of the basic elements of professional activities, tasks, duty and obligation. Another term is "Ethics Talk— in Profession". Here it involves the question of desirability, right, good, duties, responsibilities, decision making knowledge as well as virtues and values in profession and professionals. It involves talk of ethical desirability or ethical worth in case of professional decision making and act involving disagreement as well as agreement. It needs practical wisdom to decide whether professional ethics comes in the domain of meta-ethics or normative ethics. Finally, he opines, "Ethics without concern of professional ethics is thus incomplete; it does not take the value of professional life seriously, and ethical concern in language is not at all serious if language is detached from complex structure of ethical life of Homo Sapiens.

The main issue of the Chapter *Professional Morality and the Principle of Justice*, by Begum Bilkis Banu, is the controversy regarding the autonomy of professional ethics. For Benjamin Freedman, it is autonomous and deserves separate ethical treatment. Some peccadilloes to morality must be permitted to them as they are working for higher utilitarian values. For example volition of *ahimsa* is permitted to a surgeon, because his act is meant to save the life of a patient. But she is of the opinion, that it is not a valid ground for declaring it autonomous as in normal case too, such breach of conduct is allowed on the name of *apad dharma*. If telling lies can save the life of a man from a killer, it is justified because it is performed for the greater good. Hence, in the case of such conflict we must see that the principles of justice is upheld whether it is done by a professional or non-professional.

At the very outset of her scholarly Chapter entitled *Theoretical Issues in Business Ethics* Dr. Archana Srivastava has tried to define Business Ethics. For her, business ethics. . . . examines ethical rules and principles within commercial context. She is of the opinion that it is a normative discipline where particular ethical standards are advocated and then applied. Since professional ethicists and supporters of business ethics have produced an array of moral theories and framed several issues for business and corporate world, she aims at examining and exploring the different issues, approaches, and conflicting interests into it. Various ethical perspectives are examined here from different points of view such as the industrialists, employees, shareholders, the trade union, companies the commercial enterprises and society as a whole. Sometimes their interests clash and give birth to typical ethical problems. Owing to these different perspectives and conflict of interests among them, various ethical issues appeared and theories emerged in the field of business ethics. Each ethical theorist tries to champion his own theory. In such a circumstance, the author tries to examine and evaluate them on theoretical and contextual business situations. After examining and analyzing different ethical theories and issues of business, she arrives at some ethical solutions and suggests certain ethical policies along with the appointment of Ethics Officer to curb fraud, corruption and abuse scandals, as it is in vogue in U S A and other western countries. However, she is sceptic and doubtful about effectiveness of *ethics officers* in the market places, because, for her, ethical business-practices result from a culture and climate that usually emanates from the top of the organization. Mere establishment or a position is insufficient to inculcate the ethical behaviour unless it gets support from general management. Finally she concludes that the foundation of ethical behaviour goes well beyond the corporate culture or the policies of any given company. At the same time, it also depends upon the individual's early moral training, the other institutions that affect an individual, the competitive business environment, the company and the society as a whole.

Journalism is also a profession today. It has to abide by its normative aspects. With the rising role of media in democratic society journalists have to shoulder lots of responsibilities of their profession in bringing out high quality of news reporting, upholding the professional standards, enhancing the reputation and trust in the news organization, so that it may boost the size of the audience it serves. But in doing so the media persons have accepted some malpractices to earn money, get popularity, serve the interests of the politicians, bureaucrats, or enemy countries. Sometimes they hurt the sentiment of the people by manipulating the news. This is the reason that Dr. Shiva Bhanu Singh in his Paper, *A Critical Appraisal of Journalism-Ethics* has enumerated code of *Journalistic Ethics* for upholding public enlightenment, establish justice and foundation of democracy. These codes are objectivity, responsibility and novelty. Since journalism is regarded as the Fourth State, its moral responsibility and social accountability has increased. Though like other business the primary aim of journalism has also become money-making instead of nation-building. He concludes, due to cut short combination among different newspapers and electronic channels, journalists are bound to follow the ethical standards and professional norms otherwise their professional existence will always be on stake.

At the very outset of his learned chapter, *Ethical Dimensions of Medical Profession* Dr. Sanjay Shukla opines that the ideal of every profession is to observe its norms and regulate its aims in an excellent and in perfect way *(yogah karmasukausalam).* It pays in the long run in terms of health, wealth and prestige, provided it is observed as a selfless service to the humanity. Today, the medical professionals have paid their attention on money only. For that they are ignoring the professional norms and their Hippocratic Oath, which they have in the very beginning of their professional career. That is why instead of being equated with God (*Vaidyo Narayanohari*) they are ironically called the brother of Death God (*yamaraja sahodara*), often greater than Him. The reason is simple. The Death God takes life once only, but the doctors, in addition to it, takes away the wealth of the patient too. (*Yamastu harantipranah vaidyah pranah dhanani ca).* He suggests six cardinal virtues for the medical professionals. These are beneficence, non-malfeasances, autonomy, justice, dignity, truthfulness and honesty. He expects from them to shoulder the great responsibility of medical health of the people and set a noble example before others in a civilized society.

Applied Ethics

Before discussing Applied Ethics in detail, it seems proper to present a brief sketch of the definition, nature and scope of the ethics itself. This will help us understand Applied Ethics in its proper perspectives. Since from the very beginning of the study of moral philosophy, ethics is being defined extensively, we do not want either to repeat the same thing here, or to discuss and define it afresh. Here we would like to lean heavily on the description and definition given in the past, in general and of John F. Mackenzie, in particular. He is of the opinion that "Ethics is the study of what is right or good in conduct. . . . and considers the action of human beings with reference to rightness and wrongness, their tendency to good or to evil." Ethics also deals with man's habits and customs, man's character, as well as the principles on which they habitually act. It also considers what constitutes the rightness and wrongness of those principles as well as good and evil of those habits. In order to understand it in a proper way, the terms right and good require a little explanation.

The term *right* means straight or according to the rules. When we say that one's conduct is right, it means that it is in consonance with the prescribed rule of that conduct. On the contrary, when we say that one's conduct is wrong, it means that the conduct is not *conforming* the rules prescribed for it or it, has violated the rules. The term *good* means valuable for some end. If we say that, his conduct is good, it means, that his conduct is serviceable for any end or ideal that he has in view. However, a careful observation of the use of term *good* indicates that it has two imports, (i) it is means to some end, and (ii) it is itself an end. At the mundane level, end varies from time to time, person to person, as for some; fame is the end of life, for others love, knowledge, wealth, etc., are the ends of life. However, on the transcendental level, supreme good becomes the *summum bonum* of life. Thus, ethics deals with some standard of judgement. After referring to it, one can say that the conduct is right or wrong or one is better than the other. So far the question of the nature of the ideal is concerned, there are some alternatives to it. (a) There is a single ultimate end, (b) there are a set of rules imposed upon us by some authority, or (c) is it an ideal type of human life, which we have enabled for ourselves ? We should discern the possible ways to determine it. Thus, ethics is the general study of ideals involved in human life

So far as the question of nature of ethics is concerned, it is normative in character; because it is related with what is good and what is right in human purpose, both action as well as standard and values of life. It deals with general conditions involved in rightness or goodness of the conduct Thus we can say that ethics is the normative science of human behaviour in ordinary business of life. It is primarily concerned with rightness or goodness of conduct, which is decided with the reference to some external standard. It also sets a goal in human life, mundane or supramundane, towards which life has to evolve. When we cast a glance on ethics and its different aspects in relation to shifting human scenario and context, we find that, broadly speaking, it is concerned with *three theories* as given below.

Utilitarianism

It is based on the belief that "all is well that ends well". Hercin the practical consequences of various policies are evaluated on the assumption that the right policy is one that results in greatest good of greatest number.

Deontological Ethics

Herein notions are built on rules. In other words, we can say that there is an obligation to perform the right action regardless of actual consequences. (*karmanyeva-dhikaraste ma falesukadacana. Gita*, II 47). In India, the *Bhagvad—Gita* has optimized this notion and in the West, Kant has done through the concept of Categorical Imperative.

Value Ethics

This has been basically derived from Aristotelian ethics and the notion of Confucius, which asserts that a right action will be that which is chosen by a suitable agent. A good action will be good not because of what it performs or effects, not by its aptness for attainment of some proposed end, but simply by virtue of the volition.

Apart from the above-mentioned three approaches, there is another modern approach of ethics which attempts to overcome smilingly the impossible divide between Deontology and Utilitarianism. It is a case-based reasoning. It is also known as *casuistry*. It does begin with any theory, rather it starts with immediate facts of real and concrete cases. However, it makes use of an ethical theory but it does not view the ethical theory as the most important feature of moral reasoning. This modern approach to ethics is called *Applied Ethics*. This is a case of application of ethics on a particular scenario. Albert John and Stefen Toulmin challenged the traditional paradigm of ethics. For them it is not proper to start with a theory and apply that to a particular case, rather it is proper to start with a particular case itself and ask what morally significant feature (including both, theory and practical considerations) ought to be considered for that particular case. It was also observed that consensus on particular problematic case often emerges when the participants focus on the fact of the case rather than an ideology or theory.

Applied Ethics is the sub-group of the classification of Philosophical Ethics. It is a philosophical search of right or wrong within a controversial scenario. In fact, popular philosophies relating to morality and ethics are built upon the act of repetitiously classifying the subcategories of classifications and then inventing metaphorical knowledge to place within the subcategory. Normally we use the term ethical, moral and right synonymously. In the same way, we use the opposite terms unethical, immoral and wrong as synonymous terms. However, we also know that these do not exist. We define what is right or what is wrong, because of the vagueness of our acts (*Gahano karmano gatih*) and latitude or flexibility of relating principles. Hence, it can be said, that classification within philosophical concept of ethics that seems to contain invented metaphysics. In other words, we can say that Applied Ethics is a sub-group of philosophical ethics. Its knowledge within its practices is more metaphorical than the fact. Hence, it requires more quantity of intelligence to invent the philosophical view that may help us choose to investigate the origin of right and wrong, not within metaphor but within real events.

The term Applied Ethics is composed of two words, "Applied" and "Ethics". Here ethics is not used in the traditional sense of the term. It is simply a logic-based set of designs and beliefs combined with a deep causation. In order to recognize right or wrong in a practical scenario, one has to derive his choice logically from the pre-established code of conduct. These codes of conduct must exist within that context, as any right or wrong that may exist is already existent in their individual foundation of logic. The reason is simple. Out of nothing comes nothing. (*nasato vidyate bhavo, nabhavo vidyte satah—Gita* II.16). A person does choose his or her nature during a scenario. The inward nature of the person exists prior to that scenario. In any situation, an observer can observe how an individual's nature will react in different circumstances. Hence, the moral judgement will be based upon individual's preestablished standard. It is another thing that the standard in the same scenario may not be the same in case of different individuals, but we will judge the change of standard itself based on pre-existing standard. A true example of the case is of Avinash Kumar Srivastava himself. He was doing pre-commissioned course of N.C.C. at Officer's Training School Kampthee, Nagpur (Maharashtra). It was a very small town. Heavily nailed wires barricaded the school. Cadets were not allowed to cross the barricade, even in emergency. Because of the poor food supply, there was a need to take milk as supplementary food to maintain their health. Milk was available about fifty yards away from the fence in a house of a milkman. Inside the school, additional milk was not available even on payment. Cadets were in practical rather existential dilemma. If they go to the milkman's house to procure the milk crossing the fence, the rule's of the school is violated. If they do not go to procure the milk, the rules are honoured but the health of the cadets is deteriorated. Ethical questions of right or wrong were at stake, because we did not have the legal permission to cross the boundary at any rate or in any situation. The cadets resolved that they would procure the milk stealthily without informing the authority or the guard. Thus, cadets continued to take milk regularly. In the above-mentioned scenario, there are four ethical problems. (i) Cadets were illegally crossing the boundary regularly, which was immoral; (ii) Cadets had taken the oath not to trespass the boundary in any circumstances. They will never violate the rules and norms of the school; (iii) It was possible for the cadets to cross the bar stealthily, procure the milk, and at the same time pretend they were inside the school and they did not break the rules. In other words, they remain disciplined in the eyes of the school administration; and (iv) A few or all cadets would have been expelled from the Officer's Training School, if caught red handed, illegally crossing the barricade or this news is leaked to the authority.

However, there was no ethical problem in the above-mentioned scenario. There was only a problem of deciding whether the weight of life and health protection out-weighed the risk of expulsion from the school and face embarrassing or demoralizing situation. In other words, one has to decide whether the desire for health protection was more important than one's honour and prestige, or career in NCC services. This example illustrates that the common usage of the terms "Ethics" and "Moral" have nothing to do with right or wrong. In fact, the concept of ethics is nothing but weighing pre-established preferences. Each individual has a preestablished weight of chosen standard. Until other desirable things do not outweigh the present standard, he will continue to behave in the same way, i.e., which ever self chosen standard appears to serve the best of the moment.

In another example, we find a person who accepts honesty as a standard in order to attain social acceptance, or he desires money as a standard for social prestige. If quantity of money and social prestige is not too great for him, then the person will remain honest. However, on the contrary, if sufficient money and/or prestige is made available to him, in such a case he may outweigh the standard of honesty. Here, the logic of his preference weighs that money and prestige is more important than honesty and social acceptance.

Thus, in Applied Ethics there is no ethics at all. It is a logic-based set of desire and belief. Here right and wrong are logically derived choices. These choices have decided and established long before a person makes a choice within a scenario. All that a scenario does is that it makes possible for a person's true inward self to know all these. It keeps a person's mind abreast of all such alternatives. Hence, any right or wrong that may exist in any scenario is already existent is already existent within an individual's foundation of logic. The individual's pre-existing standards choose to follow what is held to be the most important. There are two alternatives, which option will protect cadet's health and life or the cadets may choose not to violate the norms and remain honest and disciplined. In the other scenario, the person has to decide between two choices, money and prestige, or honesty and social acceptance. All choices are influenced by the pre-established foundational choice. The choice may be focused inwardly or outwardly, but the strings of self-chosen standards are the logical choices. These are in agreement with the foundational standards. The Applied Ethics illustrates through the scenario, how self-chosen desires react in the real world. However, it does not have any potentiality to discover what is right or what is wrong.

Applied Ethics is, basically, a by-product of Western Ethics or Western Philosophy. Hence, it has to follow the typical traits of Western Philosophy, while propounding the normative principles through observations as western thought is primarily based on observations. It is simply a rational explanation of the events or of the world. Newton first saw apples falling on the ground. He observed it minutely in different contexts. Thereafter, based on those observations, he invented the Law of Gravitation. In the same way, standards of right or wrong were propounded by observing events in different scenarios. For the answer of why any act is right or wrong, one has to rely on the first hand observation of the conduct, context, and person performing the act and the situation or scenario under which this was performed. Thus, the sequence of logic runs as follows.

1. The question is what is right and what is wrong.
2. It is unknown.
3. Without knowing right or wrong western ethics speaks of a scenario of human events, real or imaginary.
4. It attempts to find, what is right or what is wrong within the scenario.

Normally, it is impossible to judge any act as right or wrong without any pre-established standard. However, the logic of western philosophy is circular in character. For it, ethics are the moral standard and morals are ethical standard. In the same way, it believes that it can discover unknown right or wrong within another unknown scenario. Now, the decision of right or wrong will define the words right or wrong. Since the reasoning is circular, it begins from nowhere and ends in nowhere. Hence, there is a need of a logical sequencing of events because each accurate conclusion is built up on an accurate previous conclusion. In fact, the right or wrong exists before man or man's scenario and the created things. Man and his scenario exist before normative principles. Hence, there is a need of a correct logical dictate for defining a thing to be known before a thing can be measured. It is fallacious to count right or wrong within scenarios. Let us take a concrete example of "abortion". For its rightness, some may argue that since: (a) Abortion helps slow the problem of over population; (b)Women have human right on their bodies. Therefore, if she likes, abortion is right. On the other hand, one can also argue that abortion is wrong because (i) Unborn child is conscious, and (ii) the foetus is a separate human being. Its killing will amount culpable homicide. Hence, it is illegal and wrong. Here both set of arguments have some validity but we are getting difference in conclusions from each valid statement. However, we cannot decide a conclusion right or wrong from any one argument if all arguments are based on correct information. In every such scenario, is it so that a person simply picks and chooses bits of data that supports his beliefs and bias ?

It is clear from above example that a person's need, belief and religious affiliations help one right or wrong of a particular event in a scenario. The person picks and chooses the fact that supports his pre-existing choice. Here, in the case of "abortion", there is no possibility of discovering right or wrong within the debate. We have to look the answers of right or wrong in the reasoning of why persons have formed the pre-existing choice. The choice for and against, of any act in question, are there. If we choose a choice to weigh right or wrong then the judgement should be of pre-existing decisions and not of a scenario. Here a question arises, "If Applied Ethics is defined as an attempt to find right or wrong in a scenario, then without knowing what is right and what is wrong before hand, how can we judge a thing, act or event right and wrong in a scenario?" If we cannot answer it positively, it means applied ethics has numerous flaws in its logic. Such as (a) It starts without any standard, i.e., without knowing the definition of right or wrong; (b) It tries to find out/define, right or wrong in a scenario; and (c) In addition, its conclusions are not unanimous rather each conclusion contradicts the other.

Thus, Applied Ethics can be distinguished from normative ethics where the moral judgement is based on pre-existing moral standard, moral principles or moral code of conduct. It is also concerned with what people should believe to be right or wrong. Applied Ethics is also different from Meta-Ethics, which concerned with the nature of moral statements. Defining it, Brenda Almond says, "Applied Ethics is the philosophical examination, from moral-stand point, of a particular issue in a private or public life that are matters of moral judgement." For him, the term "Applied Ethics is used to describe the attempts to use philosophical methods to identify morally correct course of action in various fields of human life. For example, Bio-ethics is concerned with identifying the correct approach to matters such as euthanasia, abortion, allocation of scarce health resources or use human embryo in research. Environmental ethics is concerned with questions, such as, duties of human toward landscape or species. . . . As such; it is a study which supposed to involve practitioner as much as professional philosophers."

The second section deals with the nature, significance and scope of Applied Ethics. It comprises of six articles. In the first article entitled "Post Modern Trends in Applied Ethics" Dr. R. C. Sinha has tried to earmark, that post-modernism is a reaction against the modern ethics, wherein Meta or master narrative is replaced by multi narratives, that can be lived or experienced with. The rise of new procedures or modes of resolving ethical disputes gave birth to moral relativism, as we cannot ignore the actual conditions experienced by the moral agents. But he is of the opinion that applied ethics and theoretical ethics cannot part company, as the former cannot thrive at the cost of the latter. However, he concludes that both the ethics applied different roles in different spheres, but there is a need of theory and application of moral principles and that theory should gain support from the consciousness reached at the applied level.

Prof. R. C. Sinha, taking a key from Mackie, explains the concepts of "right" and "duty' and links them with utilitarianism. For him good or duty is possible in the social context alone. He is of the opinion that utilitarianism consists of "greatest good in greatest number" rather than "greatest happiness of greatest number" and this makes a difference. He says that right and duty can be understood in two different senses, legal and ethical. The legal sense of the term is the subject matter of jurisprudence, as in this case, court has every right to intervene. On the contrary, moral right is justified by the ability of an individual to assert it for the "common good". A man who is not living in the society has no meaning of such terms like right, good, duty, etc., as these are social constructs. This is the reason that he says, "Right is a justifiable claim in a community, and a duty is the duty to fulfil that claim". Individual rights involve another individual's duty.

In the next part of his learned essay, "Right, Duty and Utilitarianism", he explains these concepts in the light of applied ethical domain of Bio-ethics. He enquires it with special reference to euthanasia, in connection with the legal riddles of "right to live" and the "right to die" as well as the sanctity of life. Further, he takes up another bio-ethical problem of "Abortion" in the light of mother's right, the right of the foetus to live and so on. Finally he concludes that man in the terminal stage or vegetative stage, must have the right to die on humanitarian ground, like a normal man. However, he is not in favour killing any handicapped person, in any pretext, as it amounts to culpable homicide. Dr. R C Sinha, in his scholarly paper, "Some moral issues in Legal profession", has tried to evaluate the lawyer-client relationship and raised two objections against it. (a) This relationship is either immoral or amoral; and (b) In this relationship lawyers treat their client in a paternalistic fashion. In the latter the client is dehumanized. For him, the former is related with "*professional differentiated behaviour*", which creates a new moral universe. Here an advocate argues for his client's issue even if it is wrong, neglecting the moral considerations. Here a lawyer becomes an amoral skilled person who evolves techniques for defending his client's even unfair issues at the cost of humanity and moral causes. It is virtually immoral to fight against the right cause and justice. But if he does not do so, professionally his act is immoral. Secondly, in the lawyer-client relationship the client is dehumanized. He is not treated with respect and dignity which he deserves. The reason is simple. The client's interest becomes dominant in relation to his personality and he tolerates the bad/sad treatment of the advocate. For Dr. Sinha, its solution should be to *deprofessionalize the legal profession*, only then the relation of equality between them can be established. This can happen only when the legal procedures are simplified and become directly available even to the lay persons.

Prof. S A Shaida in his very scholarly paper on *Some Features of Husserl's Life-World* informs that Husserl during the formation of this concept was influenced by Dilthey's concept of 'Life-nexus' as well as the concept of 'Being-in-the World' of Martin Heidegger. This concept was further developed by Maurice Ponty, Jan Patoeka and Alfred Schutz, students of Husserl. Explaining the meaning and the content of 'Life-World' Husserl says, "In what ever way we may be conscious of the world as a universal horizon, as coherent universe of existing objects, we, each "I the man" and all of us together, belong to the world as living with one another in the world; and the world is our world, valid for our consciousness as existing precisely through the "living together"! We, living in the wakeful world, consciousness are constantly active on the basis of our passive having of the world. . . . Obviously this is not only. . . . for me, the individual ego; rather we in living together, belong to the world as world for all, pre-given with the ontic meaning. . . . The we subjectivity. .(Is) constantly functioning."(p. 108-109) Thus "life world" may be conceived as a universe of what is self evident or given, a world that subjects may experience together. For Husserl the life- world is the foundation of all the epistemological enquiries. As a matter of fact, this concept of "life-world" has its origin in biology and cultural Protestantism. This concept has been used particularly in the field of social sciences, sociology and philosophy. It emphasises a state of affair wherein the world is experienced and the world is lived. In Husserl's tradition, the life world is a pre-epistemological stepping stone for Phenomenological analysis. He is of the opinion that life-world is not a small or a minor problem for theoretical sciences, but its universal problems can be understood in different ways, such as (a) pre-givenness, (b) temporality, (c) sedimentation, (d) returns and advances; and (e) science of the life-world.

On the basis of the above discussions the author observes, "Everybody knows and realises that the present day science has been too much developed and Husserl is worried about the negative or harmful role of science". The so called self sufficiency of scientific objectivism is "false self consciousness". It has dehumanised and is shorn of all anthropocentric considerations. It is a real crisis and has resulted into ignoring the life-world. The author has tried to explain his views' under following subheading

Historicity

Husserl accepts the historicity of all knowledge and understanding as well as the mode of understanding, at the same time. In order to provide decisions for radical understanding we have to reflect back in a thoroughly historical and critical fashion. Historical reflection has to be seen as our "necessity as historical being who 'not only have a spiritual heritage but have become what we are thoroughly and exclusively in a historical-spiritual manner". The historical reflections of the both, philosophers and scientists, lead to knowledge. Husserl applies the historicity in a wider field. Here all that is individual, social and psychical are rooted in their historicity. Thus the application of historicity is not restricted to what one accepts or rejects, rather it can be extended even to unacknowledged legacies which has, without our consent, shaped us as what we are, our historicity and tradition. To sort out the things we can apply the method of 'epoche', but how can the unknown world be brought to be bracketed or epoche, is not known. The content of the life-world is subject to change and variation but its general structure is not, as it is not relative. For Husserl life-world has its own ontology, its own ontic meaning. Life-world is the product of past cultural traditions, sedimented within it. However, future experience can revise it or even reject it. Dr. Shaida explains in detail the aspects of pre-givenness of the life-world. Later on he discusses the role of prejudices within the horizon of life-world. For him, Husserl's approach to life-world is described as theoretical praxis, which can be understood and classified only through a critical understanding of the total unity of our history. He also compares the views of Gadamer and Husserl with regard to prejudice, pre-givenncss, self-knowledge and others and finds affinity between Husserl's 'Life-world' and Gadamer's 'Situation', 'Horizon'. Dr. Shaida is of the opinion that Husserl's approach toward scientific objectivism finds its echo in Gadamer's distrust in historical objectivism which conceals the involvement of the historical consciousness itself in effective history

Dr. Shaida, in his learned paper "*Postmodernism and Ethics*" opines that global consumerism and impact of information technology have destroyed the mode of human relations. The traditional-based culture is overtaken by superficial commonality employed by the unified culture propagated by the electronic media. This gave birth to post-modern conditions that displaced unified ways of analysing good, values and obligations and recommended multiple standered as morality is not independent of particular interests and concern of the moral agents. Thus it marks a total paradigm shift from theoretical and conceptual foundations of ethics to specific issues and problems involved in practice of virtues that are embedded in our traditional as well as in the geo-political situations surrounding us.

The sixth and the last chapter of this section, '*What is Applied Ethics'* by M. P. Chaurasia, is an attempt to explain the nature and scope of the subject matter in a very simple way, so that even a common man can understand it properly. For him Applied Ethics is a broad term. It covers a wide spectrum of descriptive, prescriptive and interactive ethics. In this context he also explains the meta-ethics, ethical nihilism and distinguishes between the applied ethics and traditional ethics. These create an essential background for applied ethical discourses. He has narrated the basic principles involved in the both, with full clarity and consistency. He has also provided a justification for concepts like right, good, justice, truth telling, individual freedom, etc. He has raised a very important question, "Can supernatural concept be good"? and explains it. The author has very nicely discussed Utilitarianism, Kantian ethics, Moral standard, etc. He draws our attention that in the light of the above discussion, what sort of conduct can be good. It is a nice explanatory essay that enables us to understand the cumbersome coinage of multi-layered, multi-meaning concepts of Applied Ethics.

Environmental Ethics

The third section of this volume is environmental ethics. It is an important part of applied ethics in the post-modern context. During 1970, it emerged as a consciously recognized area of philosophical enquiry. It is another fact that there had been much substantial and influential work on philosophy of environment much earlier. Henry David Thoreau, Albert Schweitzer and Aldo Leopold have authored very important essays on "Land Ethics". However; it could form a part of a concrete programme among the professional philosophers to investigate the environment as a field of philosophical concern. But it is again a fact, that later on, it received a sustained attention by professional philosophers. Thereafter, it developed dialectically and progressively. In other words, we can say that the subsequent work was built on the foundations supplied by the subsequent work. This movement continued to advance further by a process of criticism and reconstruction. In fact, the environmental philosophy, which emerged in 1970, was in direct response to a widespread belief that the world was in throes of environmental crisis. This belief was partially fostered by the writings of scientists and policy makers. In 1962, Rachel Carson published his book, '*Silent Spring*', wherein he apprised the world about insidious dangers of pesticides and other synthetic chemicals on human health. The book of Steward Udall, Secretary of interior in John F. Kennedy administration, '*The Quite Crisis*,' was published in1963. Herein he excoriated the *raid on the natural resources* and the *rape of the natural beauty* of South America. Through his book Udall insinuated, though rhetorically, that quite crisis could have proved to be more disastrous than cold war's threat of nuclear holocaust. These writings and others created an atmosphere of fear of destruction of this planet if proper measures are not taken to curb it through self restraint. It was also felt that environmental problems are basically social problems. It begins with people as cause and end with people as victim. It is people who create a bad environment and bad environment brings out worse in people. Hence, the reason and remedy of the impending environmental tragedy has to be searched in the human nature itself. That is why there is a need of environmental wisdom to be in the centre of the agenda of the contemporary humanity.

As it has already been mentioned, that environmental ethics is a branch of Applied Ethics. It has emerged from the contemporary interest of applying and exploring certain ethical concepts, precepts, principles and position to a set of concrete situation, which modern man is confronting in the life, concerning human relationship with nature, natural entities and the members of the biotic community. However, ethics cannot be applied until we have the clear understanding of the underlying concepts of human beings, their ends and their normative values along with the understanding of the object.or the situations to which the situations pertain. From the point of view of the methodology the problem of environmental ethics can be treated at these three levels.

Meta-ethical level

Here the meaning of the ethical terms are clarified through linguistic analysis

Metaphysical level

Here a fundamental premise of the nature of reality is examined.

Normative level

Here ethical norms and actions and attitudes are formulated. In order to understand environmental ethics in its proper perspective, we must have a grip on the above mentioned three levels of understandings. Now it is clear, that environmental ethics is related to environment. Here the term ethics is related to a comprehensive and coherent set of principles of obligation and values. It is concerned with questions like duties of humans towards landscape and species. When an ethics becomes environmental ethics it must satisfy these two conditions : (a) It must hold that there are non human beings which have moral standing; and (b) It must hold that of those beings which have moral standing, are larger than the class of conscious beings. A being has moral standing, if and only if, we morally ought to consider how is it affected by a given action or policy. Such beings are morally relevant, but conditions are fulfilled, only if such beings (other than human beings as well as other conscious beings) are capable of being inherently valuable. In another words, they must have values independent of any conscious being. If any ethics lacks it, it cannot be an ethics of environment. However, it can be ethics for environment. Here, the former can be termed to be the environmental ethics. Thus the concept of environmental ethics is set forth involves postulating that non conscious natural objects can have value in their own right, independent of human interest. Now a thing is right, when it tends to preserve the integrity, stability, and the beauty of the biotic community. It is wrong when it tends to be otherwise. The above discussion entails that environmental ethics is not a narrowly focused view consisting of ethical principles only, about the treatment of animals, forest and other natural entities. It includes principles pertaining to all those beings which have standing of their own. Explaining the nature of applied ethics Louis P. Pojman says "Environmental ethics is the fullest extension of objective ethics, extending the moral thoughts beyond one's community and nation to include not only all people everywhere, but also animals and whole of nature, the biosphere, both now and beyond, the imminent future to include the further generation. Global environmental ethics, through logical extension of traditional ethics, is revolutionary in that, it calls on us to think and act in the ways we hardly imagined, subordinating our policies, economics and technology to a holistic global understanding of how we function with the ecosphere. It calls us for a new deeper moral consciousness. (*Global Environment Ethics*, Mayfield Publishing Company, London, 2000). As it is indicated earlier that environmental ethics can be thought in these two different ways as below.

Firstly, it is a sort of subdivision of applied ethics, wherein the application of well established conventional moral philosophical categories is done to the emergent practical environmental problems. Secondly, Environmental ethics is a creative enterprise where we explore an alternative moral and even metaphysical principle in order to tackle the new emerging environmental problems. The latter is more ambitious, as the task of the environmental ethicists here, is that of theoretician or of a philosophical architect, which is more difficult and problematic. The reason is simple. A moral philosopher, in the latter sense of the term, has not to apply the traditional moral principles on the new emerging environmental problems. Since it has become a separate discipline an environmental ethicist has to explore, examine, analyze and apply the concepts that are symptomatic of the world view that causes environmental pollution, the aesthetic degradation of nature, human over population, resource depletion, and ecological destruction and abrupt massive specie's extinction.

Today, environmental ethics has arrived at the fourth decade of its continuous journey. It is experiencing itself to be at a curious cross road. The reason is simple. It has produced an array of moral theories. All of them attempt to extend ethics beyond its traditional human domain. Their arguments demand moral consideration for non-human beings as well as ecosystem. Further many leading environmental ethicists are inclined to restrict their pluralistic position. For them even the narrow set of theoretical approaches is sufficient for generating an adequate environmental ethics. Some ethical theorists are of the opinion that a coherent environmental ethics must embarrass a restricted set of properties like non-anthropocentrism, moral monism or holism and perhaps, a commitment to some form of intrinsic value. However, we should not discourage the ethicists for insisting that one approach of environmental ethics is better than its other competitors. Instead, we should encourage sober but vigorous assessment of competing moral position.

All twelve chapters of three section are dedicated to this job wherein the need, reason and remedy of the impending environmental tragedies has been explored. Not only this, these environmental ethicists have also tried to suggest alternative normative principles along with the code of conducts as found in our religio-philosophical moral traditions resonate to our problems. They have also tried to redefine these in the light of new emerging environmental situations, by providing them a new scientific, empirical and naturalistic edifice. One thing that has emerged out of their discussions is the need of environmental wisdom (ecosophy) that may create an eco-friendly bent of mind, which will not only help us preserve nature and natural entities, rather this feeling will help emerge environmental consciousness in us. This makes us feel that humans are related to all other creatures, as we all have the same origin in so called non-living matters. However, this kinship itself is of no concern to one who does not believe that non-living can have moral standing. If the non-humans are inherently valuable and environmentally conscious, an attitude of respect, admiration and love towards nature and natural entities (living and non-living both) is entirely appropriate.All the twelve Papers of this section are given to environmental ethics.

The chapter on *'Need for an Environmental Ethics'* by Dr. Sarita Kumari, can be treated as an introduction to this chapter. Sharing with Avinash Kumar Srivastava, she opines that environmental crisis is really a social problem. It emerges with people as cause and ends with people as victim. After painting a disastrous picture of man made ecological degradation, in terms of nuclear holocaust and other destructive modes of pollutions, which may destroy the entire human civilisation and the ecosystem, she opines that it is the result of anthropocentric ethics, wherein entire nature is meant for human pleasure. Now there is a need of '*cosmo centric ethics*' wherein nature and natural entities are subject of moral concern. If the entire ethics is oriented from nature's point of view, we can never be aggressive towards nature and eco-friendly attitude may emerge. But in doing so a proper precaution has to be taken, as even in framing out a nature-centric ethics, man's interest comes from the back door. She has prepared a comparative chart which categorically shows as to how cosmo-centric or nature-centric ethics serves the human end.

Dr. Shiva Bhanu Singh in his article, *Nature and Scope of*

Environmental Ethics, opines that the entire eco-crisis is due to man's aggressive attitude towards nature which is the result of Christian Weltanschauung that holds that entire nature and natural entities including birds and animals have been created for human pleasure. Man is at liberty to use and misuse them. This anthropocentric western ethics told very heavily on this planet earth. On the contrary, Indian ethics is cosmo-centric wherein natural entities, including flora and fauna, have their own intrinsic value and right to live. Being the highest evolutes of creation, man has the duty to care and share it. The rites and rituals of the Hindu religion is framed in such a way, that it not only protects natural entities from decay, but also from the human encroachment and aggression and thus, strengthens man's harmony with nature.

Dr. D.C. *Srivastava* in his chapter on *Deep Ecological Consciousness*, enters into a debate initiated by Arne Nass, what should be the moral concern, man or the nature. It results in formation of two ecological theories, Shallow and Deep. The Shallow Ecology is anthropocentric. According to it nature has to be protected and preserved for human consumption. On the contrary, the deep ecological theory holds that natural environment should be protected because they have independent value regardless their usefulness to humanity. The Shallow Ecology is the outcome of Christian religion. Because the Book of Genesis, the early part of the *Bible*, says that the world is made for human use and pleasure. The Deep Ecological concern has found its first genuine expression in Hindu religion. Millennia ago, the Hindu thinkers looked upon life (*jiva*) as omnipresent universal expressed in particular units Even the human mind is increasingly the perfect aspect of Universal mind. All living beings are the members of ecological community bound together in the network of interdependence. This new perception gives birth to a radically new system of ethics. This is the demand of the day as anthropocentric ethics has brought the entire universe on the brink of disaster. The nature-centric and holistic deep ecology can generate in us eco-friendliness or universal wisdom.

Dr. Sanjay Kumar Shukla in his learned chapter entitled '*Need of Ecosophy in Technocratic Society*' points out, that how knowledge and competence combined with folly (lack of wisdom) made a mistaken separation of man from nature, which has resulted in rapacious exploitation or destruction of the nature in the name of development. Hence, ecological wisdom (*ecosophy*) is necessary for our proper negotiation with the environment. This has given birth to different models of environmental ethics, having somewhat different moral values. These eco-centric ethical values are independent of human purposes. For it, all species of the world have the equal right to live and blossom. Sanjaya observes that this egalitarian view is also deplorable. In such a situation, even harmful bacteria and dangerous virus causing disease and death, will also be considered equal to human and other animals, birds and many other non-injurious species of the world. This will create a problematic situation. In order to avoid the evils of both the ethics, he sought for a sort of ecosophy that can harmonise the materialistic outlook, which is responsible for environmental degradation, with the spiritual one, that delineates on values of love, piety and sacrifice as well as visualise the spirit of companionship between man and the nature.

Dr. Kakoli Basak in her learned chapter on '*Ecological Ethics: Indian Metaphysics and Ethical View Point*' observes, that ecological ethics aims at sustainable development. Ethics that developed in the west is anthropocentric one, whether it is the virtue ethics of Socrates, value ethics of Aristotle, Deontological ethics of Kant or teleological ethics that refers to Utilitarianism of Bentham and J. S. Mill. From the environmental point of view, these all are shallow ethics. It is another thing they all fight pollution and resource depletion, but are oriented towards human interest. On the contrary, Deep ecology is eco-centric. According to it, all living beings are alike in having values of their own. Here, ecological community forms the ethical community. For her, Indian moral system (normative) has metaphysical background wherein the entire universe is the manifestation of the *Brahman* and is identical with the cosmic self. Hence, the nature and natural entities including man, an animal, birds, biotic and abiotic have equal moral values and thus forms a holistic ethics. Here every thing has to get perfection; every thing has intrinsic as well instrumental value. Here the question of environmental degradation and encroachment of natural resources for human pleasure does not arise. It aims at the perfection of all men, animal and nature.

Dr. Sucheta Shukla in her chapter on "*The Role of World Religions in Environmental Crisis,*" observes that the Christian religion gave birth to anthropocentrism in ethics. With the rise of science and technology man exploited the nature for his development and comfort. It resulted in environmental degradation and ecological imbalance. If we take into account all the religions of the world we will be able to frame a Cosmo-centric ethics. It will save the nature from human encroachment and help us upgrade the environment. She tries to show that contrary to the Christianity, other religions of the world advise us to care and share the nature. For that she quotes stanzas of religious scriptures that refer to the unity of the man and the nature.

Dr. Mritunjay Kumar in his chapter on '*A Philosophical Vision of Environment*", concentrates on the Cosmo-centric character of Indian religion, that establishes human nature unity and generates in us regard and respect for nature and natural entities. For the *Vedas* the divine normative principle *Ṛta* is controlling the cosmos and its movements. Natural entities have their own intrinsic value independent of human interference. Human encroachments against nature have brought the world on the brink of disaster. Only by observing the rules of nature, *Dharma,* we can protect the universe and save the human life. (*Dharmo raksati raksitah*) If it is engrained in human mind, it will give birth to love, and respect for natural entities. That is why in the age of yore, the dwelling place of students and *Risis* were forests, wherein the great epics were authored, and history was created and thus had been a source of inspiration for profound relation between man and the nature. Even in this present age, old spiritual wisdom can save the world from ruination.

Dr. Avinash Kumar Srivastava in his chapter on "*Do Trees have Right of their Own: A Buddhist Reply*", warns us regarding environmental tragedies and comedies that are born out of our disastrous acts. To avoid these, he suggests forming a nature-centric ethics in place of anthropocentric one, wherein even trees will have the right for its survival and against their encroachment. Here, he tries to spotlight the legal status of a tree as a right holder from different angles. He comes to the conclusion that like human beings, more specially a child and a senile old man or institutions, trees must accrue right in the eyes of law and that has to be protected. Any sort of injury caused to it must be treated as punishable offence and compensation to it must go for its benefit. For the Buddha all biotic beings including trees, animals and men, have the same origin and are made up of the common elements, i.e., *rupa dhatu* and *arupa dhatu*. Hence, they all must have equality before law and require equal protection of the law as well as equal rights of their own. Buddha has made a provision of *pacittiya dosa* as punishment for those who causes any injury to the tree. Dr. A. K. Srivastava is of the opinion that Buddhist religio-ethical directives have to be taken into consideration, in formation of the law rules and act of any country. Law making is a continuous process. It has emerged out of customs, rituals and the rules of the tribes. If Buddha's teachings are interpreted, utilised, analysed and applied for the environmental causes, laws regarding right of trees must emerge and thus the antiquity of Buddhist religion and ethics may provide protection to trees and their rights.

The learned chapter on, '*Built-in Environment: An Integral Part of Environmental Ethics*' jointly authored by Dr. Protima Ganguli and Mritunjay Kumar talk of two types of environments, natural and Built-in (man made). The latter is detrimental to the human existence as we have destroyed the natural environment for our short term benefits, without visualising the long term harms. After presenting a comparative chart of both the eco-systems and their good and bad results, they have tried to show that by introducing environmental ethics, we can protect nature and maintain the ecological balance. At the same time, they also point out that both types of environment are the integral part of environmental ethics. Built-in environment takes care of human development on physical level (Material uplift and industrial development) and the natural environment maintain the life supporting system. Hence, we must develop eco-friendly attitude in all the spheres of life, social, material, spiritual and natural.

Dr. M.P. Chaurasia in his learned chapter, '*Ecosophy: An Overview*', observes that due to human folly (lack of ecological wisdom or love for it) men exploited the nature mercilessly to feed their greed and brought the planet on the brink of disaster. To save it we have to develop a proper ecosophy (ecological wisdom) in the common mass. It will help us recognise the intrinsic value of nature, grow non-exploitative vision towards natural resources and restore ecological equilibrium by developing eco-friendly attitude.

Prof. Nirbhai Singh in his scholarly chapter '*Environmental Ethics and Indian Culture*' opines that environmental ethics of the West is an abortive attempt for healing the ailing humans. It is the illegitimate by-product of science and technology, that has given birth to too many incurable diseases. It has created a post-modern era, wherein human destiny is sitting on the melting volcanic portal of material values. Contrary to the Western philosophy, Indian value system has developed a non-anthropocentric view point, based on the truth that both human beings and nature have equal values of life. Value creation carries out through self cultivation, which is the crux of Indian culture. Here, nature (*dharma*) serves as source, for the sublimation of life's unification of man and nature. There is no dichotomy and enmity between the two as it is free from anthropocentrism.

The humble effort of Sri Shiva Nath Prasad, in his essay entitled, '*Osho Rajneesh and his Eco-concern*' is to unearth some of the hidden aspects of Osho's philosophy. Generally, Rajneesh is famous for his controversial speeches, like "From Sex to Super Consciousness", logical arguments and concocted stories in support of his stands. But Sri Shivanath Prasad is of the opinion that following the footsteps of the great Indian seers and religious-philosophical texts Osho too, was concerned for the multi-dimensional predicaments afflicting the mankind, besides, discussing classical problems like *Nirvana*, God, Soul Theory of *Karma*, etc. Today environmental problems are tormenting the human mind, as it has brought the entire universe at the brink of disaster. No one as yet has tried to explore the preaching and teachings of Rajneesh in this perspective. Sri Prasad through his essay, has tried to spotlight the reason and remedy of the impending environmental tragedy in the light of philosophy of Rajneesh. He explains that it is evident from the early account of his student life that he left Banaras Hindu University and got his admission in Sagar University, Sagar, only to live in unison with nature's rich bounty, which provides peace of mind and heart. Knowing it well that trees and vegetations are the primary source of life saving gas, Oxygen, he imagines of a state, wherein men have cut all trees and burnt the entire vegetation. This would read to a situation wherein all living beings will die due to suffocation in the absence of oxygen, the life savings gas. This is the reason that he speaks of living relationship between man and nature. This will never allow anyone for deforestation, as deforestation invites dooms day, which may destroy the entire planet, without any nuclear holocaust or world war. He then speaks of conservation of nature that will lead to conservation of the earth and in turn conservation of life. Rajneesh ask us to change our aggressive mind-set toward nature and advises us to make it eco-friendly. He is of the opinion we are dependent upon the nature for our needs and even our greed. We must also, in return, restore the damages caused to it in terms of reforestation and by taking strong steps to bring a halt to deforestation, as well as by developing a non-encroaching attitude towards nature. Only these may create an ideal state of ecological balance. Like modern environmentalists, Osho also suggests, to avoid the use of poly bags and the waste of toxic, as these will pollute the water, air and earth up to the extent that this planet will not remain a congenial place for living. If we do not realise the gravity of the problem, dooms day will not wait for the change of our vision. Finally Sri Prasad, on the basis of the analysis of Osho's view on environmental crisis and ensuing ecological tragedies and comedies, as well as its reason and remedies, observes that, Rajneesh proves himself an arch priest in the temple of nature.

Avinash Kumar Srivastava

Section – I

BUSINESS ETHICS

Chapter – 1

The Necessity of Professional Ethics in a Business Concern of the Present Age

Prof. Nityanand Mishra

In the ancient days, business transactions were either two-person or a few-person affairs and they were not at all competitive by and large. The sellers certainly charged some extra amount as profit which served their livelihood. But they never compete among themselves in a profiteering spree. The dealings used to be neat and fair by and large in those days.

But the situation is very different these days. Well, we very well know that the world today has become what is called a global village. What happens in, say, the United States of America at this moment does affect India immediately after. The fluctuations in the Stock Markets are clear indices of such changes. Rises and falls in prices do not remain confined now within a small region, nor they remain limited to just a few persons. They give rise to global effects, if I may say so. Furthermore, people of today have become much clever in many different ways. They have started now showing their progress extraordinary cleverness now in profiteering. "I am the richest person in the world, and my name should be recorded in the Guines Book." This has become the new ideal as it were.

Now can riches be enhanced and multiplied today in any other way, if not by making more and more profit in business? Gone are the days when people used to occupy foreign territories by force and became wealthier than others. But then, if to become wealthier businessmen start competeting race in chargin of more and more profit who are the ultimate sufferers in such competitions? Obviously the consumers, who these days are spread over the entire globe. Even a small item of modern consumption, say a torch, might happen to be made in China, but it would come *via* the United States market and also to the Indian market and also to the markets of other countries as well. And in this odyssey the world, the consumer good concerned would become a convenient tool for earning increased profits. Well, quite automatically now a question arises; why should not one follow the Socratic maxim of seeing how many things we can do without or for that matter the Indian maxim of non-possession, called in Sanskrit *aparigraha*? We all know that the twenty-fourth and the last Tirthankar of Jainism, Lord Mahavir became ultimately a Digambar (one having the sky as his dress). He was an *aparigrahi* par excellence. Now, would you accept that all persons throughout the world should become total *aparigrahis*? True, there are persons even today who remain naked even in cold winter seasons. But I do not think that his should be adopted as an ideal way of living. Take another custom, not to be vaccinated against small-pox. Should an attack of small-pox be taken as an appearance of a goddess? In older days, hundreds and thousands of human lives met death due to an attack of the small-pox disease. Should a vaccination against small-pox be avoided? Two types of people would answer this question in the affirmative, first those who take this disease as an appearance of the goddess Shitala. And secondly, those who would disapprove of the use of manufactured goods as was done by our own Mahatma Gandhi. It is a common knowledge now that due to rise and development of science and technology quite a number of life-saving and life ameliorating drugs have been and are being manufactured all over the world and are becoming available for consumption. Well, if they are life-saving and life ameliorating, should they even then be avoided and not consumed? The reasonable answer is clear enough. The truth before it that what were luxurious before have now become necessities of life. Even the Mahatma preferred to use only natural goods and even instead of factory-made medicines, did use a a time-watch, and when he went out on a journey he kept the watch hanging near his waist. And he undertook railway journeys, also he travelled in third class always. Is not a time-watch manufactured good? Is railway train a gift by Nature? It is very obnoxious to say that people should see how many things they can do without, and also that they should altogether avoid the use of manufactured goods. I would here beg to differ from both Socrates and the Mahatma.

Well, making a watch or for that matter any manufactured good is not ordinarily a single-man affair. Most manufactured consumer goods of the modern times are products of big business concerns in which hundreds and even a thousands of workers may happen to be engaged. And in order for them to to give good results they need also to be organised in a hierarchical organisation. To run such organisations has become the profession of those who can afford and also want to run them.

Well, the term profession is a very wide term and it does not signify only business profession. In Hindu society right from the very ancient times, there happens to be a class of people who would conduct sacramental rites; such people are called '*Purohits*'. These *purohits* have to be given *dakshina* at the end of such rites. This offering of *dakshina* forms part of the ritual itself. Well, whatever religious merit such offering might-happen to have, one thing is crystal clear that they serve very well in so far as livelihood of *purohits* is concerned. We can very well say that the *purohits*' *pauruhitya* is their profession. But this does not imply that one who adopts *pauruhitya* runs a business. Similarly, physicians, lawyers, teachers, media persons, etc., do not run a business to earn their livelihood, we take 'business' in the sense of a corporate organisation for manufacturing consumer goods.

Now, when we talk about 'Professional Ethics" we take with reference to the above list of professionals also. These professionals are as much vulnerable to corruption as the business professional are. I do not, however, want to say here that all professionals without any exception are corrupted. There are honourable exceptions in all professions. But experience does show that all professions these days have in them more sinners than saints. So some Professional Ethics is a very necessity for all professions now. But here, I shall deal only with one profession, namely, the profession of running a commercial business corporation.

Now, the very first question that arises in respect of a commercial business concern is profit earning? And surely, the present answer is that profit-earning is the very soul of a commercial concern. Indeed, why else would such a concern getstarted at all? Would a capitalist or a company of share-holders invest their money in any business just to incur loss or at best to keep its investment on a par with itself. How is such a concern related to Melton Freidman of Chicago University, USA has opined that the aim or objective of a business concern is to earn as much profit as it can. Keeping prices within proper limits is not the job of a business concern. That job is automatically performed by mutual competition amongst the business concerns themselves. So, why should a business concern bother about any increase in prices? They should bother only about the earning as much profit as they can.

But then ethics does enter into the scene here. It is true that a human being has to amass as much wealth as he can quite irrespective of what he actually needs. But should this be regarded as right attitude? The resources of the world are in fact limited and the number of human beings depending upon them is quite very large. Should a single individual deprived of the available resources? Or should even a group of individuals be so deprived? If the answer is "yes", I would like to know from that "yes man" about how would he react to the same reaction of somebody else. I am sure his answer would be one of disappointment. Amassing of wealth for one's own self or just for one's family is wrong in principle and it must surely be avoided and even be banned. For, otherwise society will go ruins. And if society goes to ruins, who will remain? Will that "yes man" himself survive then?

Let us now take the present issue from a different angle. Business corporates manufacture goods for the use of consumers. If the goods are not useful for the consumers, will the latter ever buy them? Obviously no. Surely, the manufacturers would produce only those goods which are useful to the buyers. And by so producing the manufacturers would in fact help or serve the consumers. But then how can this rendering of service to the people by the manufacturers go with their harassing and torturing the same people by charging unjustified profits? Logically, both helping and torturing cannot dance in tango. And this is true not only in respect of a business profession but also in respect all other above mentioned professions. So what is urgently needed is *proper professional disciplining*. And that is what Professional Ethics meant for.

Now Professional Ethics never says that a business concern must not charge any profit. It is true that there are many corporate organisations which trade on "no-profit-no-loss" basis. And this type of trading is certainly not a committing of crime. If such a business is done just for the sake of pleasure of doing it or for the sake of doing a service to humanity, it is surely welcome. It would deserve what is called supererogatory praise. But even if a business concern earns a reasonable profit by selling goods, it does not go against any moral maxim at all. Well, business corporates do have to maintain and keep satisfied a large hierarchy of employees and they have also to maintain themselves and their family members in very decent way. And if their capital money is contributed by the shareholders they too have to be paid handsome dividends. Can all the above demands be met by the business heads without charging appropriate profits while selling their goods? Charging a reasonable profit is remaining within the ethical boundary.

But trouble arises, when the business leaders cross the ethical boundary. Professional Ethics would never permit such crossing. We have already pointed out that extracting unreasonable prices from consumers is downright torturing anybody; and torturing anybody is the very opposite of being moral. The ultimate criterion of all morality is just the doing good to the entire existence, to humanity. And if in respect of beneficiary, any preference needs to be exercised, it is humanity that has to be preferred no doubt.

Here, I would very much like to refer to La Rue Tone Hosmer's analysis of the topic of our present concern. He has analysed this topic from the point of view of (1) economics, (2) law, and (3) philosophy. The economic approach lays stress on maximum profit-earning because such an earning is the very motive of a business concern. In legal approach profiteering is regarded as illegal and hence punishable in accordance with the law of the land. But the philosophical approach which is neither instinctive nor authoritative but it is holistic, takes into consideration the basic character of human beings. It links the profession of corporate business with enlightened conscience of human beings. Let us dwell upon this matter in somewhat greater detail. Before we do this, we must grant *a priori* that what we ought to grant *a priori* is that a thing is what it is and if it is self-conscious, it does not try to "true" to itself. You do not accuse a tiger if it devours your cow. You accuse either your fate or your lack of skill for the proper upkeeping of domestic animals. And properly speaking, it is surely the latter which ought to be lamented. But then why so? Because you are a thinking being and you could have very well prevented the cow being devoured by the tiger. Had your cow been kept within a safe boundary, she could not have been devoured by the tiger. Bountiful Nature during her onward evolutionary march endowed the animal species with thinking capacity, so that it could be able to adapt and adjust in a better way. And this evolved what is called Homo Sapiens. So, even if you are still an animal, you are a thinking being besides. This was pointed out for the first time by Aristotle in Western culture and by Kapil of Samkhya Philosophy in Indian culture. This philosophy says that *Prakṛti* evolved *mahat* or *buddhi* in course of its evolution.

Well, I have taken the above detour merely to point out and emphasize the fact that a human being is not just an instinct-borne animal, but he is also a rational thinker. Here then, a very pertinent question arises. If a human being is both an instinct-borne animal and also a rational thinker, it is surely within his choice to follow this instinct and discard being rational. Why should not his instinct prevail over his reason. Now, if in the evolutionary march of Nature, reason is added to animality its being so added could not have been without any purpose. Acting rationally must have to be reckoned as superior to behaving instinctively reckoned. And the very existence of the possibility of a choice here is itself defamatory instinct and appreciatory of reason.

Now, let us come back to the topic we were discussing earlier in connection with profit earning by a business concern.Well, we have already conceded that every business corporate is perhaps justified to earn "legitimate" profit. But if our own long discussion about the basic nature of a human being is correct no business corporate has the moral right to charge even a whit more than the legitimate profit. I had better quote here a very erudite writer about business ethics, Rajiv Kumar Mishra. He in his book *Business Ethics* says, "According to Milton Freidman, Business has only one Social responsibility to use resources and engage in actions designed to increase its profits so long as it remains within the rules of the game, which is to say, engage in open and free competition, without deception and fraud".

"Conventional business leaders feel that there is no commonality in the two objectives. While the objective of a business is to maximise profits and shareholder's money, ethics are perceived as benevolence, charity, and social responsibility."

"However, the holistic meaning of ethics is much wider and covers the entire gamut of business operations transparently on principle. Ethical practices are deeply embedded in business plans and form the core of business strategy." (*Business Ethics* — Rupa & Co, New Delhi, 2006, p. 41)

This above remark of R.K. Mishra is a clear advocacy of the

principle that business concerns must be grounded on ethical foundations. But then there are thinkers galore who think otherwise. They say that if in a business concern profiteering is not resorted to they are bound to die out sooner or later who would dare run a business incurring loss, or at best by incurring no loss but earning no profit either.

But then, a sound ethics would not stipulate that a business concern must not earn any profit at all. We have been stressing all the time that earning reasonable profit is ethically sacrosanct. We recognise that leaders have to meet not only the cost of manufacturing of the goods, but also that of maintaining the corporate workers to their utter satisfaction. Further, they have to pay quite a number of taxes, and also have to care about for the increase of shareholders dividends. And apart from all these liabilities they have to maintain themselves and their families in a decent and dignified way. They are, therefore, logically and ethically entitled to charge as much profit as is adequate to meet all the above-mentioned excuses.

Now, it needs to be very much emphasized that those who think that ethical business dealings cannot earn any profit are wrong. And what I am saying is borne out by actual findings. I shall give below just an example in order to authenticate what I have just said. This example is taken from R.K. Mishra's above mentioned book itself. He narrates here his findings in his own study of the company Wipro Limited which has hub at Bangalore. He writes, "The phenomenal growth of the company is not always in the best of business environment and with no risk. It has faced all the difficulties and ethical dilemma of a fast growing company. . . . But in spite of these risks and tough business environment to succeed company has always played fair game. The fair treatment given to the workforce shareholders, and society is worth appreciating. The company has hardly resorted to poaching professionals from other companies nor adopted unethical practices of damaging others' reputation".

"Azim Premji (the Chairman of Wipro) has tried to incorporate work ethics and social responsibility as the core business strategy. He has not publicised the causes Wipro has undertaken and high moral values they represent. Indeed they implemented the *niskama* way of running the Largest Infocom Company. Rendering near perfect service quality to the entire overseas customers with sincere efforts to be ethical and transparent without bothering for immediate results and gain has paid rich dividends." (*Ibid.*, p. 192-93) Well, it is quite clear from R.K. Mishra's statement alone that Wipro even being ethical is not all a losing concern but is rather a profit-earning one so much so that it pays to its shareholders rich dividends.

Now, before I close my article, I would also like to acquaint my readers to the present trend of thinking on the part of the business leaders in respect of their business-related aims and objectives. And for this, I shall just reproduce here, Mark Gender's report which appeared in the *Times of India*, Patna, dated 14th September, 2007, under the title 'Let's Make Markets Friendly'. The report is "In 2006, we drew together a team of leaders from organisations such as ABB, Alcan, Amnesty International Group, BP, Dr. Reddy's, Ford, International Institute for Sustainable Development, Infosys Technologies, KPMG, McKinsey and Standard Chartered. We challenged them in particular to look at the role of global business in society. Inevitably, such a team has differences, not always along a line separating business from civil society. But they all agreed on their findings.

"Their opening statement was unexpected. We all believe that for companies to succeed into the future they must play a greater role in contributing to solving the problems that society faces, including environmental degradation, poverty and the abuse of human rights."

This report does not say, "The prupose of business is to create shareholder value". It says the purpose of a global company is "To provide ever better goods and services in a way that is profitable, ethical and respects the environment, the individuals and the communities in which it operates".

Now, if it is clear that ethics is a necessity for a business profession, it is no less necessity for such other professions a dire necessity as medical practice, teaching by teachers, legal practice, press-reporting, etc., etc., as well. I shall not go here into any detail about the low level of degradation to which those professions have come to. Most of us are already aware of this. But I must stress one specific point here that the only remedy for all these fast deteriorating professions is Professional Ethics. But then, any ethical norm whether professional or individualistic must not be entertained just mere conceptually, but it must be made an integral part of the very mode of one's behaviour.

Chapter – 2

Profession and Ethics—Talk in Profession

Debashis Guha

The nature of contemporary ethics is such that even an old fashioned philosopher having a heavy leaning on pure normative discussion and a more modern philosopher thinking it smart to deal in meta-ethics would like to think twice before they stick to their passions in an orthodox way. Though there have been a great hullabaloo by meta-ethicists, particularly of Ayer's legacy and by some old hats in norms to stop a growing menace (or confusion) called, "applied ethics", it has nevertheless solidly set its foot within ethics. Yet, what is within ethics was not in full view until another one mushroomed called, "professional ethics", and as usual there has been philosophical din and bustle going to the extent of stopping this nuisance. Alas! It has established its worth by now. Yet, fading relics of heat should be extinguished for skeptics are not so good people to bear them for long. Let me take up this task to establish the worth of "ethics talk in profession" in some possible ways that I have in store. Well, that attempt makes moderners proud as far as it is within meta-ethics, and, therefore, we may call it a case of *justification of ethics—talk in profession*. However, it is primarily important to know what we mean by "ethics-talk in profession". For that purpose, we should know the meaning of "profession" which is another aim of this chapter to unfold.

Taking an oblique turn first, we may know what "profession" is not. It is not to be confused with business, that is, to think that a profession amounts to be involved in some business to earn profit. Business is one among many full time activities or engagements. Professional engagements unlike commercial business activities do something more rather than mere financial profit making. Professionals have engagements to achieve different *ideals* or *service based ideals*. This is top or primary in their agenda in life rather than to eke out a living or earn as much as they can. In that sense, although many professionals might have commercial ideals but that is not equivalent to earn or to make profit (limits unknown) rather, to "serve" the public, the nation or the international community. However, in doing so none is so foolish as to disregard his or her well-being. It is clear, therefore, that "profession" may be understood too narrowly as mere business engagement to earn a living to make profit, or too widely to mean serving the masses by abnegating self. As earning and profit do make some sense in profession, they may be understood differently as far as earnings are in terms of fixed salaries and incentives, which is, *institutionally limited*, checked and balanced. Also true is that such professionals imply several *restrictions* on themselves in terms of profits even if they may have ample opportunities to cut loose (never mind some people habitually doing so because truly speaking they are not professionals). Yet, "profession" carries with it the sense of duties in the sense of "due" and this in turn involve "right" or "legal claims" to what they owe, and obviously they may raise voice, fight and seek justice. Speaking about "profession" would involve basing charges upon the time, energy, skill and rightfully expect to get back what they should. Hence, "profession" for an understanding involves intrinsic and extrinsic limits to earning, and dues and rights as well. Thus understood, "profession" is clearly neither merely an occupation nor business, it is "something more".

To carry on the clarification of meaning of "profession", we come to know that a profession demands an accurate or at best near accurate knowledge of the basic elements of professional activities or tasks or duties and obligations. The knowledge need not be dormant rather, it should be dynamic or practical. That is not sufficient, as an amateur may be as knowledgeable as a professional about these things is and be very dynamic. We know some of our next-door neighbours who are revered amateur teachers. Yet, they do not have a teaching profession or are not professionals for they are not "members permanently engaged in a specialized group activity". Amateurs like professionals may not be permanent in terms of dedication and application. Even if they are so, most of the time they may be doing some extra work to earn more or to satisfy one's academic interests or even work for personal dignity and rewards. They do not have any servicebased ideal as has been gifted to them by an agency or institution. If one argues that we do have selfless teachers not appointed or covenanted, who life long teach for teaching's sake or to spread knowledge to commoners without even taking a pence and may be thus at a state to beg for living, for he or she does not have another occupation or business or profession, is still not comparable to the professional teacher. The reason is simple, we have stated that an appointment, a covenant, a contract along with fixed duties, rights and earning would be necessary to conceive of a profession and there is no reason to imagine them as self-sacrificers. In that case, the example of our great amateur would be pointless. Moreover, amateurs often commit errors in judgements, decision making and remain scot-free for there are no regulation in principle to check them or correct or punish them. One may still argue that professionals (even best ones) do commit errors (also knowingly) and remain scot-free. The point is that in principle, they are expected not to do such things, and a hawk eye, a deterrence in the form of rules or statutes is there. Quite often then not they are punished in cases of derogation of professional life.

It is due to this that "profession" involves both care for "quality of life" and "quality of work life" within realms of well-defined duties, obligations, rights and profits. In fact, lot of confusion in our minds may be due to *derogatory sense* of "professional". We often think that to have a profession is to have "capacity of opposites" like, a doctor either saving or killing a sick person. A professional is thus taken as a cunning person who would go to any extreme as some businessmen do to gain profits and/or to just neglect duties. We often say that "he is a very professional teacher" in this derogatory sense without knowing that we have done a blunder in using the term in such a manner. Why should "professional" be taken as "most cunningly done self motivated activities" when we have been pressing the point that a service based ideal is supreme to it with certain checks, and now knowing that a care for "quality of life and quality of work life" is needed? Hence, a doctor who kills is what we call a "killer" and not a "professional" doctor. They are treated accordingly in the legal field. On the other hand a "professional" footballer may earn a lot and yet have a noble ideal to entertain the masses by virtue of skilled play forgetting damages to his body (often insured) and to be sure, the person does have a qualitative work life and care for quality in social life (Games and sports does contribute to it). Interestingly, the person is well paid by an agency or organization through a contract and is thus in no sense an amateur footballer or a crooked businessman.

With this, we come to realize that it would be wise to talk about clients and their interests and welfare when we talk about "profession" and "professional". In view of clients a profession carries with it sense of *care for internal and external goods*, the former being the uniquely desirable thing for the client, whereas the latter is the beneficial thing for the client. For instance, for a teacher, the clients being pupils, the former good is "finding out proper methodology of teaching a subject", whereas the latter is to contribute to "good results in terms of marks or percentage" for the student. Often amateurs and business-oriented teachers might not take care of both or any one.

Another matter, a little debated is, "profession" truly so-called, needs to be activities covering those which are more than or exceeding duties bestowed on them, called "supererogatory" actions. Prof. J. O. Urmson[1] calls such professional "Saints and Heroes" in a "non-religious" sense but does not agree that "supererogation" has a deontic sense rather, it is purely *exceeding act* we prefer to do in the spirits of disinterestedness and fearlessness in "being a little more generous, forbearing, helpful or forgiving"[2]. However, Professor Mike W. Martin[3] does not agree on this "non-deontic" standpoint to say that "profession" does cover "supererogation" with a clear "deontic" import. They are "responsibilities" or "genuine responsibilities"[4] which ought to be taken by all professionals in a judicious way. Whatever may be the outcome of the squabble, we come to know that speaking about "profession" would involve "beyondness of duties" (may be, it is to go 'beyond' individuality to sociality and then to transcendentality). A person having a "profession" may be thus understood as the one who apart from other things, transcends the corporeal duties to cover welfaristic and more than that, the ideal of liberation of souls in bondage. Great it may be but not so, if we believe Urmson that in considering notions of "supererogation", spiritual / religious imputations won't do, there is otherwise a category confusion. Any way, this is not a place to settle this dispute.

It is time now to reflect on the meaning of "ethics-talk in profession". It is simply considering the question of desirability, right, good, ought, duties, rights, obligations, responsibilities as well as virtues and values in professions and of professionals. If we think carefully, such 'talk' would involve several professional decision-makings and acts for their desirability, goodness and so on. In this regard, it is but natural that there will be major controversies regarding the justificatory part or the reasons in favour or disfavour of something being desirable and so on in a professional field. Hence, precisely, "ethics talk in profession" would involve, "talk of ethical desirability or ethical worth" in cases of professional decision making and acts involving disagreements as well as agreements.

The meaning of "ethics talk in profession" being clear as we imagine, we further ask, why at all is it necessary? What happens if in ethics, we, the ethicists do not consider such "talk" as meaningful? Further, what happens if in such "talk" professionals are not a party? These are *skeptical* questions, which may be best jokingly, replied as if both parties do not participate in such "talk" they are perhaps not doing *something within ethics*, and that is a great harm to that field. The staunch skeptics unperturbed would retort "In fact, the 'something' (professional ethics) is 'something bogus' which some of you have discovered to save the case of ethics as useful but without it, everything will remain fine". This is in reality skeptic's full circle, returning to pooh! pooh! Professional Ethics and even Applied Ethics.

One way of justifying why "professional ethics" is within the field of ethics and not an unnecessary or imaginary task undertaken by some ethicists of "non-analytic interest" is that having "non-analytic interest" in ethics have been looked down as "improper" by the logical positivists and many snob analysts who think that ethics ought to focus on analysis of concepts and ethical language and nothing more. It is not our business as ethicists to interfere in professionals' diverse fields in the name of ethicality and bring it within the field of ethics. Rather, we should be restricted to analysis of ethical language and to the question of justification in ethics. For our poor non-philosopher professionals the message is that they are competent enough to do good for themselves and it would be needless to either take help of ethicists or academic ethics in order to glorify the case of professional ethics. What they have is unique professional *ethos* and working knowledge of good decision-making and, therefore, needs no academic ethics.

If we take the case of ethicists championing the case of normative ethics, applied ethics and professional ethics, there is absolutely no point in thinking that meta-ethics has been sorted out. However, when we imagine a professional doctor coming across an assertion: "organ donation is just or right" or that when he himself asserts in that way, hopefully, he has his own way to explain the notion of "just" and "right" without any idea about academic meta-ethics. Equally true is that the person might naturally speak about a norm or norms like well-being, benevolence or duty to explain why he uses "right" and "just" with "organ donation" as an intentional decision of a donor. This he does without any academic idea about norms of ethics. More interesting in that the person might debate at length about the justification of one norm over others to enable others in his professional coterie to take a practical decision regarding organ donors in their organizations or institution, which they would allow as ethically right and just. With this, they have applied their ethical norms in intersubjective discussion and corroboration of views without any idea about practical ethics.

Not so naive are the ethicists or a non-philosopher professional *trained* well in ethics. However, equally true for them is to engage in all these three things, the meta-ethical, the normative and the practical. Ethicists might go a step forward to show that "right" and "just" are notion not to be logically defined for such and such reasons, and, therefore, for their meaning we need more clarifications, may be in terms of duty or benevolence or utility and argue at length to show why such and such explanation holds good, thus supporting a particular normative view. These trained people would be more academic and logical than the naive doctor to show why "right" and "good" needs to be explained for their meaning. However, any treatment of ethical language by the trained ethicist has some connection with normative assertions as far as such language has a strong and historically long normative anchor. This becomes particularly evident when ethicists or even naive professionals are pressed upon with "why" questions. It will be needless to say that analysis of ethical language for their truth and meaning need not depend purely on the non-cognitive basis because we have seen the difficulties of the orthodoxy of ethical language being functional in one particular way. In a sense the cases of both naive doctors and trained ethicists justifies the close association of meta-ethical and normative discussions within ethics. Taking the case of resolution of value-laden practical problem by the ethicist or the doctor or both would further involve an ethically oriented debate, that is, about "why" decisions like "organ donation" is right and just and so on, and what exactly needs to be done which has a human face not merely a pragmatic value. Such debate leads the parties to further consideration of norms. In naive cases, unknowingly norms are called upon by virtue of ethical knowledge one has through ethical experience in teeming biotic society one lives; whereas in trained cases, this may be done more consciously by virtue of both ethical experience and academic knowledge. In any case, *artificially* as in latter case, or *naturally* as in former case, norms are into service. There is no doubt that such application of ethical knowledge raises questions of justification, which is meta-ethical in nature. And in considering a case of ethical debate, natural unfolding of the meaning of "desirability-language" is made possible. Hence, naively or scholarly, any way, ethics involves all the three things not one. For the present purpose, 'ethics-talk' becomes important in professions as a whole involving all three components not any one. It is thus pointless to argue that 'ethics-talk' in profession is either meaningless or beyond ethics proper because it is not purely analytic in nature rather, cares for the non-analytic practical adventure. A sweeping remark to follow is that wholesome ethics is in essence not purely analytic, it does have strong practical inclination. It is for this main reason that 'ethical discussion' in profession does make a sense or that we may sensibly imagine an "ethics-talk in profession".

Now, let us imagine two worlds—one in which there are professionals (non-philosophers) having concerns for desirability questions and practical urgencies of value resolution and another one in which there are no such concerns in the name of the 'ethics'. In the first world, ethics-talk is possible and in the second, it is ruled out. What happens if following the clarion call of our analysts we disregard professionals and ethicists having ethical concerns? Nothing more and nothing less than that we live in a world where either ethicists are imagined as self declared *gurus* or chauvinists taking up all practical concerns of value or that there are no such people as there are no value-laden problems.

The first alternative is ruled out as for the ethicists or for the non-philosophers, practical concern of value makes no sense to our analysts. Yet, if our analysts rule out chauvinists they need not rule out practical concern for value because such concern is possible without chauvinism. It may be made possible through ethical dialogue and consensus. The second alternative of imagining a world devoid of value-laden practical problems poses serious problems if we take that to be true because value-laden problems or raising questions of ethical value or those of should or ought in moral sense are not there because ethicists think so or that some professionals impute that sense rather, they are intrinsic to some decision-making in professional life. The intentional decision-making and subsequent acts in professional life raises serious questions for the professionals and others in the society (for they are influenced by such decision-making and acts) in the sense of: "why should we or should we not take some such decisions irrespective of the mere facts that there is a rule or something has been followed or something is customary or something has been thus far found beneficial to such and such people"? In our world where our intentional decision-making and acts influences a large part of the entire ecological community, we cannot and need not abstain from facing such questions as such tendency may be itself immoral for many reasons we already have. The world of our analysts will thus bereft of people who take care of should and ought in decision-making. It may well be that they stop asking, why should such things be treated as a duty or right or obligation or responsibility? A world bereft of such things rules out with it the questions of norms, debating about norms and their possible or actual applications. Tragically, in that world, an analyst will carefully look into truth and meaning of ethical language completely detached from life of decision-making or public life of value concerns without imagining that concern for ethical language can never be free from actual concerns in ethical life and ethical dialogue. Ethics without concern for professional ethics is thus incomplete; it does not take the value of professional life seriously, and ethical concern in language is not at all serious if language is detached from complex structures of ethical life of Homo Sapiens.

REFERENCES

1. Urmson, J. O., "Saints and Heroes", from *Ethics: History, Theory and Contemporary Issues*, (Eds) Steven M. Cahn & Peter Markie (Eds), Oxford University Press, Oxford, 1998.
2. *Ibid.*, p. 703.
3. Martin, Mike W., "Personal Ideals and Professional Responsibilities" in *Applied Ethics in a Trouble World*, (Eds) Edgar Morscher *et al.*, Kluwer Academic Publishers, The Netherlands, 1938.
4. *Ibid.*, pp. 173-703

Chapter – 3

Professional Morality and the Principles of Justice

Begum Bilkis Banu

Ethics is the discipline concerned with what is morally good and bad, right and wrong. The subject of ethics deals with issues relating to practical decision-making and its all embracing practical nature, links it with many other areas of study including anthropology, biology, economics, history, politics, sociology and so on. However, ethics remains distinct from such areas of study in that it is occupied not so much with factual knowledge as it is with values. It is occupied with human conduct as it ought to be rather knowledge as it actually is. There are certain principles or code of conduct usually regarded as the general code of conduct. Some such principles are — "You ought to tell the truth", "You ought to keep your promises". We have certain professional code of conduct relating to each profession and as such we have what is called legal ethics, medical ethics, business ethics and the ethics of a teacher. "Physicians ought to save human life whenever possible". "Teachers ought to encourage and develop the intellectual curiosity and inquiry" are the principles of medical ethics and educational ethics respectively.

Mike. W. Martin in his article on professional ordinary morality makes the following distinctions between *professional morality* and *ordinary morality*—

(1) Professional morality consists of the standards endorsed by professional or professional societies. Ordinary morality is the set of standards people endorse in their non-professional private life.

(2) Professional morality is the set of binding moral obligations to which professionals ought to be committed because of their special skills, function and working milieu, etc. Ordinary morality is the set of valid moral considerations and morally correct judgements considered in abstraction from special context of the profession and specific moral obligations of the professionals.

(3) Ordinary morality in some sense emanates from or has its origin in basic features of the human conditions. Whereas professional morality emanates from the special roles of professionals.

(4) Professional morality is a set of valid moral principles which sometimes requires acts that are immoral for anyone except persons having professional status. Ordinary morality is the set of considerations which would make the acts immoral in the case of non-professional agents.

Using these definitions it is plain that there are professional moralities and there are non-professional moralities. A professional is committed to both professional code of conduct as well as to general code of conduct. Now the questions—what a professional ought to do if there is a moral conflict between professional code of conduct and the general code of conduct? The principle, "One ought to tell truth" may come in conflict with the medical code of conduct that "Physicians ought to save human life". Should the physicians be truthful to his critically ill patient when the patient's knowledge of his condition will make his recovery unlikely or impossible? Here, although it appears that to honour one principle is to violate the other yet it is not the case. When the physician tells a lie to save the life of a critically ill patients, it does not imply that he is upholding a professional code of conduct and is thereby violating the general code of conduct. "One ought to save human life" is also the principle of general morality. Morality demands that human life ought to be saved at any cost. If this type of conflict arises before a non-professional then in that case also a non-professional is expected to save human life at the cost of telling a lie. The principle that "Human life ought to be saved" is the code of conduct both for the professionals as well as for non-professionals. In order to uphold this principle, sometimes one may have to go against the principle that "One ought to tell the truth". The physician ought to tell his patient an uncouraging untruth. All moral philosophers excepting Kant would argue for saving the patient's life. Moral principles allow for exceptions otherwise it leads to moral fanaticism. Only a morally fanatic person will uphold the principle that one ought to tell the truth at the cost of a person's life. "Moral fanaticism results from misapprehending the nature of ideals, moral nihilism from failing to recognize the primacy of duty"[1].

There are some people like B. Freedmen and Alan. H. Goldman who believe that professional ethics is independent of general ethics and that professional ethics is autonomous and deserves a separate ethical treatment. Benjamin Freedman says, "We sometimes attribute to professionals a morality of their own, attached to their own, attached to their professional role. By that I mean that professionals are more constrained by their professional values than are non-professionals and conversely take into less account those considerations which ordinarily apply.[2] Freedman means to say that professionals by joining a profession acquire an obligation and they are more obliged to their professions than they would be were they not professionals. Professional morality places professional values at a higher position in the ethical hierarchy. It gives them greater ethical importance than does ordinary morality. According to Freedman, professional morality is autonomous because there are cases where it is morally right for a professional to act in a ascertain manner, whereas it is immoral for a non-professional to act in that way. For example, it is immoral for an ordinary man to perform open heart surgery but is permissible for cardiovascular surgeons to perform them and this is because of their particular professionals status. However, the example given by Freedman in support of his view that professional morality is autonomous is inadequate. Since a cardiovascular surgeon is an authorized member of medical profession, therefore, it is morally right for him to perform an open heart surgery and anyone who is an authorised member of that profession can do the same. This in no way imply that professional morality is autonomous or that it is independent of general morality.

Freedman has another reasons for holding the thesis that professional morality is autonomous and the reason is that professional morality can justify peccadilloes. He says that it is permissible for a teacher in professional role to commit reaches of manners in pursuit of professional values (these might be education or pursuit of truth). It is permissible for news reporters in pursuit of their value to breach social customs as well.

However, as against Freedman it may be said that professional morality cannot be said to be autonomous simply on the ground that it allows for breaches of manners in pursuit of professional values. The fact that professional morality allows for breaches of manner in pursuit of truth does not give professional morality an independent status. Professional morality allows for breach of manner or breach of ethical codes so long as it is understood in terms of greater good or so long as it has a good consequence. Not only professional morality allows for breach of conduct but general morality also allows for breach of conduct so long as it has a good consequence.

Russell says, "Every system should allow loopholes and exceptions, for if it does not it will in the end crush all that is best in man".[3]

Any profession whether it is a legal, medical or teaching profession or any other profession is concerned with people and is a kind of public service. Since in any profession other people are involved, therefore, whenever any conflict arises, we always have to ask whether the action that we are doing would be just to them. Would the action violate their right? Our general morality demands that we recognize that other people have legitimate claims on us. They recognize their claim is to accept the basic principle of justice. Thus the concept of justice is fundamental in morality. The principle of justice must be upheld by all whether professional or non-professional. In order to act on justice sometimes a professional has to act in professional context on the general ethical norms. Professional morality like ordinary morality consists in a readiness to do justice to all.

REFERENCES

1. H.B., *Kant, Moral Philosophy*. 1970
2. Benjamin Freedman: "A metaethics for professional morality". *Ethics* Vol.9 No.1986.
3. Edited by Robert E. Egner. *The Basic Writings of B. Russell*, p. 442

Chapter – 4

Theoretical Issues in Business Ethics

Dr. Archana Srivastava

Business ethics is a "form of applied ethics that examines ethical rules and principles within a commercial context; the various moral or ethical problems that can arise in a business setting; and any special duties or obligations that apply to persons who are engaged in commerce". Generally speaking, business ethics is a normative discipline, whereby particular ethical standards are advocated and then applied. It makes specific judgements about what is right or wrong, which is to say, it makes claims about what *ought* to be done or what *ought not* to be done. While there are some exceptions, business ethicists are usually less concerned with the foundations of ethics (meta-ethics), or with justifying the most basic ethical principles, and are more concerned with practical problems and applications, and any specific duties that might apply to business relationships.

Conflicting Interests

Business ethics can be examined from various perspectives, including the perspective of the employee, the commercial enterprise, and society as a whole. Very often, situations arise in which there is conflict between one or more of the parties, such that serving the interest of one party is a detriment to the other(s).

For example, a particular outcome might be good for the employee, whereas, it would be bad for the company, society, or *vice versa*. Some ethicists (e.g., Henry Sidgwick) see the principal role of ethics as the harmonization and reconciliation of conflicting interests.

Ethical Issues and Approaches

Philosophers and others disagree about the purpose of a business in society. For example, some suggest that the principal purpose of a business is to maximize returns to its owners, or in the case of a publicly-traded concern, its shareholders. Thus, under this view, only those activities that increase profitability and shareholder value should be encouraged. Some believe that the only companies that are likely to survive in a competitive marketplace are those that place profit maximization above everything else. However, some point out that self interest would still require a business to obey the law and adhere to basic moral rules, because the consequences of failing to do so could be very costly in fines, loss of licensure, or company reputation. The economist Milton Friedman is a leading proponent of this view.

Other theorists contend that a business has moral duties that extend well beyond serving the interests of its owners or stockholders, and that these duties consist of more than simply obeying the law. They believe a business has moral responsibilities to so-called stakeholders, people who have an interest in the conduct of the business, which might include employees, customers, vendors, the local community, or even society as a whole. They would say that stakeholders have certain rights with regard to how the business operates, and some would even suggest that this even includes rights of governance.

Some theorists have adapted social contract theory to business, whereby companies become quasi-democratic associations, and employees and other stakeholders are given voice over a company's operations. This approach has become especially popular subsequent to the revival of contract theory in political philosophy, which is largely due to John Rawls' *A Theory of Justice*, and the advent of the consensus-oriented approach to solving business problems, an aspect of the "quality movement" that emerged in the 1980s. Professors Thomas Donaldson and Thomas Dunfee proposed a version of contract theory for business, which they call Integrative Social Contracts Theory. They posit that conflicting interests are best resolved by formulating a "fair agreement" between the parties, using a combination of (i) macro-principles that all rational people would agree upon as universal principles, and (ii) micro-principles formulated by actual agreements among the interested parties. Critics say the proponents of contract theories miss a central point, namely, that a business is someone's property and not a mini-state or a means of distributing social justice.

Ethical issues can arise when companies must comply with multiple and sometimes conflicting legal or cultural standards, as in the case of multinational companies that operate in countries with varying practices. The question arises, for example, ought a company to obey the laws of its home country, or should it follow the less stringent laws of the developing country in which it does business? To illustrate, United States law forbids companies from paying bribes either domestically or overseas; however, in other parts of the world, bribery is a customary, accepted way of doing business. Similar problems can occur with regard to child labour, employee safety, work hours, wages, discrimination, and environmental protection laws.

It is sometimes claimed that a Gresham's law of ethics applies in which bad ethical practices drive out good ethical practices. It is claimed that in a competitive business environment, those companies that survive are the ones that recognize that their only role is to maximize profits. On this view, the competitive system fosters a downward ethical spiral.

Rushworth Kidder developed a fascinating way to address ethical conflicts. He calls it a "trilemma". Instead of feeling stuck in a choice between violating your ethics and doing something painful but ethical, he suggests exploring if there is a third, unexplored option.

Corporate Ethics Policies

Many companies have formulated internal policies pertaining to the ethical conduct of employees. These policies can be simple exhortations in broad, highly-generalized language (typically called a corporate ethics statement), or they can be more detailed policies, containing specific behavioural requirements (typically called corporate ethics codes). They are generally meant to identify the company's expectations of workers and to offer guidance on handling some of the more common ethical problems that might arise in the course of doing business. It is hoped that having such a policy will lead to greater ethical awareness, consistency in application, and the avoidance of ethical disasters.

An increasing number of companies also requires employees to attend seminars regarding business conduct, which often include discussion of the company's policies, specific case studies, and legal requirements. Some companies even require their employees to sign agreements stating that they will abide by the company's rules of conduct.

Many companies are assessing the environmental factors that can lead employees to engage in unethical conduct.

Not everyone supports corporate policies that govern ethical conduct. Some claim that ethical problems are better dealt with by depending upon employees to use their own judgement.

Others believe that corporate ethics policies are primarily rooted in utilitarian concerns, and that they are mainly to limit the company's legal liability, or to curry public favour by giving the appearance of being a good corporate citizen. Ideally, the company will avoid a lawsuit because its employees will follow the rules. Should a lawsuit occur, the company can claim that the problem would not have arisen if the employee had only followed the code properly.

Sometimes there is disconnection between the company's code of ethics and the company's actual practices. Thus, whether or not such conduct is explicitly sanctioned by management, at worst, this makes the policy duplicitous, and, at best, it is merely a marketing tool.

To be successful, most ethicists would suggest that an ethics policy should be:

- Given the unequivocal support of top management, by both word and by example.
- Explained in writing and orally, with periodic reinforcement.
- Doable....something employees can both understand and perform.
- Monitored by top management, with routine inspections for compliance and improvement.
- Backed up by clearly stated consequences in the case of disobedience.
- Remain neutral and non-sexist.

Ethics Officers

Ethics Officers (sometimes called "Compliance" or "Business Conduct Officers") have been appointed formally by organizations since the mid-1980s. One of the catalysts for the creation of this new role was a series of fraud, corruption and abuse scandals that afflicted the U.S. defence industry at that time. This led to the creation of the Defence Industry Initiative (DII), a pan-industry initiative to promote and ensure ethical business practices. The DII set an early benchmark for ethics management in corporations. In 1991, the Ethics Officer Association was founded at the Centre for Business Ethics(at Bentley College, Waltham, MA) as a professional association for those responsible for managing organizations' efforts to achieve ethical best practices. The membership grew rapidly (the EOA now has over 1,100 members) and was soon established as an independent organization. Another critical factor in the decisions of companies to appoint ethics/ compliance officers was the passing of the Federal Sentencing

Guidelines for Organizations in 1991, which set standards that organizations (large or small, commercial and non-commercial) had to follow to obtain a reduction in sentence if they should be convicted of a federal offence. Although intended to assist judges with sentencing, the influence in helping to establish best practices has been far-reaching.

In the wake of numerous corporate scandals between 2001-04 (affecting large corporations like Enron, WorldCom and Tyco), even small and medium-sized companies have begun to appoint ethics officers. They often report to the Chief Executive Officer and are responsible for assessing the ethical implications of the company's activities, making recommendations regarding the company's ethical policies, and disseminating information to employees. They are particularly interested in uncovering or preventing unethical and illegal actions. This trend is partly due to the Sarbanes-Oxley Act in the United States, which was enacted in reaction to the above scandals. A related trend is the introduction of risk assessment officers that monitor how shareholders' investments might be affected by the company's decisions.

The effectiveness of ethics officers in the marketplace is not clear. If the appointment is made primarily as a reaction to legislative requirements, one might expect the efficacy to be minimal, at least, over the short term. In part, this is because ethical business practices result from a corporate culture that consistently places value on ethical behaviour, a culture and climate that usually emanates from the top of the organization. The mere establishment of a position to oversee ethics will most likely be insufficient to inculcate ethical behaviour: a more systemic programme with consistent support from general management will be necessary.

The foundation for ethical behaviour goes well beyond corporate culture and the policies of any given company, for it also depends greatly upon an individual's early moral training, the other institutions that affect an individual, the competitive business environment the company is in and indeed, society as a whole.

NOTES

Above the Bottom Line: An Introduction to Business Ethics, Robert C. Solomon, Harcourt Brace Jovanovich, 1983

Business Ethics : A Kantian Perspective, Norman E. Bowie, Blackwell, 1999.

Business as Ethical and Business as Usual, Sterling Harwood, Belmont, CA: Wadsworth Publishing, 1996.

Companies With A Conscience, 3rd Edition, Howard Rothman and Mary Scott, Denver, CO: Myers Templeton, 2004.

De George, Richard T. (1999). *Business Ethics*. Prentice Hall.

Essays on Ethics in Business and the Professions, Jack N. Behrman, Engelwood Cliffs, NJ: Prentice Hall, 1988

Ethical Dilemmas in the Modern Corporation, Gerald F. Cavanagh, Prentice-Hall, 1988.

Ethics and the Management of Computer Technology: Proceedings of the Fourth National Conference on Business Ethics, National Conference on Business Ethics (4th: 1981: Bentley College) Cambridge, MA: Oelgeschlager, Gunn & Hain, 1981.

Knight, Frank (1935/1980). *The Ethics of Competition and Other Essays*. Univ. of Chicago Press.

Perspectives in Business Ethics, Laura Hartman, Burr Ridge, IL: McGraw-Hill, 2004

The Right Thing: Conscience, Profit and Personal Responsibility in Today's Business, Jeffrey L. Seglin, Spiro Press, 2003.

The Excellence of the Efficiency of the Learning Organisation that is the Hellenic Features of Current Economics Moral. Lea B. Virághalmy, Budapest, 2003 (Abstract)

Chapter – 5

A Critical Appraisal of Journalism-Ethics

Dr. Shiva Bhanu Singh

A human being is a rational, responsible, multi-relational and free agent who cannot remain indifferent to the consequences of his conduct. He can act in a good and right manner that is conducive to general well-being. On the other hand he can act in a harmful and undesirable manner. This requires regulation of his act and norm-prescription. In these circumstances ethical consideration becomes meaningful since they tell us about the rules and regulations to be adhered to and prohibitions to be avoided. Man lives in society and interacts with other members of society. His multiple needs and aspirations need different professions and vocations since every human being cannot undertake all the vocations and perform all the works of every profession. In order to regulate human conduct 'Professional Ethics' is established for every profession. Media-ethics, a sub-division of professional ethics deals with the ethical norms and standards of different forms of media like broadcast media, film, theatre, print media, electronic media, internet, etc. Media-ethics also deals with certain controversial issues related with media like sting-operations, yellow journalism, pornography, mass-journalism, telecasting blue firms, cyber crimes etc. Media ethics propagates values like Truth, Accuracy, Freedom of expression, etc. The ethical codes incorporated in media-ethics are promulgated by the (quasi) governmental agency responsible for licensing a profession. Violation of these codes may be subject to administrative (e.g., loss of license), civil or penal remedies. A code of ethics is a formal statement of organisation's values on certain ethical and social issues. Ethical codes are distinct from moral codes that may apply to the culture, education and religion of a whole society.

Journalism ethics is a part of media-ethics which aims to aid journalists in dealing with many ethical dilemmas, they may encounter. From highly sensitive issues like national security, to everyday questions, such as accepting a dinner from a source, putting a bumper sticker on one's car, publishing a personal opinion blog, a journalist must make decisions taking into account such things as the public's right to know, potential threats, reprisals and intimidations of all kinds, personal integrity, conflicts between editors, reporters and publishers or management, and many others such conundrums.

Freedom of speech is one of the most important features of media-ethics. Freedom of speech is the concept of the inherent human right to voice one's opinion publicly without fear of censorship or punishment. The right is enshrined in the United Nations' Universal Declaration of Human Rights and is granted formal recognition by the laws of most nations. None-the-less the degree to which the right is upheld in practice varies greatly from one nation to another. In some authoritarian forms of government overt government censorship is enforced while among liberal democracies, censorship has been claimed to occur in a different form and there are different approaches to issues such as hate speech, obscenity, and defamation laws. The United Nations Universal Declaration of Human Right, adopted in 1948, provides, in Article 19, that :

> "Everyone has the right to opinions without interference and to seek, receive and impart information and ideas through any media and regardless of frontiers.'

However, the rights provided in above article is subject to certain restrictions, but these shall only be such as are provided by law and are necessary : (a) For respect of the rights or reputations of others; (b) For the protection of national security or of public order, or of public health or morals. The right is further qualified by Article 20 which prohibits war propaganda, incitement to violence, and certain forms of hate speech. As far as Constitution of India is concerned, it guarantees freedom of speech to every citizen and there have been landmark cases in the Supreme Court of India that have affirmed the nation's policy of allowing free press and freedom of expression to every citizen. In India, citizens are free to criticize policies, politicians, bureaucracy and government organizations.

Journalism ethics and standards include principle of ethics and of good practice to address the specific challenges faced by professional journalists. The Fundamental codes and canons commonly appear in statements drafted by both professional journalism associations and individual print, broadcast, and online news organizations.

> "Every news organization has only its credibility and reputation to rely on."

Like many broader ethical systems, journalism ethics include the principle of "Limitation of harm". This often involves the withholding of certain details from reports such as the names of minor children, crime-victims' names or information not materially related to particular news, reports, release of which might, for example, harm someone's reputation.

The principles of good journalism are directed toward bringing the highest quality of news reporting to the public thus fulfilling the mission of timely distribution of information in service of the public interest. In case of violation of Journalism ethics, the journalists may face dismissal for ethical failures. Upholding professional standards also enhances the reputation of and trust in a news organization, which boosts the size of the audience it serves.

News manipulation is an important area of journalism ethics. News can manipulate and be manipulated. Governments and Corporations may attempt to manipulate news media; governments, for example, by censorship, and corporation by share ownership. The methods of manipulation are subtle and many. In the same way manipulation may be voluntary or involuntary.

The guidelines of journalism ethics lays emphasis that the journalists are expected to report the truth but they have to take care of public interest also. Sometimes truth may conflict with public interest and privacy. For instance, revelation of military secrets and over sensitive government information may be contrary to the public interest, even if it is true. In the same way right of privacy may conflict with free speech. Thus it can be said that publications of any news is not necessarily justified simply because that information is true.

Sometimes violation of regulatory norms are done by journalists for the sake of their vested interests or for cheap popularity and for promoting the sale of newspapers. Media ethics restrains the depiction of violence and sex and the presence of strong language. Again in the name of art, sometimes established values are neglected. In the name of art, media may deliberately attempt to break with existing norms and shock the audience. The extent to which this is acceptable is always a hot bed of ethical controversy. Again, audiences have different reactions to depictions of violence, nudity, coarse language, or to people in any other situation that is unacceptable to or stigmatized by the local culture or laws (such as the consumption of alcohol, homosexuality, illegal drug use, scatological images, etc.). Even with similar audiences, different organizations and even individual reporters have different standards and practices. These decisions often revolve around what facts are necessary for the audience to know.

The code of Ethics, generally accepted by the society of

professional journalists states : "Public enlightenment is the fore runner of justice and the foundation of democracy. The duty of the journalist is to further those ends by seeking truth and providing a fair and comprehensive account of events and issues. Conscientious journalists from all media and specialities strive to serve the public with thoroughness and honesty. Professional, integrity is the cornerstone of a journalists credibility.

The primary themes common to most codes of journalistic standards and ethics are the following :

(a) *Objectivity*— The journalists that maintain unequivocal separation between news and opinion. The reporters must avoid conflicts of interest and they should not accept bribes for reporting stories that affect the reporters' personal, economic or political interests. Again competing points of view must be presented in a balanced and unbiased manner. Persons who are the subject of adverse news stories must be given a reasonable opportunity to respond to the adverse information before the story is published or broadcast.

(b) *Accuracy*— Reporters are expected to be as accurate as far as possible, given the time allotted to story preparation and the space available and to seek reliable sources. The reporters must adhere to factual reporting after verifying facts through more than on eye witness. Controversial facts must be reported with attribution. Defendants at trial must be treated only as having "allegedly" committed crimes until conviction. The journalists must see that, corrections are published when errors are discovered.

(c) *Confidentiality*—The reporters must maintain confidentiality of anonymous sources. Pictures, sound and quotations must not be presented in a misleading context. Simulations, re-enactments, alterations and artistic imagings must be clearly labelled us such, if not avoided entirely.

(d) *Privacy*—Private persons have privacy rights that must be balanced against the public interest in reporting information about them, public figures have fewer privacy rights. The journalists are expected to recognize that private people have a greater right to control information about themselves than do public officials and others who seek power influence or attention, only an overriding public need can justify intrusion into any one's privacy.

(e) *Responsibility*— To serve the public's need to know, the journalist must take responsibility for scrutinizing the force of power in society, government and business among them — whose actions and decisions can materially affect our lives. On another level, the journalist must take responsibility for the facts that he/she reports and the conclusions he/she reaches.

(f) *Novelty*—Novelty is what attracts many a journalists in his or her career. A journalist is generally in search of novelty everywhere or, at least tries to find a new angle of view at old things in order to attract his reader or listener or spectator.

The journalist throughout the world are expected to follow the above ethical standards and guidelines but many a time complaints are lodged against the journalists for their careless reporting, biased and partial reporting, manipulated and articulated reporting due to certain influences, pressures or other vested interests. The root cause of such inaccurate, sensational and manipulated news items may be pressures applied by advertisers, government, political organizations, business and other powerful institutions — including the press itself. The role that sensationalism plays in selling a news product be it a newspaper or a television broadcast, is certainly another important factor.

The moral responsibility and social accountability of journalists increase in a democratic state because journalism is regarded as the Fourth Estate. Journalism has become an important institution of democracy through transparency and freedom of information. However, like so many institutions of democracy, journalism is also not free from common institutional evils such as unbridled ambitions, petty politicking and corruption. Like any other business, its primary aim is money-making and not nation building. This development has affected the flowering of true democracy and justice. In the present circumstances due to cut throat competition among different newspapers, and electronic channels, the journalists are bound to follow the ethical standards and professional norms otherwise their existence will be at stake. The social and political awakening of common people also has become a strong sanction for the journalists.

Chapter – 6

Ethical Dimensions of Medical Profession

Dr.. Sanjay Kumar Shukla

I

The present world scenario is marked by globalization which demands the specialised professionals in almost all walks of life. The emergence of new and newer professions is a quite natural phenomenon to cope with the rapidly changing and transforming socio-economic structure. A. human being is a responsible, free agent who is rational and discriminative as well. He, therefore, cannot remain indifferent to the consequence of his conduct. This requires regulated conduct and norm prescription. Ethics is the branch of philosophy, which studies human conduct to determine standards of good conduct. There can be as many professional ethics as there are professions. The human existence is multi-faceted and. multi-relational. Human needs and aspirations are also multiple and, therefore, all these require a variety of professions and vocations. It is due to the limitation of human genius that no individual can perform all the work of every profession. So human conduct in this regard needs regulation, both intra-professional and inter-professional. A professional ethics is basically a management ethics. It pertains to the management of a profession in the sense that it regulates the knowledge, will, skilful performance and distributive enjoyment of results, of that profession. The ideal of any profession is and has to be excellence which reminds us the ideal of *Bhagwad Gita* — *Yoga* is perfection in action (*Yogah Karmsu Kosalam*) Although every profession has to work out its own norms and regulations keeping in view the ultimate goal of excellence or perfection, but still we can point out general prerequisite of any profession as competence, commitment and punctuality.

II

Thousands of years ago, when human civilization was in its infancy, people attempted to help a fellow being who was ill or injured and thus the practice of medicine was born. Later, as the science grew, it became a full time occupation and doctors had to be specially trained in the art and science of medicine and it became a 'profession'. The medical student are asked to take the Hippocratic Oath — which originated in Greece. This oath is basically to keep them true and sincere to the good of humanity at large. This oath, being administered to medical practitioners before they are given licence to start practicing as physician, is a perfect: idealistic moral code for Doctors of Medicine. The medical profession is indoctrinated with the principle that medical treatment is based on compassion towards beings and it is not primarily meant for earning money or fulfilling other worldly desires. In Vedic India and even later for many centuries, physicians were told that medical practice was never fruitless; it always gave some benefit or other for the doctor, not necessarily material or momentary. It is clearly stated that sometimes *punya*, sometimes friendship, somewhere money, somewhere else fame guided medical profession. Often knowledge and experience forms its norm but never is treatment without its fruits (Kacid Dharma, Kacid Maitri, Kacid Vittam, *Kacid Yashah/ Kacid Arthavbodhasch Cikitsa Nasti Nisphala//*). Today, what we are witnessing in medical profession is that ethical motivation is replaced by monetary consideration. The selfless, dedicated service to humanity has become commercialized and turned into lucrative profession. The aim and purpose of medical science is also very clearly defined. "The 'physician-ness' of a physician consists in understanding the nature of the disease and in relieving of distress. The physician is not the lord of life." Vyadheh Tatvaparijnanam Vedanayasch Nigrah/ Aitad Vaidyasya. Vaidyatvam Na Vaidyah Prabhurayusah//). It is really a beautiful definition of the physician's duties and also his limitations. It emphasizes great skill and teaches humility too.

It is pertinent to raise the question that, are these values observed or upheld today? Apparently not, as the recent years have witnessed a change in this scenario. Gradually there has grown an increasing tendency amongst doctors to adopt measures that are not always for the good of the patient. This has produced in the public mind a mistrust of the medical profession. Why has this happened? It is due to the lack of emphasis on ethical values during the training of doctors or due to the absence of an efficient watchdog — institution that could guide and control doctors, or is it due to a general growth of *adharma* that is being reflected in the medical profession. It is obvious that the chief motivation of young people today to enter the medical profession is the desire to earn money. The medical profession is seen by them and their parents and by the public as a safe and lucrative avenue of affluent life. This is supported by the fact that parents are willing to pay large amount of fees and donations or even adopt malpractices to get their sons and daughters admitted into medical institutions. It is because of this initial handicap, we should not expect from the young doctors to be noble and altruistic. Strangely, over the past two decades there has been in our country a swing towards materialism, a tendency opposed to our own culture of simplicity and *dharma*. At every turn the present generation of doctors meets with crass materialism, opportunism and corruption from the lowest to the highest levels of society. The pursuit of wealth and material gain seem to be the sole aim that motivates individual and society. To expect the medical profession alone to be pure milk in an ocean of salt water is unrealistic. Still, as the medical profession has to deal with the life and death of human beings, it has to raise itself to an acceptable level of ethics, so that the public will repose confidence in the profession.

III

The medical profession is still considered to be the noble profession in the eyes of public. A good doctor is even now equated with God (*Vaidyo Narayano Harih*) and respected. Of course, there have been many situations when a different attitude is exhibited when medical help fails to achieve the desired result either due to negligence or incompetence doctor is called as lord of death—Yama's brother. (*Yamaraja Sahodara*). It is ironically stated that doctor being brother of *Yamraja* with the difference that *Yamaraja* only takes off the life while Doctor life and money too. (*Vaidyaraja Namastubhyam Yamaraja Sahodarah/ Yamastu Harati Pranan Vaidyah Prana Dhanani Call*). Hence, it is in fitness of things to analyse the code of conduct regarding the medical profession. It is pertinent to raise the question how accountability can be ensured in the medical field in case of several malpractices prevalent in this noble profession as spurious drugs, reckless surgery, illegal sex determination test, abortion, euthanasia, private practice even by government doctors and professors of medical college. The application of consumer protection act to the medical profession has created a situation where it has become necessary to re-examine and reassert various facets of the problem of medical ethics. The pressing need is to evolve a sound and efficient professional ethics of medical profession so that public may or will repose confidence in that profession which is intimately connected with human life.

I will be making here an attempt to sketch the *modus operandi* of doctors for material gains. They sometimes manipulate the condition of patient to be serious and critical so that more money can be extracted. They actually make money out of fear psychosis of both patient and attendant. It is seen that in some cases unnecessary clinical tests like Ultra-Sound, CT-Scan and MRI of patient is advised as there is fixed commission of doctors for each prescription to he paid by diagnostic centres. It is sometimes seen that lack of proper care and negligence of doctor and nursing staff during treatment may cause death of patient. Although sex determination test is legally banned but still in private nursing homes it is done in clandestine manner for which heavy foees is charged. Similarly abortion involves moral issue which is feetus killing either for unwanted child or preference for male child. We often come across in newspaper and magazine about drug rackets manufacturing spurious drugs and supplying them to medical dispensary and drug shops. It is heinous crime against humanity as poor public purchase the medicine with the hope and expectation that he or she will be cured. There is new trend of Doctor-Medical Representative clique in which some cases the doctor prescribes the newly launched medicine for material gains either in cash or gifts. Even though the private practice is legally banned and doctors get non-practicing allowances, still doctors and professors of medical college engage themselves in it for amassing huge wealth. The plight of primary health centre is deplorable as government doctors are often unwilling or reluctant to serve in rural areas which shows lack of dedication and devotion to their medical profession. Stringent measures are, therefore, necessary to ensure minimum five years rural service for new doctors so that casualties may be minimised in villages. The shocking news of trading human organs in which the involvement of some doctors is quite obvious clearly reflects that they are crazy about money. It is sometimes observed that blood transfusion to patient without careful matching makes his condition critical and even risk life. We find that in some cases patients die due to careless surgery by doctors. The postmortem report of doctors is very vital in case of murder trial but sometimes they provide fake report and thereby mislead the administration of justice for monetary gains. In euthanasia (right to die), the role of doctor becomes crucial as he has to ultimately decide whether patient has any chance of survival or recovery in future with advancement of medical research. He should not collude with relatives of patient if they want to kill. The patient for selfish purpose. We can also conceive the situation in which doctor conspires with the relatives of a person to make the death of that person a natural death. Doctor is after all the saviour of life and should not never act contrary to it.

IV

Medical ethics is the discipline of evaluating the merits, risks and social concerns of activities in the field of medicine. It comprises set of principles of—

1. *Beneficence :* A practitioner should act in the best interest of the patient. (*salus aegroti suprema lex*).
2. *Non-maleficence :* It lays down the principle of "first do not harm". (*primum non nocere*). It reminds a physician that he or she must consider the possible harm that any intervention might do.
3. *Autonomy :* The patient has the right to refuse or choose their treatment (*voluntas aegroti suprema lex*).
4. *Justice :* It concerns the distribution of scarce health resources, and the decision of who gets what treatment.
5. *Dignity :* The patient and the person treating the patient have the right to dignity.
6. *Truthfulness and honesty :* The patient should not be lied to, and deserves to know the whole truth about his/her illness and treatment.

The medical profession has long subscribed to a body of ethical statements developed primarily for the benefit of the patient. The principles adopted by the American Medical Association are not laws, but a code of conduct which define the essentials of honourable behaviour for the physician—

1. A physician shall be dedicated to providing competent

medical care, with compassion and respect for human dignity and rights.

2. A physician shall uphold the standard of professionalism and remains honest in all professional interactions.
3. A physician shall respect the right of patients, colleagues, and other health professionals, and shall safeguard patient confidences and privacy within the constraints of the law.
4. A physician shall continue to study, apply and advance scientific knowledge, maintain a commitment to medical education, make relevant information available to patients, colleagues, and the public, obtain consultation, and use the talents of other medical professionals.
5. A physician shall recognize a responsibility to participate in activities contributing to the improvement of the community and the betterment of public health.
6. A physician shall, while caring for a patient, regard the responsibility to the patient as paramount.
7. A physician shall support access to medical care for all people.

Teaching of medical ethics of undergraduates every alternate year of the medical courses, repeated refresher course in medical ethics for post graduates and practitioners, and strengthening of the powers of the Medical Council with a will to act are the necessary immediate requirements for making a medical profession really a noble profession. Ethical or *dharmic* values are essential for the existence and for the progress of any society and have to be preserved and practiced if human civilization has to progress. Since the medical profession deals with the problem of life and death, this argument is untenable that corruption is a universal phenomenon of society, the doctors belonging to elite noble profession must shoulder greater responsibilities. Hence, it is truism to say that the doctor and the teacher have to set a noble example before others in any civilized society.

Section – II

APPLIED ETHICS

Chapter – 7

Post-Modern Trends in Applied Ethics

Ramesh Chandra Sinha

In this chapter, I have attempted to give an account of post-modern relativistic ethics. In applied ethics, the ethical principles are required to be applied to practical moral problems. It is application of principles to human situations. Post-modern trends in ethics is relativistic. It is neither analytic nor universalistic. Post-modernity is against abstraction. Modern Philosophers of ethics love objectivity and analysis of language. Post-modern Philosophers are not impressed with objectivity and linguistic analysis Kant's 'Categorical Imperative' is under question. The conception of ethics is facing new challenges in the hands of post-modernists. Applied ethics provides relative frameworks within which practical moral problems can be solved. In recent times, there is growing awareness of the many moral, social and political issues which beset the post-modern world. There are burning problems of terrorism, poverty, social injustice and inequality. On the one hand, society is faced with crime and corruption; on the other hand, we find moral controversies and indifference. There is apparent lack of moral knowledge and sensitivity. In contrast to traditional and modern ethical theories, a new post-modern morality is emerging in the twenty-first century, as seen by changing attitudes towards sex and various rightist movements. New problems have also been created by scientific and technological changes, including the many issues of bio-ethics which focus on matters of life and living beings.

Post-modern philosophical problems have been evoked in twenty-first century due to various moral conflicts and controversies. It also results in clash of civilizations and disruption in society. In ancient times, we find that there were agreement about matters of right and wrong conduct. Ordinary people also have a sense of commitment of doing what was considered right in a particular cultural backgrounds. Traditional moral philosophers, therefore, shared many beliefs about the rightness or wrongness of particular acts. On the contrary applied philosophers concentrate on finding moral principles which would serve to resolve moral conflicts and ethical doubts. In post-modern era, there is little agreement on moral issues. The problem of moral philosophy is not so much one of justifying moral beliefs already known or assumed to be true. The problem is to work out a methodology and its application in order to solve the problem.

In modern age, the work of moral philosophers has focused more on problems of logical construction and analysis of language than on problems of application. The most dominant trend of the twentieth century philosophy has been linguistic analysis. It understands philosophizing as conceptualizing. Strawson in his book *Analysis and Metaphysics* adheres that concepts are clothed in language. So in order to understand philosophical problems, we have to analyse language. The analytic philosophers focus attention on philosophy of language. In fact, most of analytic philosophers could not address practical issues. Some of logical positivists like Ayer has questioned the efficacy of moral truth. The emotivists, for example, have taken the position that there is no such thing as moral truth. Intuitionists have argued that moral truth cannot be discovered by reasoning. Post-modernists in turn, have claimed that morality is a matter of cultural perspectives. Despite the emergence of linguistic philosophy in the mid twentieth century, there are philosophers who have proposed normative ethical theories. Some of the philosophers have questioned the distinction between meta ethics and normative ethics. Kant argues that moral rules can be established on the basis of universal applicability and respect for persons. Utilitarians argue that the rightness or wrongness of actions is determined by the values of its consequences. Moral philosophers propound conflicting ethical theories. It has created the impression that philosophy has little to offer in the way of solutions to everyday practical problems of life.

In the early 1970s, philosophers have been addressing post-modern ethical problems. The chief characteristics of post-modernism are post-structuralism and anti-intellectualism. In the nineteenth and early twentieth century, philosophers concentrated on structuralism and rationalism. The post-modernism does not subscribe to logicality, centrality and rationality. Post-modern philosophers of ethics are lovers of multi-narratives instead of "Grand narratives". The new fields of applied ethics have developed in the post-modern era of twenty-first century. In the past twenty years, there has been numbers of conferences, societies, journals, texts books and institutions devoted to the subject of applied ethics. Recent Indian professional philosophers have been taking keen interest in applied ethics.

In post-modern age, new models have been developed to provide procedures for making practical decisions and resolving disputes. Peter Singer observes. "To an observer of moral philosophy in the twentieth century, the most striking development of the past twenty years would not be any advance in our theoretical understanding of the subject nor would it be the acceptance of particular ideas about right and wrong. It would, rather, be the revival of an entire department of the subject: applied ethics".[1]

It is quite important to investigate the relation of theoretical ethics to applied ethics. We have to view this problem not only from the point of view of what philosophers have to offer to the solution of practical problems, but also from the point of view of seeing how philosophical ethics itself might be improved by considering problems of application. By applied ethics. I understand the question of the applicability of a theory to solve the practical problems of human existence. Applied ethics is concerned with theory's ability to resolve practical disputes. D.D. Raphel observes, "The best way to understand the nature of philosophy is to have some experience of doing it".[2] Ethical principles are abstract without moral practices. Philosophizing is theorizing. Ethical theorizing and the application of moral theory in practical moral judgement is not limited to moral philosophers. Even an ordinary man without having philosophical background theorises about values. People may use or do use moral theories of one kind or another to justify their activities to resolve moral dilemmas of actual existence. Scientists are apt to theorize. Economists do theorize about economic structure. Psychotherapies are founded upon ethical theories as various as hedonism and perfectionism. Scientists, economists and psychotherapists are prone to apply ethical principles in their respective fields. Even medical practitioners, business men and other professionals do apply ethical principles. Social scientists and theoreticians in other disciplines, assume the truth of one ethical theory or another without critical evaluation. Philosophers attempt to justify the theories they propose. Hindu ethics is supposed to fall within the province of religion as well as philosophy. In Hindu Philosophy, ethics and religion both are inter-mixed up. The term *dharma* is expressive of this notion. Religious practitioners are apt to assume that principles expressed in their codes are true. Religious practitioners sometimes attempt to justify religious beliefs on philosophical grounds. Normally, ethics is concerned with rightness or wrongness of human conduct. Therefore, when one seeks answers, not only of what is right or wrong in particular case, but also of questions of correct principles, it seems only natural to turn to philosophy for answers.

The problems of applied ethics arise when man begins to reflect upon his or her moral practices. Moral philosophy questions the justification of actions or the reasons for judgements. In classical ethics, we find discussions on different standards of moral judgement. Difference of opinions are the source of philosophical reflections. This is a typical post-modern trend. Difference is the watchword of Derrida's Philosophy. In his books entitled *Positions* and '*Margins of Philosophy*' Derrida highlights differences. In actual human situation it also arises when people are genuinely perplexed about what they should do or what they should not do. In their attempt to resolve a moral dilemma, they seek philosophical reasons for or against-particular moral actions. In so doing they often appear to personal codes or socially accepted norms. However, such rules or norms may also be disputed. In actual existence, there is always a sort of disagreement about the norms of behaviour. The accepted ethical norms seem to be conflicting. Some accepted norms of society may also seem inapplicable to concrete human situation. It may not be clear which judgement the rule requires. When ethical norms are in question, the next step is to move to ground realities. The ground realities of life and its prevalent practices help us to resolve moral conflicts. It determines the range of their application. It justifies exceptions or clarify their meanings. Moral reasoning does not always proceed in this way, of course, for persons may begin by appealing directly to accepted moral principles. Moral values are contextual. Moral values are not opinions. Values take shape in course of social interaction.

Historically, moral philosophers have attempted to examine and defend ethical theories in order to guide actions. Principles enlighten moral judgement. The justification of moral action or beliefs are being done on moral theories. The major difference between popular opinions on ethics and theories is that philosophers usually try to clarify their positions and demonstrate their truth. Philosophers apply logical tools and reasonings to ascertain truth. Philosophers use logic to test moral principles. Philosophers also tend to give explicit attention to the methodology employed in their examinations of moral principles.

Ethical theories are influenced by philosophical heritage and historical background. Moral philosophers also come to their positions by analyzing the values of societies in which they live. Moral values are product of inter-personal relationship. Values are not static. Values do change in changing circumstances. Philosophers, therefore, tend to reflect basic cultural views. Culture is cultivation of values. Values are product of social dynamics. We are expected to find Christian ethics among Christians or Hindu ethics among Hindus. Philosophies influence the beliefs of their adherents. The difference in the moral beliefs of different cultures have, in fact, led many people to believe in the general relativism of values. Post-Vedic Hindus were well aware of the cultural diversities and ethical relativity among people of different ages and regions. The *dharmasastras* and epics point out how the ways and customs of people of North and South India differ from each other. Customs are an important source of norms of conduct (*acara*). Customary patterns of *acara* are generally defined as that which has been handed down by earlier generations. The *Ramayana* and the *Mahabharata* assert that the injunctions of *Vedas* cannot be applicable to all people alike. Cultural relativism starts with the empirical fact of cultural diversity in moral beliefs. A belief in cultural or individual relativism, however, is not peculiar to post-modernism. It is a form of moral relativism which finds expressions in all periods of Indian history.

The reasons which many philosophers have advanced to cut short post-modern relativism are very simple. They have argued that there must be universal and objective principles discoverable by reason otherwise moral judgements and moral controversies would not make any sense. Post-modernism explodes the myth of objectivity and universalism. It upholds that logicality leads to abstraction. Critics of post-modernity would say that there is no point in having a moral relativism, or in disputing the opinion of others, unless one had reason to suppose that opinions could be either correct or incorrect. Moral opinion is mere opinion about nothing, if there is no standard to determine the correctness or incorrectness of opinion. In the twentieth century, logical positivists and emotivists like Ayer and Stevenson have claimed that moral judgements are not logically justified. They uphold that moral judgements are simply expressions of feelings. Hence, moral judgements are not judgements at all. Critics of relativism say that standard of moral judgement must be objective. In order to judge actions as right or wrong, we must have some uniform standard of morality. Post-modernism does not subscribe to this view of logical positivists. Hindu ethics believes in plurality and not in uniformity.

Many philosophers have upheld that ultimate moral principles cannot be proved by deductive reasoning for, if they could be so proved, there would have to be still higher principles. But if there were higher moral principles, the principles being proved would not be ultimate, and the same argument applies to any higher principles. This leads us to fallacy infinite regress. However, this argument ignores the possibility of establishing principles in other ways. For example, moral principles might be established by intuition, or by showing that the principles in question really are ultimate. According to teleological theory of morality, that a given value or set of values function as an ultimate end, and one may even try to show why it is ultimate by citing certain facts about the world, or certain characteristics of human nature. Plato argues that there is no higher principle than goodness itself because it bestows value on all other things. Hedonists have argued that when all is said and done the only reason anyone could give for thinking anything valuable is that it gives pleasure. There is no ultimate standard or principle. There are several principles and various standards of moral judgement. The celebrated American pragmatist namely John Dewey upheld that there are different values in different contexts. Values which function as ends in some context function as means in others. In a system which has more than one principle, it is thought that some method needs to be devised for resolving possible conflicts in principles. Thomas Aquinas appeared to believe that ultimate ends need not conflict, for he thought that a person could always be positively oriented towards several ultimate goods without ever acting in opposition to any of them.

The question is : What makes right action right or wrong actions wrong? whether actions are right or wrong independent of our reasoning about them or whether they are right or wrong because they correspond to right reasoning? In the twentieth century, objectivists such as act-deontologists and intuitionist H.H. Prichard, have argued that actions are right or wrong in and of themselves. Actions are right or wrong regardless of how anyone might reason about them, G.E. Moore also seems to agree with this view. Intuition or reasoning is thought to be a way of finding out which actions are right. But intuition or reasoning does not make them right. Butler observes, ".... Any plain honest man, before he engages in any course of action, ask himself, or this I am going about right, or is it wrong or....".[3]

Some of the champions of applied ethics do not subscribe to objectivists' view on moral standard. Moral judgements are prescriptive in nature and not simply descriptive. They must issue from some authority, even if the authority is of reason itself. However, in many ancient and medieval accounts, the authority of reason was not limited to human reason, for the entire universe was thought to have a rational structure to which human reason is subordinate. In theological ethics, the standard of morality is determined by God's reason. God was supposed to have conferred his goodness upon man and his world. Such moral theories were ontological in the sense that being and value were understood to be correlative terms. Things have value according to their level of being in a hierarchy of nature, and things could be evil, or lack value, only by failing to actualize their potentialities, or by failing to achieve the perfection of the species to which they belong. Such reasoning has been the basis of self-realization theories offered by a number of philosophers from Plato to Aristotle and Augustine to Aquinas. Many ethical theories do not have logical or ontological foundation for they are often quite relativistic. They do not presuppose a belief in essential nature or transcendental values. It does not transpire that all traditional moral philosophers are idealistic or perfectionists. Epicureans in Greece and Carvaka in India were materialists who believed that *summum* bonum of human existence is pleasure. There is nothing transcendental. The end of life is to seek pleasure. Pleasure is the be all and end all of human existence. The standard of moral judgement is hedonism and not perfectionism. The stoics believed in a natural law based upon one's place in the universe, but they were more concerned with attaining peace of mind by controlling their feelings and sensuality. In India, Samkara and Sri Aurobindo were concerned with self-realization. The rationalists and idealists were influenced by Platonism. The British empiricists were influenced by Epicureanism. Hobbes developed a social contract on the basis of a hedonistic philosophy.

According to Platonic and neo-Platonic theory, our ability to know what is right or wrong is guaranteed by the Divine illumination of human understanding. Modern school of rationalistic philosophers such as those of Descartes, Leibniz and Spinoza believed in innate ideas. A belief in innate ideas need not be based on faith in God. Kant claimed that there is a first principle of practical reasoning implicit in moral reasoning. Kant conceived God as secondary postulate of morality. Kant upheld that moral laws are maxims which can be universally applied.

Kant was agnostic but rationalist. He opposed empiricists. Epicureans thought that morality could be founded on human sentiments. Bentham and Mill did not deny Kant's principle of universalizability as they did amend and supplement it by arguing that moral reasoning requires a consideration of the consequences of actions, and that consequences, in turn, can be evaluated only on hedonistic grounds. Bentham and Mill in tune with Kant hoped to lay foundations for a science of ethics by uncovering the logic of moral reasoning. Kant believed that his moral rules applied to all human beings. Kierkegaard accepted Hegelian idea of an Absolute, but he declined to accept Hegelian rationalistic account of ethics. According to Kierkegaard, man is united with God not by reason but by choice. Marx accepted Hegelian dialectic process. Marx turned Hegelian dialectic process upside down. Marx was materialist and Hegel was idealist. Marx conceived that morality is class-bound. John Dewey was influenced by Darwin. Dewey modified Marxian deterministic notion of historical process in favour of individual freedom.

As a matter of fact, Marx can be termed as the representative thinker of modernism. Marxism, pragmatism and existentialism are prominent philosophies of modern age. However, a new type of analytic philosophy was introduced by Russell, Moore, Wittgenstein and Strawson. Analytic ethics in concerned with the meaning of ethical terms. Traditional philosophers of ethics have been concerned with moral reasoning and language. A new distinction was drawn between meta-ethics and normative or substantial ethics. In *Principia Ethica*, Moore claimed that the primary question of philosophic ethics is the meaning of good, not what kind of things are good. The debates which followed during the first-half of the century were largely debates on meta-ethical questions. Moore contemplated that the meaning of good was the central question of ethics. He argued that good could not be proved by any other property. Goodness cannot be proved by any process of reasoning. That is what Moore meant by saying that goodness must be intuited, but he thought that other moral properties, such as rightness, could be derived from goodness by a process of utilitarian reasoning. Deontologists thought that rightness or obligatoriness was the fundamental moral concept. H.H. Prichard held that the rightness or wrongness of each and every particular act must be intuited. The reason is that there is no other properties which make acts right. Sir David Ross also upholds that rightness is fundamental, but he thought that moral principles, not particular instances, must be intuited, since he believed that moral rules cannot be derived from any higher principle. Thus much of the debate focused on whether good or right is the basic concept of ethics and whether particular acts could be justified by rules or principles.

Logical positivism rejected the basic assumption of intuitionism that moral terms refer to moral properties. The Logical Positivist like Ayer argued that the primary function of value terms is to express human emotion and that because of this, moral utterances are neither true nor false. Logical positivists made a fundamental distinction between facts and values—between cognitive, fact–stating propositions and non-cognitive evaluations—which has plagued moral philosophy ever since. Jean Paul Sartre argued that moral judgements could not be determined by principles. Values are created by choice. Thus, following World War II, moral philosophy seemed to be dominated by the metaethical positions of emotivism. They restricted the place and function of reason in ethics. These views had a powerful influence upon traditional theories like Utilitarianism and Rigourism. J.J.C. Smart used emotivism to support his preference for utilitarianism. R.M. Hare combined the Sartrean idea of choosing moral principles with a Kantian requirement to universalize that decision. In the 1950s and 1960s a new version of utilitarianism developed and a distinction was made between rule-utilitarianism and act-utilitarianism. Rule utilitarianism holds that ".... An act is right if and only if it conforms to a set of rules general conformity to which would maximize utility; the other that an act is right if and only if it conforms to a set of rules general acceptance of which would maximize utility, where acceptance of a rule is thought of as falling somewhat short of conformity to it. Of course to make his normative ethics complete the RU must tell us which rules fulfil his stated requirements".[4] Moral rules according to intuitionist like Ross were justified by the principle of utility. Rule utilitarianism is a two-staged theory in which at the first stage, moral rules are justified by utility and, at the second stage, particular actions are justified by means of the rules.

It is appropriate to ask for reasons in ethics. Moral evaluation is not simply a matter of intuition, emotion or choice. The distinction between facts and values was also under question because it seemed that actions could be justified by social practices. Values can be derived from facts. John Rawls proposed a social contract theory, according to which principles of justice are based upon fair consent. Rawls's theory evoked interest in ethics which extended beyond philosophic circles. The development of game theory of Wittgenstein, utility theory of Mill and social welfare theory of John Rawls also added new dimension and techniques to ethical analysis. Fox and Joseph observes, "Applied philosophy is concerned with clarifying moral issues and determining how general principles can be applied to concrete cases."[5] Traditional normative ethics is abstract. Some of the issues of applied philosophy were in fact raised, the new student demonstrators who in the late 1960s and 1970s demanded "relevance" in higher education. They called for classes in world peace, environmental issues, social justice and human rights. Problems of bio-ethics and professional morality also began taking interest in applied ethics. This trend has assumed enormous importance in the recent syllabus of Indian universities.

The growth of applied ethics has posed a problem to theoretical ethics. Theoretical ethics are normative in character. Neither normative ethics nor virtue ethics play effective role in solving practical problems of life. Fox and Joseph states that "Theoretical ethics also appears to be threatened by the possibility that applied ethics may continue to grow and prosper without theoretical guidance, for the issues of applied ethics are sometimes argued within the contexts of popular debate without any explicit attempt to apply theories at all. Theories are applied mechanically without any attempt to determine whether they are appropriate or inappropriate."[6] In the post-modern conditions, there is need for coupling theoretical and applied ethics. The application may prove to be a means of testing and improving theory. It may enable applied ethics to rise above mere application to the level of philosophy itself. Applied ethics has not benefited from recent developments in ethical theory. The ethical theory has not yet been improved by considering problems of application. John Stuart Mill and John Dewey address social issues. They are not consistent with post-modern ethical trends. In the modern age, philosophers have been concerned primarily with abstract issues concerning the objectivity of moral judgements.

True that science influenced our ethical world-views in the wake of modernism. Science gave the models for truth. Scientific claims are tied to observable data. The logical positivists argued that the very meaning of a proposition is dependent upon its possible verifiability or falsifiability through experience. They viewed ethical statements as being non-scientific. Ethical statements being emotive are not descriptive. A.J. Ayer in his book *Language, Truth and Logic* has mentioned that ethical statements are emotive. They can't be verifiable. They are non-cognitive. Hence they are meaningless.

Post-modern trends in applied ethics anticipate cultural relativism. They questioned universal moral principles. Post-modernists called attention to multiplicities of moral practices. Cultures have sub-groups cultures. Post-modernity envisaged plurality and differences. There are individual differences within groups. Cultural relativism contemplates that each culture or individual has opinions about what is right or wrong, but the theory provides no basis for claiming that any opinion is or even could be objectively true.

It is generally upheld that science is deterministic. Post-modern trends are in conflict with deterministic nature of science. Ethics postulates freedom of will. In other words, causal determinism conflicts with the ethical supposition of freedom and responsibility. Marxism relegated ethics to a deterministic process. It holds that ethical theory is an instrument of class exploitation. The post-modern philosophic views of Jacques Derrida have challenged the positivist thesis that scientific knowledge is directly linked to observation. Fox and Joseph observe, "The objectivity of science seems to rest more on good reasons, the consistency of shared date and interpersonal agreement than upon uninterpreted observations."[7] The post-modern views on science have created a new climate of multiple opinions in which ethical theory can be re-evaluated and reassessed. If the theoretical interpretation of data plays an important role in science, then one may suppose that it may do so in ethics as well without any apparent loss of objectivity. Human aspiration, reason and agreement may be regarded as elements which give ethics an objective grounding. Ethical theories requires to be tested in concrete human situations.

Linguistic analysis of ethical terms has lost its charm in post-modern world. I think, mere analysis and clarifications of meaning of ethical terms are not enough. Man is not content with words and its meanings. He loves actions and applications in concrete human situation. The application of moral principles in life and society is very important. Mere analysis is abstract. The striking development in post-modern ethics is practical application of moral principles in varying human situations. Peter Singer rightly observes, "To an observer of moral philosophy in the twentieth century, the most striking development of the past twenty years would not be any advance in our theoretical understanding of the subject nor would it be the acceptance of any particular ideas about right and wrong. It would, rather, be the revival of an entire department of the subject : applied ethics".[8] I think life is larger than logic. The myth of universalism has been exploded in post-modern age. Relativism has become order of the socio-moral thought under the impact of post-modernism. Cultural relativism and difference cannot be brushed aside. Abstract idealistic moral principles and scientific deterministic theories which threatened the assumption of human freedom now appear to be incapable of explaining many human activities.

The demand for applied ethics has come in the post-modern society which is full of tension and disruption. The substantive ethics seems to be losing its ground and giving way to applied ethics. Post-modern philosophers are prone to do applied ethics. Some of the philosophers of post-modern age are trying to deconstruct the edifice of grand system of ethics. They are trying to resolve a variety of vital issues. Their position is that of relativist. They uphold that there is no widely accepted single theory to support their investigations. The domain of ethical theory, its methodology, and its relationship to application are pluralistic and relativistic in nature.

In the modern age, the emphasis was on ethical theory. In the post-modern age, the insistence is on application of moral principles to living existence of human beings. The twentieth century having background of objectivity and analytical inclinations to determine the meaning of ethical terms have lost its glamour. It also lost continuity with changes in society and in the various sciences. It also lost much of its continuity with traditional theories. Social sciences like economics developed sophisticated models of rationality and choice independently of philosophical ethics. Philosophical theories ignored post-modern trends and development. It appears that philosophers need to develop a sense of cultural relativism of post-modern age. *A Theory of Justice* by John Rawls published in 1971, was an exemplary attempt to construct a substantive ethical theory of justice. The theory lays down basic principles and a methodology of its application. In his method, Rawls identifies firmly held convictions, such as the rejection of slavery, as data against which theory can be tested. Such convictions may be modified by the theory, but as part of a process of mutual interaction between theory and convictions. In general the work of Rawls signalled (1) a new confidence in substantive theory; (2) reworked conceptions of objectivity and data in ethics; and (3) a view of ethical theory as a way of ordering basic conventions. Most importantly, from the standpoint of applied ethics, his theory seemed to lend itself to a wide variety of applications from medicine to business and law.

Critics may say that Rawls theory of justice appears to suffer from shortcomings. First of all, the theory is presented in a highly abstract form. This is typical of traditional ethical theories but the abstract principles of traditional theories could be given more specific interpretations because they usually reflected the social practices of their times. By contrast, Rawls defends his principles on the basis of assumptions which diverge widely from current practices. For example, he assumes full compliance with the principles he lays down, although in practice such compliance cannot be assumed. He leaves key terms undefined or inadequately defined. The questions of standard of morality is ignored. It assumes that application takes place instantaneously. Rawls theory is not easily applied, at least as it currently stands.

In the modern times, ethical theory has not been developed with a view to application. It seems that ethical practices is not guided by theory. In economics, application has been guided by theory. Amartya Sen has tried application of ethical principles in economics in his book *Ethics and Economics*. Most of applied economics is based upon similar theoretical foundations in micro-economics. Different schools in micro-economics tend to use similar styles of presentations and argumentations and economists often refer to the same basic data when defending interpretations and theories. In philosophic ethics, there has been a significant gap between theoretical ethics and applied ethics. There is little agreement about principles, the relevance of data, the appropriate methods of theory construction and testing.

The post-modern demands for the application of ethical theories prepares the ground for constructing new theories. It attempts to modify older theories in post-modern conditions. In recent past, we find that "Gandhivada" has been transformed into "Gandhigiri". The visual communication is in touch with the masses. "Gandhivada" was theoretical and idealistic but "Gandhigiri" is applied Gandhism. Though the expression is not very happy one for traditional Gandhiates but we can't evade visual media which is very powerful. I think "Gandhigiri" is post-modern expression. The term "Gandhigiri" was used by the visual media keeping in view the tone and temper of post-modern age. Similarly, the term "Netagiri" has been converted into "Netagardi" which stands for true picture of present day political society. Likewise the expression "Hindutava" in place of Hinduism is post-modern expression which is laden with meaning in a changing context. These expressions indicate post-modern conditions. The post-modern ethical theories may be tested by their ability to resolve problems of existence. In modern perspective, ethical theory has potential for generating agreement based upon rational considerations, objective data, and accepted principles of action. Such ethical theory would enable persons to form basically similar patterns of approach to the solution of practical problems. In the post-modern ethical trends, internal consistency would not be sufficient. Difference, multiplicities and relativity are key concepts of post-modernity. Post-modernity does not believe in "Grand Narratives" but in "multi-narratives" in ethical theories. The post-modern view is that theory may provide adequate guidance for application in the near future. In post-modern conditions, theory would be used to resolve difficult cases. It ensures consistency in application of moral principles. It provides guidance in action. It also provides relative standards of morality which can be easily applied to judge moral behaviour in day-to-day life.

But work in the fields of applied ethics cannot wait for theory to advance to the point of providing clear guidance. Indeed, theory will probably not advance unless current investigations into practical issues reveal areas of agreement and principles on which philosophers can rely in reconstructing their theories. It may be the case that a plurality of approaches to ethics is required. On the one hand, modern philosophy of ethics may need to continue their investigations in abstract ethical and meta-ethical theory but with the idea of application in mind. On the other hand, application for post-modern ethicists may need to proceed without dependence on existing theory. Modern philosophers were concerned for the universality and certainty of their moral arguments. The concern of post-modern ethicist is application. There is a remarkable shift from high level theoretical principles to practical ethics.

Applied ethics, unlike theoretical ethics, cannot ignore actual conditions. Applied ethics is directed towards the solution of controversial issues. It must assume disagreement. Hence, it seeks procedures for moving from disagreement to agreement. Applied ethics, therefore, must address the question of practical life of post-modern world. However, the problems of a practitioner, such word as health care professional, are different from those of an applied philosopher. For the practitioner faces such constraints directly, whereas the philosopher can consider how such constraints may be weakened or removed. In considering problems of application, the philosopher cannot simply assume existing or ideal states of affairs, for he must consider how actual conditions can be changed to bring about desirable results. Emphasis on actual conditions points out a need for interaction between philosophers, social scientists and practitioners in other fields.

In the end, I uphold that theoretical ethics and applied ethics are not likely to part company. Applied ethics cannot thrive at the cost of theoretical ethics. Theoretical ethics and applied ethics may perform different roles in different spheres but there is need for integration of theory and application. Theory should gain support from consensus reached on the applied level. Applied ethics should be benefited from the extension of accepted principles to controversial cases. The question boils to the point as to how moral principles can be applied in actual living condition. I think, theory prepares the background for successful application of moral principles. Fox and Joseph observe, "In general, theory needs to become more responsive to the complexities of genuine moral problems, and application needs to benefit from the general understanding rational consistency, and coordination of judgements which ethical theory can provide".[9]

REFERENCE S

1. Singer, Peter; *Applied Ethics*, Oxford University Press, Oxford, 1986, p.1.
2. Raphel, D.D., *Moral Philosophy*, Oxford University Press, Indian edition, 1986, p.1.
3. Butler, Joseph; *Five Sermons*, New York, Liberal Arts Press, 1949, p. 45.
4. Frankena, William K.; *Ethics*, Prentice-Hall of India Pvt. Ltd., New Delhi, 1988, p.40.
5. Fox, Richard M. and Demarco, Joseph P; *New Directions in Ethics*, Routledge and Kegan Paul, New York, 1986, p.11.
6. *Ibid*; p.12
7. *Ibid*; p.14
8. Singer, Peter; *Applied Ethics*, Oxford University Press, 1986, p.1.
9. *Op. cit.*, p. 18.

Chapter – 8

Some Moral Issues in Legal Profession

R.C. Sinha

The recent rise of interest in "*Professional Ethics*" has prompted me to dwell on "Some Moral Issues in Legal Profession". I contend that exploring the moral issues that arise within the legal profession can be valuable both for philosophers and lawyers.

I have been greatly benefited by studying the book entitled "Ethical Issues in Professional Life" edited by Joan C. Callahan I may be failing in my duty if I do not mention the name of Dr. Tziporah Kasachkoff of New York, U.S.A. who presented and sent the book by post to me. My views have been greatly influenced by reading her published as well as large number of unpublished articles which she made available to me from time to time.

Ethics is the important branch of philosophy. It is philosophical study of morality. As a field of philosophical inquiry, ethics is generally understood to include three conceptually related enterprises. First is normative ethics, second is meta-ethics; and third is applied ethics. The task of applied ethics is to resolve specific moral issues. It is applications of philosophical principles to concrete human situations. The task of applied ethics as opposed to normative ethics is to resolve specific moral issues and morally problematic concrete cases which arise in different areas of life. Applied ethics borrows insights from meta-ethics and theoretic normative ethics. Legal ethics is one area of professional ethics. Legal profession does seem to include a strong normative component. It requires extensive training. Lawyers attend law schools for three years. They undergo years of training with the established lawyers. The legal profession involves intellectual component. The trained ability of lawyer provides an important service to society. As a matter of fact, lawyers provide services to society which less experts do not.

Here I have tried to examine two moral problems of legal profession. The problems are raised by rational philosophers who are not in legal profession. The problems are concerned with lawyer-client relationship.

A philosopher is tempted to raise the first problem which centres round the lawyer's stance towards the world at large. The charge framed by a philosopher is that the lawyer-client relationship renders the lawyer at best amoral and at worst immoral in his or her dealings with rest of mankind. The second charge by an existential philosopher is that is the lawyer-client relationship which is morally objectionable because it is a relationship in which the lawyer treats client in paternalistic fashion. The relationship suffers from inequality. Sometimes it dehumanizes the client.

In the first issue, the primary philosophical question is: whether there is adequate justification for the kind of moral universe that comes to be inhabited by the lawyer as he or she goes through professional life. It is an a moral one and more than occasionally perhaps, an overtly immortal one. The behaviour that is involved is, to a very significant degree, what I call "profession-differentiated behaviour". Some illustrations will help to make clear what I mean by "profession-differentiated behaviour". The profession-differentiated behaviour creates a new moral universe.

In every human culture, the parent is involved in role differentiated behaviour. In Indian culture, a parent is entitled to prefer the interest of one's own children over those of others. It is regarded as morally appropriate for a parent to allocate excessive goods to his or her own children, even though other children may have substantially more pressing and genuine needs for these items. If Mrs. Semona is trying to decide what the right way is to distribute assets among a group of children all of whom are strangers to herself, the relevant moral considerations would be very different from those that would be regarding her own children. In the role of a parent, the claims of other children *vis-á-vis* Mrs. Semona's own are, if not rendered morally irrelevant, certainly rendered less morally significant. In short the role-differentiated character of Mrs. Semona alters the relevant moral point of view enormously. Similar is the case in "profession-differentiated behaviour".

The plausible and even thoroughly convincing arguments exist for the desirability of the "profession-differentiated behaviour" and its attendant neglect of what would otherwise be morally relevant considerations. To be a professional is to be enmeshed in profession-differentiated behaviour. Mr. Disoja's role as a lawyer alters his moral universe. Mr. Disoja as professional lawyer has a client whose interest must be attended to. The role of Mr. Disoja is to protect and prefer the interest of the client over those of other individuals. In case of the pleader-client relationship the point of view of the pleader is different from that which would be appropriate in the absence of the pleader-client relationship. Hence, pleader-client relationship is quite different from ordinary relationship. Once a lawyer represents a client, the lawyer has a duty to make his expertise fully available in the realization of the end sought by the client. Advocate works irrespective of the moral worth to which the end will be put or the character of the client who seeks to utilize it. The major consideration before lawyer is to evaluate that the end sought is not illegal. The lawyer is, in essence, amoral skilled person whose peculiar skills and knowledge in respect to the law are available to those with whom the relationship of client is established. The question is whether this particular and pervasive feature of professionalism is itself justifiable.

In order to seek answer let us focus upon the criminal defence lawyer. The most familiar aspect of the profession-differentiated character of the lawyer's activity it that of the defence of client charged with a crime. The accepted view within the profession is that having once agreed to represent the client, the lawyer is under moral obligation to do his or her best to defend that person at trial. It is both appropriate and obligatory for the attorney to put on as vigorous and persuasive a defence of a client to be guilty. But part of the difficulty is that the irrelevance of the guilt or innocence of an accused client by no means exhaust the altered perspective of the lawyer's conscience. In the course of defending an accused, an attorney may have, as a part of his or her duty of representation, the obligation to invoke procedures and practices which are themselves morally objectionable and of which the lawyer in other contexts might thoroughly disapprove.

It is important to point out strikingly amoral behaviour limited to the lawyer involved with the workings of the criminal case. Most of the client take the lawyer's assistance because lawyer is professionally competent. Suppose Mr. *X* wants to dispose off his property in a certain way at death. Mr. *X* wants to contract for the purchase or sale of a flat in Mumbai. Mr. *X* desires to set up a company which will manufacture and market a new product. Mr. *X* wishes to minimize his income taxes. In such circumstances, Mr. *X* needs the legal assistance of the professional lawyer, for he alone has the special skill which will make it possible for the client to achieve the desired result.

In such circumstances, the profession-differentiated character of the lawyer's way of being tends to render irrelevant what would otherwise be morally relevant considerations. Suppose that old client desires to make a will, disinheriting his elder son from first wife and transfer the property to younger son of the second wife. The question is : should the lawyer refuse to draft the will because the lawyer knows that this is unfair to disinherit one's eldest son? Suppose a client can avoid the payment of taxes through a loophole only available to a few wealthy tax payers. Should the lawyer decline to the client of a loophole because the lawyer thinks it is unfair advantage for the rich person? Suppose, a client wants to start a company that will manufacture, distribute and promote a harmful but not illegal substance, for example, wine. Should the lawyer refuse to prepare the draft for the company? In each case, the accepted view within the profession is that, these matters are just of no concern to the lawyer. The professional obligation is to work for the client. The lawyer has no moral binding to represent a client, but there is nothing wrong with representing a client whose aims and purposes are quite immoral from the point of view of standard of the morality. If the lawyer refuses to take up the case of the murderer, then it will frustrate the end of justice, because the case of the murderer will remain unrepresented. Once the lawyer agrees to take up the case, he has professional obligation to provide the best possible legal assistance and fulfil the legal obligation. Here professional morality transcends the considerations of wrong or right. The lawyer provides the best possible assistance, without regard for his or her disapproval of the objective that is sought. Richard A. Wasserstrom observes : "The lesson, on this view, is clear. The job of the lawyer so the argument typically concludes, is not to approve or disapprove of the character of his or her client, the cause for which the client seeks the lawyer's assistance, or the avenues provided by the law to achieve that which the client wants to accomplish. The lawyer's task is, instead, to provide that competence which the client lacks and the lawyer as professional possesses".

In this way, the lawyer as professional comes to inhabit a universe which is amoral. In everyday life, a lay man may not be convinced of going beyond the conventional moral universe. A lawyer cannot be very objective or detached in his attempt to work the problem on certain occasion. A lawyer may find it uncomfortable to represent an extremely unpopular client like Mr. Ramalinga Raju who is the master mind of Satyam Scandal. A lawyer may feel ill at ease invoking a rule of law or practice which he or she thinks to be unfair or undesirable one. Nonetheless, for a group of twenty-five eminent lawyers have stood to defend Mr. Ramlinga Raju knowing fully that he is the mastermind of the Satyam fraud. Most of the lawyers most of the time, pursue the interest of the client, because this gives them professional satisfaction just because the moral world of the lawyer is a simpler, less complicated, and less ambiguous world than the moral world of ordinary man. The job of the lawyer is not to judge the character of the client. It is his professional obligation to defend the interest of the client as best as he can. Role-differentiated behaviour changes the moral universe. The lawyer's behaviour is profession-differentiated because the lawyer qua lawyer participates in a complex institution which functions well only if the individuals adhere to their institutional roles. For example, when there is a conflict between individuals or between the state and an individual, there is a well-established institutional mechanism by which each side is represented by a lawyer whose job it is both to present his or her client's case in the most forceful way and to seek to expose the weaknesses and defects in the case of the opponent.

When an individual is charged with having committed a crime, the trial is the mechanism by which we determine the quantum of punishment in our society. Just imagine what would happen if lawyers refuse to represent persons whom they thought to be guilty. In that case Mr. Ramalinga Raju the ex-chairman of Satyam, the main figure of Satyam scandal will not get a lawyer to represent his case. But the existing fact is that Mr. Raju has got twenty-five eminent lawyers to defend his case. In a case where the guilt of person seemed clear, it might turn out that some individuals would be deprived completely of the opportunity to have the system determine whether or not they are in fact guilty. "The amorality of lawyer helps to guarantee that every criminal defendant will have his or her day in court". It is necessary that there should be lawyers who would play their appropriate, professional, institutional role of representative of the client's cause. The amorality of the professional role of the lawyer is not restricted to the defence of these accused of crimes. If lawyers were to substitute their own private views of what ought to be legally permissible and impermissible for those of the legislature, this would constitute undesirable shift from democracy to oligarchy of lawyers.

The amoral behaviour of the criminal defence lawyer is justifiable. But the justification depends at least as much upon the special needs of an accused upon any more general defence of a lawyer's role-differentiated behaviour. It is quite likely that the profession-differentiated amorality of the lawyer is almost certainly excessive and at times inappropriate.

From the above discussion, I draw four points. *First*, all of the arguments that support the profession-differentiated amorality of the lawyer. To the degree to which the institutional rules and practices are unjust, unwise or undesirable to that same degree is the case for the role-differentiated behaviour of the lawyer weakened if not destroyed. *Second*, it is clear that there are definite character traits that the professional such as the lawyer must take on if the system is to work. The role-differentiated amorality of the professional lawyer is justified on the pragmatic rather than principal grounds. *Third*, there is a special feature of the role-differentiated behaviour of the lawyer that distinguishes it from the comparable behaviour of other professionals. It seems far less plausible to talk critically about the amorality of the doctor, for instance, who treats all patients irrespective of their moral character than it does to talk critically about the comparable amorality of the lawyer. The doctor's concern is to cure those who are ill. The lawyer's behaviour is different in kind from the doctor's. The lawyer and especially the lawyer as advocate-directly says and affirms things. The lawyer makes the case for the client. The client's cause prevails. The lawyer lives with and within a dilemma that is not shared by other professionals. Actors in a play take on roles to say things that the characters, not the actors, believe. But we know that it is play and that they are actors. The law courts are not, however, theatres. The lawyers and judges both talk about justice. *Fourth*, the profession-differentiated character of the lawyer's way of thinking and acting is ultimately deemed to be justifiable within the system on systematic instrumental grounds. It still remains the case that we do pay a social price for that way of thought and action.

I

The profession-differentiated behaviour of the professional also lies at the heart of second problem of the two moral issues involved in legal profession. The problem that we want to examine here is that the relationship between the lawyer and the client is morally defective one in which the client is not treated with the respect and dignity that he or she deserves. The defects that flow from what might be regarded as the lawyer's excessive pre-occupation with and concern for the client. How the lawyer qua professional can at the same time be taxed with promoting and maintaining a relationship of dominance and indifference *vis-á-vis* his or her client. The problem of the inter-personal relationship between the lawyer and the client is itself another feature of the underlying issue of the role-differentiated life of the professional. The lawyer is concerned with the interest of the client and at the same time fail to view the client as a whole person. There is relationship of inequality. The pervasive feature of the relationship between lawyer and the client is in some sense a relationship of inequality. The relationship of inequality is intrinsic to the existence of professionalism. The lawyer is always in a position of dominance. The client is in a position of dependence on lawyer. The client can often decide whether or not to enter into a relationship with a lawyer. The client has the power to decide whether to terminate the relationship or not. But the significant thing is that while the relationship cannot be a relationship between equals. It must be one in which it is the lawyer who is in control. This is a necessary and not merely a familiar characteristic of the relationship between professional and those they serve. This is a fact that professional is the possessor of expert knowledge of a sort not readily available or easily attainable by ordinary members of the community at large. Hence, the client is dependent upon the professional's skill or knowledge because the client does not possess the same expert knowledge. Moreover, virtually every profession has its own technical language.

The terminology of lawyer can only be understood by another lawyer and jury. The presence of such a technical language plays the dual role of creating and affirming the membership of the professionals within the profession and of preventing the client from fully discussing or understanding his or her concerns in the language of the profession. The client is in a poor position to evaluate how well or badly the professional lawyer performs. In this professions, the lawyer does not look primarily to the client to evaluate the professional's work. The assessment of professional competence is something this is largely a matter of self-assessment conducted by the practicing lawyer The assessment is carried out not by client but by other members of the profession. It is significant to discover to what degree the professions are self-regulating. The lawyer's community determines the performance and not the client. This means that clients will necessarily lack the power to make evaluation and criticism of the way the lawyer is responding to the client's case. The client lacks the perspective necessary to pursue in a satisfactory way his best interest. The client is personally concerned but lawyer is detached.

The one question that is raised is whether it is a proper and serious criticism of the legal profession that the relationship between the legal professional and the client is an inherently unequal. One possible view is that there is nothing at all wrong with inequality imposed. It may be argued, this kind of inequality is wholly unobjectionable because it is fitting, desired, or necessary in the circumstances. It may be urged, whatever undesirability does attach to relationship by virtue of their lack of equality is outweighed by the benefits of role-differentiated relationship. The inequality is inevitable in any professional relationship. It may even be desirable. The criticism focuses upon the fact that the professional lawyer often interacts with the client in both a manipulative and paternalistic fashion. The professional lawyer does not treat the client like a person but an object. The lawyer does not accord the client the respect that he deserves. It is genuine moral defect in any meaningful human relationship. The suggested solution is to deprofessionalize the legal profession. We have to weaken those features of professionalism that produce these kinds of morally defective relationship.

True that the language of the court is technical. The technical language does help to maintain the distinctive status and power of the legal profession. The professionals tend to develop their own technical language has a lot to do with the "depersonalization" of the client. This also holds for the lawyers. The lawyer can and does talk to other lawyer and judges but not to the client. The lawyer goes out of his way to do it. It is satisfying to lawyer and judges. It is exercise of power. The ability to communicate in technical language is on the things that distinguishes persons from objects. The liability of the client to communicate with the lawyer in the lawyer's own tongue surely helps to make the client less than a person in the lawyer's eyes.

In response to this criticism, one can say that the paternalistic and impersonal ways of behaving with client are exceptional rather than the visual characteristics of the lawyer-client relationship. One can argue that a minor adjustment in legal education aimed at sensitizing prospective lawyers to the possibility of these is all that is required to prevent this. One might have a view that, at least in moderation, relationships having these features are a very reasonable price to pay for the very appreciable benefits of professionalism. The impersonality of a surgeon, for example, may make it easier rather than order for his or her to to a good job of representing a client. The paternalism of lawyers may be justified by the fact that they do in fact know better — at least within many areas of common concern to the parties involved what is best for the client. It might even be claimed that clients in his own interest cannot resist to be treated in this way. One may argue that inequality between lawyer-client relationship is the normal phenomenon. But this is morally objectionable features of the lawyer-client relationship. The one suggested way to solve the problem is to "deprofessionalize" the legal profession. Moreover, knowledge and competencies of lawyer really help people and serve the society. Excellence and competency further the maintenance of the legal profession. Significant social goods cannot be delivered without excellence in profession. There are special competencies and knowledge of laws and they are valuable. The important question is how to weaken the bad consequences of the role-differentiated lawyerclient relationship without destroying the good that lawyers do. The desirable change in legal profession could be brought about to simplify the legal language which creates a gap between client and lawyer. The use of technical language makes the legal process mysterious. The simplified legal procedure should be directly available to lay persons. The way the law works now, it is very hard for lay persons either to understand it or to evaluate or solve problems of legal profession.

II

In the end, I do not know whether the lawyer-client relationship is morally defective nor do I know to what degree role differentiation is the cause of this moral defects. I do not know very precisely what "depersonalization" would be like. I do not know whether 'depersonalization' of client is good or bad. But I am sure that law and morality is a topic worth taking seriously. My contention is that moral universe of the professionals is different from the moral universe of the ordinary man. My suggestion is that technical language of lawyers which is the major cause of exploitation requires to be simplified so that the ordinary man understands and participates in the legal process. The role-differentiated morality is accepted in society because it serves the cause of well-being of society, In nutshell, this chapter contends that morality is not universalistic but it is role-differentiated behaviour. Aristotle contemplates in his book *Nicomachean Ethics* that law is needed if the moral virtues described in the Ethics are to be nurtured. The dependence of morality on law is insisted upon in the closing page of Aristotle's *Nicomachean Ethics*. But the opinion in a Post-modern liberal democratic society upholds that (i) morality cannot be legislated; (ii) there is no morality objective enough to justify legal enforcement; (iii) morality depends upon role-differentiated behaviour; and; (iv) the moral universe of the professional is different from those of common man. Therefore, I contend that standards of professional morality do not necessarily correspond with those of ordinary morality.

NOTES

Joan, C. Callahan (ed.); *Ethical Issues in Professional Life*, Oxford University Press, New York, 1988.

Wasserstrom, A. Richard; *Lawyers as Professionals : Some Moral Issues*, incorporated in the book "*Ethical Issues in Professional Life*" edited by Joan C. Callahan, Oxford University Press, New York, 1988, p. 61.

Ibid., p. 62.

Chapter – 9

Rights-Duties-Utilitarianism : A Perspective of Applied Ethics

R.C. Sinha

This chapter on, "Rights-Duties-Utilitarianism: A Perspective of Applied Ethics" attempts to analyse the problem from a new perspective of the old problems of Rights and Duties. First of all, I have tried to analyse and understand the meanings of two terms namely Rights and Duties in traditional way. In the second part, I have attempted to discuss the concept of "Right to Life" and its bearings in the field of Applied Ethics. I have taken up the problems of Euthanasia and Abortion. My views have been greatly shaped by studying the book entitled, *Ethics* by J.L. Mackie. My approach can be termed as Rights-Duties Utilitarianism. By the expression Rights-Duties-Utilitarianism, as I understand two concepts Rights and Duties are inter-linked to social well-being. By applied ethics, I mean that ethical principles applied to concrete human situation.

Rights and duties can be understood in two senses. One is *legal* and another is *ethical*. My contention is that rights and duties are inter-related. Above all, both rights and duties imply society. Hence, I have linked rights and duties to utilitarianism. In broad sense, utilitarianism takes general human well-being as in some way the foundation of morality. I have taken utilitarianism as the greatest good of the greatest number instead of the greatest happiness of the greatest-number. The greatest good of the greater number is the criterion of right action.

According to Oxford Dictionary, a right is justifiable claim on legal or moral grounds to have or obtain something or to act in a certain way. A right may be a legal right or moral right. Legal conception of right is a matter of Jurisprudence. In the matters of legal right, court enforces but in moral right, court of law does not interfere. For example, the right of an old man to get support or respect from his offspring. What are the moral grounds on which the claim to enjoy moral rights are justified? The simple answer is that moral right is justified by the fact that ability of an individual to assert it is for the common good. We talk about rights and duties of human beings living in society. Rights and Duties imply society. The man who lived like Robinson Crusoe on a desert island would have no rights on that land. The right depends on the social life. Robinson Crusoe's power to use the things of island is a matter of might and not right. Right is always bestowed by society. It is born out of the inter-personal relationship.

The common good is the basis of right. It is for the good of the community that cetain rights, like the right to property, should be so enforceable. But the right to respect is not enforceable by law. A teacher cannot attempt to secure the respect of his students by compelling him to do it. He may get the outward signs of respect on the part of his students. Respects cannot be commanded or demanded. If respect is being demanded, the result is not for the general good of the society as a whole, because students respect teacher out of fear. The fact that a person has a right does not mean, that the person who has it, ought to assert it in every case. For example, right to speech is the fundamental right but one is not free to abuse others.

The word "duty" like the word "right" has more than one use in applied ethics. Ordinarily we say that a good action is our duty to do it. The action which we consider our duty to do differs from a right action. Every right action is not our duty to do it. It implies that only one action is right for us at the particular point of time in question. If two alternative actions are equally right to do, then we are in a fix to decide. We would not be able to say of either of them that is our duty to do it. Duties are right actions, but every right action is not duty. The most prominent good effects of duties are on people other than the doer of the action. Duties arouse sentiments of moral approval in way that merely right actions do not. The word "duty", however, is used in more specialized way as the correlative to the word "right". "If a right is a justifiable claim in a community, a duty is the obligation to fulfil that claim". A duty is the obligation of an individual to satisfy a claim made upon him by the community in the name of the common good of the common man. The child has a right to education. It is the duty of his parents or of the state to provide him all facilities of education. An ordinary contract like the purchase of Air Ticket to London shows how rights and duties are relative to each other. the Air India has a right to get the payment of the fare.

The passenger has the duty of paying the exact fare. If the passenger Mr. *X* has purchased the Air Ticket, the traveller has the right of being conveyed from Indira Gandhi International Airport to Heathrow Airport of London. The Air India has duty of providing that facility of conveyance. The obvious relation between rights and duties in a contract has given plausibility to the view that morality depends on 'social contract'. Individuals living in a society has agreed to perform certain duties because by doing so, they also acquire certain rights. A right involves a duty in two ways: (1) If one individual has a right, some other individual or individuals have the duty of satisfying the claim which is recognised by the right. The child's, right to education implies a duty on the part of his parents or of the state to provide him with that education. In some cases the duty related to a right is not so obvious, because it is largely a negative duty or a duty of abstaining from something. A man's right to the use of his own property implies a duty on the part of the neighbours to refrain from encroaching on that property. If an individual has a right, it is his duty to use that right for the common good of society. It is, for example, the duty of a child to use his education in such a way that he may become a useful member of society. This is an aspect of right which is not enshrined in the laws of a state. In ordinary circumstances, the individual has the right to do what he likes but law courts have maintained that individual's freedom is limited. One is not free to misuse his freedom of speech. As a matter of fact, duty involves moral obligation. If rights are not followed by duties, then society will go astray.

II

Now we will discuss the applied part of the rights and duties. We can speak a right to life only as a claim-right correlative to a duty not to kill others. Right to life is a fundamental right of an individual. But right to life is not absolute. The right to life has a corollary, the right to end's one's life. But this right to end one's life is not absolute. Others may have claims that tell against suicide. It may be preferable from the agent's own point of view, but other relatives and society will not approve the act of suicide in the fit of frustration. There is not difficulty in describing circumstances in which euthanasia would be permissible. The principle of right to life would allow euthanasia. When someone is terminally ill and really wants and seriously asks to be killed. It is a difficult question, whether it is ever legitimate to act on someone's merely presumed desire for his life to be ended. The grounds for euthanasia need to be very strong. J.L. Mackie observes, "Where, however, someone can be kept half alive only by the continued use of elaborate support mechanism or by repeated operations, and where the life thus maintained is plainly of no value to him it will be right to let him die".

The question of euthanasia is highly controversial. Further, J.L. Mackie observes, "But I think that they should be considered neither in terms of slogans about murder and the sanctity of life nor in terms of an attempt to calculate the effects of actions on the total general happiness, but more concretely in terms of the values, rights and dispositions involved, our understanding of these being taken over from more normal and less controversial cases". These matters should not be left for doctors to decide privately, we do not want medical experts to shield us from moral choice. I think euthanasia involves hard moral choice.

The problem of Abortion is another controversial issue of Applied Ethics. There are three important reasons that are upheld to justify abortion. *First*, it may be needed to prevent a grave risk to the mother's life. *Secondly*, there may be good reasons to expect that if the child is born it will suffer from some serious permanent infirmity. In such case mother may not want a handicapped child. *Thirdly*, unmarried mother may be reluctant to give birth to a child which she conceived as a result of rape. It may be argued that she has a right not to have her body used by or for what she does not want. The basic argument against abortion is that the unborn child is already a human being, a person, a bearer of rights. The abortion is, therefore, murder. Life in the womb is sacrosanct and to end life in the womb is morally unjustified. Hence, abortion cannot be permitted. The unborn child has been accorded a right to life. Social philosophers and progressive activists may favour the case of abortion and argue that unborn child is not a person and has no right to life, the baby just before birth has no right to life. The matter is complicated because the arguments of both supporters and opponents are quite cogent. It puts us in a fix. The ground of abortion is valid in early pregnancy. The mother's right to the control of her own body then outweighs the child's right to life. But this is not applicable in late pregnancy. The first ground, however, according to the graveness of the risk to the mother's life, might be valid at any time up to birth. The *second* ground, the likelihood of serious permanent defect, also seems to be valid at any time upto birth. In saying this I presume that it is much against the interest of the parents and the other members of the family that the child should survive. But it is also against the child's own interest of course this brings us back to the question of euthanasia. If a child is born as handicapped, should it then be allowed to be killed. We regard a newly born child as a person. It is surely not yet conscious of itself as itself, as a distinct and potentially continuing being. If the child is mentally retarded and physically unfit to live, in this case progressive humanity would require that the child should be allowed to die. This would be seen as the deliberate killing of an independent human being, not at his own request. This cannot be treated as case of mercy killing. Even the worst handicapped person does not want to be eliminated. Here birth is a salient point. It is popularly acceptable ground of distinction. Abortion is seen as different from the killing of what is now a separately existing human being.

In the end, I plead that if someone has right to life then he has also right to die when he leads a painful and vegetative life. I endorse to euthanasia but not suicide or killing of the physically handicapped persons. The elimination of the terminally ill cancer patient who is suffering and leading a painful life has right to die on simple humanitarian and utilitarian grounds.

NOTES

Lillie, William; *An Introduction* to Ethics, Methuen & Co., Ltd. London, First edition, 1967, p. 263.

Mackie, J.L., *Ethics*, Penguin Books Ltd., England, 1977, p. 196-7

Ibid., p. 397.

Chapter – 10

Some Features of Husserl's Life-World

S.A. Shaida

It is widely held that Husserl's early stages of thought could not answer several questions which he had in mind in relation to the transcendental subjectivity as well as the nature, scope and ground of scientific understanding. The foundations of knowledge which Husserl always sought to discover and explicate could not be classified and established with the help of phenomenological reduction. Rather, he was himself feeling more and more uncomfortable by the realization that complete relativism and subjectivism were possible consequences which were glaring at him. The programme of presuppositionless philosophy could not yield a proper stand point to start with. He was conscious of the fact that his theoretical attitude (and, for that matter, anyone's) must follow a "natural primordial attitude"- one of "original natural life".[1] The Crisis of European Sciences and Transcendental Phenomenology translated by David Carr, Northwestern University Press, Evanstion, 1970, hereafter Crisis. But what is the "natural primordial attitude" and how is it to be grounded ? Whether transcendental reduction leaves anything concrete to build upon any viable project of scientific understanding or is one left merely with transcendental subjectivity which brackets everything except itself ? How to understand scientific knowledge and its rootedness in some form of awareness before any theorizing starts ? Is there anything pre-scientific without being completely unscientific or anti-scientific ? And how and where to start from ? How to demonstrate or establish its historical journey ? Can some sort of relativity of all knowledge, including scientific knowledge, be incorporated without falling into the trap of full blooded relativism and subjectivism ? These are some of the issues and problems which Husserl was grappling with during the later stage of his life and the Crisis is the fruit of his deliberations and meditations on these.

As is known to every student of Husserl's philosophy, the most important concept or theme in Crisis is that of life-world (lebenswelt). But the 'life-world' is a response to certain situation which. has partly been pointed out above, but which needs some clarification. Before we take up a few specific points to elaborate, we may say a few words about the first part of the title which understandably forms the *raison detre* of his entire project.

The crisis of European sciences does not lie in its progress and development which was much too phenomenally rapid and globally respected. The mathematization of natural sciences had almost reached the stage of achieving a universal language where complete objectivity was established. There is no need to enumerate the well-known strides of achievement objective science had made. The problem which seems to have bothered Husserl is the lack of human concern which science universally showed and is still showing. Husserl was indeed bothered about the negative or harmful role of science. The self-sufficiency of scientific objectivism was seen by Husserl as a false self-consciousness in which science is embedded. Husserl felt that science has been thoroughly dehumanized as it has become shorn of all anthropocentric considerations. The crisis of meaning is the real crisis of science. It is the complete objectivism of science which was in vogue since Galileo's mathematization programme that was found to be the main reason behind the crisis and hence the attempt to find it in the *a priori* of the life-world. With the assumed self-sufficiency of objectivism grew the fallacy of ignoring the life-world within which any theorizing and meditating takes place. This, however, does not commit one to subjectivism — he had before him the Kantian model of erecting an objective edifice of ethics and aesthetics on the subjective foundation.

In the entire corpus of Husserlian writings "life-world" is one of the those very few concepts which in one book *Crisis* has been described in so many different ways that sometimes one finds it difficult to characterize it with even a tentative precision and exactness. In our attempt to bring some order to the mass of descriptions, we may put them under certain categories for discussing it. It may be pointed out that these features are also, in our view, the more significant senses in which Husserl tried to employ in his later phase of philosophizing.

(a) *Historicity :* For Husserl it was necessary to remember the historicity of all knowledge and understanding which is at the same time the mode of self-understanding. He says :

> What is clearly necessary. . . . is that we reflect back, in a thorough historical and critical fashion, in order to provide before all decisions, for a radical self-understanding (*Crisis*, p. 17).

As philosophers, he thinks, our task is to know 'only through a "critical understanding of the total unity of history — our history" (p. 71). Obviously, Husserl's philosophers also include scientists. It is also, therefore, a call to science to be aware of its own roots which can only be located in the logical or phenomenological space which is the life-world. In some generic sense it can be said to be a development or evolution, with added qualities and functions, of the natural world or the surrounding world (Umwelt) of Ideas. The beginning of historical reflection must be seen as our necessity as historical being who "not only have a spiritual heritage but have become what we are thoroughly and exclusively in a historical-spiritual manner" (p.71). For philosophical and scientific reflection and understanding, it is necessary that those who are engaged in it must think critically on the history of such knowledge in order to do it effectively.

Explicating the notion of life-world, Husserl observes,

> . . . . the everyday surrounding world of life is presupposed as existing — the surrounding world in which all of us (even I who am now philosophizing) consciously have our existence; here are also the sciences, as cultural facts in this world, with their scientists and theories. In this world we are objects among objects in the sense of the life-world, namely, as being here and there, in the plain certainty of experience, before anything is established scientifically. . . .
>
> *(Crisis, pp. 104-5)*

Husserl in his earlier works *Formal and Transcendental Logic and Cartesian Meditations*[2] had emphasized the history or temporal genesis of any conscious life or ego. In "Cartesian Meditation" he says that "the ego constitutes himself for himself in the unity of a history". In the Crisis the historicity is applied in a much wider field which is almost coextensive with the life-world where all that is individual, social and psychical must be seen as rooted in its historicity. Husserl is also aware of the situation wherein, the tradition or historicity in which we are rooted includes not only what one accepts or rejects but may also extend to unacknowledged legacies which had, without our consent, shaped what we are — our history and tradition. There are prejudices which passively or actively have influenced our thinking and attitudes which can be recognized by unearthing them and subsequently these can be bracketed. But bracketing can be applied to those prejudices and assumptions which we are aware of. Unacknowledged and unknown cannot be brought under the purview of bracketing or *epoche*. The elements or various constituents and constructs which go to make our natural attitude or the life-world can be bracketed — the contents of the life-world could be subject to change and variation but not the "general structure" of the life-world (p. 139) which is not relative. As life-world, the world has the same structure that the objective sciences pre-suppose. The Crisis, as David Carr[3] observes, "reveals a radical discovery which changes the character of phenomenological investigation". Since the life-world is a historical-cultural world, many life-worlds are possible. This is a view which was also held earlier by Husserl[4]. For Husserl, the life-world has its own ontology and as a pre-scientific world its ontic meaning is the presupposition for any theoretical and practical activity. As he says,

> What is actually first is the "merely subjective-relative" intuition of pre-scientific world-life.
>
> *(Crisis, p.125)*

Husserl's emphasis on the life-world's own and constant ontic meaning for beings who live in it suggests that he thematizes the problem of the manner of being of the life-world which would indicate what kind of "scientific" tasks. i.e. tasks to be resolved with universal validity, arise in respect to this world's own manner of being. (p. 123). The knowledge of the objective scientific world is grounded in the self-evidence of the life-world and, as he says, "we as scientists are among the components of the life-world" which exists as pre-given; hence "all science and we are pulled into the 'subjective-relative' life-world". (p.131) One is reminded here of Gadamer's and Schleiermacher's concepts of understanding but we will touch upon Gadamer later. For Husserl, each one of us is "something of" the world of which we are constantly conscious as a horizon,

> We are conscious of this horizon only as a horizon of existing objects; without particular objects of consciousness it cannot be actual. The world. . . . exists with such uniqueness that the plural makes no sense when applied to it. Every plural and every singular drawn from it presupposes the world horizon.
>
> *(Crisis, p. 143).*

Such a pre-given world surrounds and limits us as a flowing.

Yet constant horizon. In other words, Husserl is interested in the effective-historical dimensions which are uniquely constructed by all the elements and forces which are real at any stage of history — either of the individual or of the group. To say that we cannot escape our history is to say that we cannot escape ourselves. Calling such a life-world subjective-relative, or "subjective-historical" (Schlelermacher's phrase) is to recognize the role of the participants engaged in the theoretical and practical activity. But it is subjective in Kantian sense and relative in Gadamerian sense The life-world functions as a constant pole around which all our mental and physical acts and movements revolve. The historical character of all our scientific and philosophical activities which Husserl seeks to emphasize is a call to make such activities historically relevant and humanly fruitful. The scientists who develop knowledge and techniques are themselves completely neutral to their uses and those who weild power and control the scientific programmes are atrociously callous and unconcerned about their employment. Historical situation, specially in the contemporary world, demand the awareness of their responsibility and accountability to humanity at large. Whether science is beneficient or 'maleficent' is a question which is generally dismissed as silly and at best it is encouraged only as a topic of essay writing at the school level. Husserl's critique of scientific objectivism should also be appreciated in this context. The mathematised idealization of science is one aspect but it is not the only approach towards our living world which is also a historical-cultural world. The universal life-world is the cradle of all cultural and scientific theories and interpretations. Science, as "a human spiritual accomplishment" presupposes the "intuitive surrounding world of life, pregiven as existing for all in common". Hence, science "continues to presuppose this surrounding world as it is given in its particularity to the scientist" (p.121). The life-world is the way ultimate reality is given to people structured by the historical practical horizons towards which people direct their lives. It is the product of past cultural traditions, "sedimented within it" that exercise their power over the present and future through the contemporary praxis they support. Historically, of course, people have lived in pre-science period. The life-world was always there before sciences as it continues in the period of science (p.123). Within the life-world the reality of particular objects is always provisional. Future experience and interpretation can always revise or reject them. Nevertheless, such revisions can only change details, not the "ontic certainty of the world" (p.143).

(b) Another aspect of the life-world which we have sparsely touched upon but is very crucial to our understanding of this concept is the pre-givenness of the life-world and a number of other related ideas which we find in the *Crisis*. Life-world is mostly referred to as 'pre-given' (p.122), presupposed, taken for granted, "pre-scientific", pre-logical, "pre-predicative", it is intuitively given and intuitively known, taken for granted, the original ground of all theoretical and practical activity (p.49), "a realm of original self-evidences", "that which is self-evidently given is experienced as "the thing itself" in immediate presence or in any other mode of intuition (pp. 127-8), world of known and unknown realities (p. 50). Husserl's emphasis on its pregivenness and other related ideas primarily aims at showing that life-world is prior to science. It is an obvious truth that scientific theories came up much after men and women lived in the world of perception which was the world of naive realism. Historically, people have lived in the epoch of pre-science. Husserl says, "that the life-world was always there before science just as it continues in the epoch of science" (p. 123). What he means by the "most general structures of the life-world' (p.142) is a stronger sense of pre-givenness. Both perception and scientific theorizing equally pre-suppose it. It is "pre-given as existing for all in common" (p.121), and even the straight forwardly perceptual is communalized (p.163). There is some ambiguity on this point in his earlier writings which shows how his various formulations move between direct realism and subjective idealism *via* conceptual realism. There is some tension in his views concerning the sphere of ownness in the context of life-world and intersubjectivity. Sometimes he suggests that we can not have intersubjectivity without the former but we can have the former without the latter. Again, despite his views concerning the *a priori* nature of the life-world, he gives it some concrete content. Life-world, as mentioned earlier, has certain cultural objects and properties. Scientists, their theories and their perceptions are elements within the life-world as sciences are "cultural facts in this world with their theories" (p.104). He says :

> The knowledge of the objective-scientific world is "grounded" in the self-evidence of the life-world. The latter is pre-given to the scientific worker . . . . as ground, yet, as they build upon this, what is built is something new, something different. If we cease being immersed in our scientific thinking, we become aware that we scientists are, after all, human beings and as such are among the components of the life world which always exists for us, ever pre-given; and thus all of science is pulled, along with us, into the merely "subjective-relative" life-world.
>
> *(Crisis, pp. 130-1)*

For Husserl, all interpretations and pictures of the life-world can never be one with it. They are views or interpretations of the life-world, not the life-world. The validity of the pre-given life-world does not depend on some purpose or goal of investigation, "every end presupposes it" (p. 382). He says that the life-world has a structure though not purposive one. But to attribute structuredness to the life-world is to presuppose a role of subjectivity *vis-á-vis* the life-world. If it is structured, consciousness appropriates it and its pre-givenness and pre-scientificality would be compromised. Perhaps, what Husserl wanted to say is that as it is given to us intuitivity, any conscious being would perceive it having some structure, however vague, immediately given to us in a purely uniterpreted way. As he points out, the pre-predicated world always remains the "constant presupposition and background for every conceptual world-view". Nevertheless, since cultural properties and ideas are included in the life-world and they, in Husserls expression get "sedimented" they may colour our perception of reality and the much-needed distinction between experience and interpretation may become difficult to make. The sedimented understanding and interpretation may sharpen the variations and changes in life-worlds belonging to different cultures and epochs.

(c) Finally, we may briefly discuss the role of prejudices within the horizon of the life-world. Along with various qualifications and descriptions that Husserl offers of the life-world, one repeatedly referred to is its status as a "horizon". It is a horizon of perceptual objects' theories, ideal constructs and our fellow men. In general, it may be said to be the totality of all that surrounds us at mental and physical levels, and which is constantly and necessarily pre-given (p.142). It is a horizon within which all other worlds are constituted and given. It is not another world but the condition and possibility of all worlds. Its "constant validity", "self-evidence" and "ontic meaning" for all beings who live in it seem to suggest the inevitable, pervasive and unsurpassable limit of our thinking and knowing. Husserl speaks of the "natural primordial attitude" as opposed to the theoretical attitude of the Greeks. In the beginning of the scientific development it may be closer to *techne* but with even the initial development of theoretical interest it gets closer and closer to praxis. Sometimes Husserl's approach to the life-world has been described as "theoretical praxis". This horizon is understood and classified "only through a critical understanding of the total unity of history — our history" (p.71). We must turn to the tradition of which we are a part so that we may look into and acknowledge historical prejudices which determine the issues and problems of philosophy. What is required is that we relive the tradition in order to bring to recognition the prejudices that are a part of the tradition. Husserl indeed often speaks of prejudices in the pejorative sense unlike Gadamer's use of it in the neutral sense. But the general tenor of his discussions also sometimes suggests that a non-pejorative neutral sense is not incompatible with his views. The turn from the neutral to the negative sense is generally a function of later theorizing and reflection. Generally speaking, the Crisis is thematically the construction of a history which reflects the philosopher's own philosophical prejudices in order to overcome or throw out those very prejudices. But one has to work through the prejudices and tradition which are a part of one's life-world in order to break through them. Husserl considers it a constant struggle against historical prejudices (which require a sustained and cautious analysis of them) to arrive at, or at least be aware of, the phenomenology of science and culture and to place them in its proper perspective. The prejudices involved here do need proper attention. To the extent that there are prejudices which are unacknowledged and deeply embedded in one's tradition, it is much more difficult to dredge them out. Still, the Crisis tries its best to make us aware of these difficulties.

Husserl's life-world is the horizon against which all things stand out and without which they cannot appear to us. As horizon life-world is unique and unitary but the term 'singular' (as opposed to "plural") "makes no sense when applied to it" (p.143). What it actually means is that one persons' horizon is unique to him for various reasons including his own history and traditions. It clearly does not mean that there is one and the same for all. Life-world is the horizon within which all other worlds—linguistic, cultural, historical, scientific, literary, artistic etc. — are given and constituted. It is not another world in addition to them.

At this point it may seem relevant to look into Gadamerian thought to locate certain ideas in Husserl which can be further widened and related to some other contemporary trends. Husserl's treatment of prejudice has been referred to above and, as pointed out, it has a negative sense. But when admitted as unacknowledged, it becomes one of the components of the life-world. In this sense it may function as a way to realize our understanding and awareness of our cultural and scientific world. It may later, however, be bracketed or reduced by some method of reduction. Gadamer, on the other hand, accepts it in his philosophical hermeneutics as a useful prejudgement or bias which constitutes our understanding. It provides an openness to the world which is a necessary constituent of our "effective history" whose structural elements are awareness of our hermeneutic situation and its "horizon". In hermeneutic philosophy, distance between past and present is bridged by tradition which is also emphasized within Husserl's concept of the life-world. For Gadamer, understanding is "placing oneself within a tradition in which past and present are constantly fused". The openness for tradition help bring about the awareness of effective-history which is "hermeneutical consciousness".[5] For Gadamer, 'all self-knowledge proceeds from what is historically pre-givens. Any historical situation contains its horizon — a view which Husserl must readily accept. Like Husserl's pre-givenness of the life-world, Gadamer also emphasizes the role of "fore-having", "fore-sight", and "fore-conception" as presuppositions for the constitution of an object. These also provide the structure of meaning[6]. Like Husserl, Gadamer also accepts the significance of historicity as an ontological one, unlike Dilthery, as it affects the very nature of what is understood. In Gadamer's thought, it is in the fusion of horizons that we approach what we understand . . . . with the prejudices which constitute the historical reality of (our) being". For Gadamer, hermeneutic reflection, like Husserl's transcendental phenomenology, is supposed to mediate between science and the life-world. And the life-world, in Heideggerian parlance, can be said to formulate or define the mode of being of the Dasein. It must not be implied here that we are equating Gadamer's views on linguistic nature of understanding with Husserlian horizon which is all-inclusive. It is only the methodological semblance which we want to bring out.[7] Gadamer comes close to Husserlian standpoint in his recognition that one's horizon of world is largely constituted by not only time and the history of being but also by the history of philosophical and aesthetic thought. Alfred Suchutz speaks of the life-world as,

> *"Arranged into fields of different relevance according to my current state of interest, each one having its own peculiar centre of density and fullness and its open but interpretable horizon".*[8]

For Suhutz, "concrete historical, socio-cultural lebenswelt"[9] within which all typifications of common sense thinking are themselves integral elements of the concrete historical socio-cultural lebenswelt within which they prevail as taken for granted and as socially approved.

Now such a life-world cannot perforce be posited against the cultural relativists. Many a writer conveniently place Husserl against Gadamer on the point of objectivity or non-relativity of the life-world and the relativity of the 'Horizon'. In the case of the life-world, Husserl admits that the results of theoretical reflections "flow into the very subsoil out of which they grow". Thus it may be difficult to distinguish between the experienced and interpreted. They can become part of the way of experiencing. Theory in sedimented form may affect the structure of the life-world. Thus life-world may differ fundamentally from one cultural group or epoch to another depending on the nature of sedimented interpretations, Some pre-given world structure may be the background for every new theoretical achievement but it may not always be the same structure that is taken for granted. This allows for a more flexible and accommodating concept of the life-world than a single, insulated one. Gadamer's fusion of horizons presupposes more open-ended horizons with an openness towards the other, Husserl would not admit it though this may be worked out in the context of his *Crisis*. Various life-worlds constitute different possible worlds, always relative to the thinker or experience, but can still be fused together.

It is also significant to note that both Husserl and Gadamer have a common concern about the relation between sciences and the realm of human understanding. Juxtaposing along with what we have earlier said about Husserl, let us attend to Gadamer's words :

> . . . . the central question of the modern age . . . is. . . . how our natural view of the world — the experience of the world we have as we simply live out our lives — is related to the unassailable and anonymous authority that confronts us in the pronouncements of science[10].

Husserl's disquiet with the fallacy of scientific objectivism finds its echo in Gadamer's distrust of historical objectivism which "conceals the involvement of the historical consciousness itself in effective history".[11] "Thus we find that there is a greater affinity between Husserl's life-world and Gadamer's "situation" and "horizon". Husserl has, at a number of places in the *Crisis*, recognized and stated that the life-world functions as horizon, i.e., the limit or boundaries of our knowledge and understanding. Gadamer also admits that (every) finite present has its limitations". We define the concept of "situation" by saying that it represents a standpoint that limits the possibility of vision. Hence, as essential part of the concept of situation is the concept of "horizon". The horizon is the range of vision that includes everything that can be seen from a particular vantage point[12].

REFERENCES

(*The Crisis of European Sciences and Transcendental Phenomenology* translated by David Carr, Northwestern University Press, Evanston, 1970., hereafter Crisis, p. 281).

1. Husserl, *Cartesian Meditations, tr.* D. Cairns,Martinus Nijhoff, 1960, p.75.
2. David Carr, Interpreting Husserl *Critical and Comparative Studies*, Martinus Nijhoff, 1987, p.91.
3. *Cartesian Meditaions*, op. cit., p. 133.
4. Gadamer, H.G.*Truth and Method, tr.* W. Glyn-Doepel, London, 1975, p. 274-75 hereafter, TM.
5. *TM*, p.285-286
6. *TM*, p.193
7. *TM*, p.245
8. Alfred Sctutz, *Collected Papers*, I. Martinus Nijhoff, 1962, p.134.
9. *Ibid*, p.149
10. Gadamer, H.G. *Philosophical Hermeneutics, tr.* D. Linge, Berkeley, 1976, p. 25.
11. *TM*, p. 268.
12. *TM*, p. 269.

Chapter – 11

Post-Modernism and Ethics

S.A. Shaida

Post-modernism is a radical way of understanding all aspects and areas of human thought and experience by uprooting and deconstructing all the myths and illusions which are seen as products of modernism and Enlightenment. The situation of man in modern age and the complexities of post-industrial and post-capitalistic socio-economic realities gave rise to equally complex ideas and beliefs. Some of these are objectivity, truth, power, authority, absolutism, universal and eternal values, absolute duties and goodness and a host of similar ideas and theories based thereon. The reaction to such a state of affair came from a formidable list of thinkers such as Nietzsche, Kierkegaard, Marx, Habermas, Derrida, Bauman, Loytard, Walzer, Heidegger, Mac Intyre, Bernard Williams, Foucault, Feyeraband, Kuhn and others.

Nevertheless, what marks them all is the rejection of modernism and all that it entails. And among the latter it is foundationalism which is most vehemently rejected by all even though they may differ among themselves on matters of detail and their respective approaches.

Foundationalism has most crucially been involved in epistemology and ethics even though it has exercised great influence in studies of culture, art, science and some other areas. But before we discuss the post-modernist approach to ethics, it may be helpful to delve into the general tenor and the overall thought-content of post-modernism.

Post-modernism can be viewed as a reaction against a naive and unflinching confidence in progress and objective scientific truth. The grand or meta-narratives of the Enlightenment period or the age of reason claimed to be a grandiose project which is seen by many post-modernists like Loytard and others as hollow and counter productive. Hence, it is rejected and replaced by *petite* narratives, i.e., by local or regional narratives. The upsurge of the dominance of the affluent Western countries, their culture, economy, sciences and polity has not only negated the value of less developed or developing societies which have also been treated as less human and less cultured. In international politics, the western countries led by the U.S. made the dishonest and false claims that true democracy, peace and progress are found only in their countries and not in the Afro-Asian world. It is not only Fukuyama or Bush who propagate such lies but they are also backed by the neo-conservatives who are in fact neo-fascists. The Kafkasque situation in the contemporary western (i.e., American) culture and politics demand a radical confrontation and post-modernism is an honest attempt in this direction.

The post-modernists situate themselves in times where some catastrophic upheavals have destroyed human faith and hope in peace, security and progress. Complete reification and dehumanization of man are operative at all levels. Western society, since the days of Bacon, has always accepted knowledge-power equation but its penetration in all areas of human life has destroyed human relations. In Foucault's analysis of this phenomenon we find the manifest, the hidden, the conscious and unconscious manifestations of complex forms of oppression and exploitation. In politics, the world is facing not only the possibility of a serious nuclear holocaust (anticipated by Hiroshima and Nagasaki) but also systematic genocide by the same demonic power which dropped the atom bombs. Most of this has happened and is happening in the Third World and in the Banana Republics which, for the U.S., house less than humans. The unipolar world has become far too dangerous for the Plebians and the Puritans.

The post-modern geo-political condition is the common background for almost all the post-modernists who react to all established beliefs and theories by negating or denying them. The skepticism or pessimism which is lurking behind such rejections may be traced to the writings of Neitzsche and Heidegger. But this skepticism is counter-balanced by the attitude of romanticism which makes them rebel against all forms of tyranny including the tyranny of truth. The all-important theme which binds all the post-modernists is the rejection of foundationalism and essentialism epitomized in the Enlightenment project constructed by Kant. Truth, for post-modernism, is always buried under manipulations, propaganda, interest or rationalization. The criteria of truth and certainty grounded in scientific objectivity, have themselves become suspect on account of competing discourses which tried to locate scientific truths within alternative paradigms. The works of men like Kuhn and Feyeraband sought to redefine the traditional concept of truth. Denial of truth is of course rejection of absolute truth and absolute reality. Contemporary human situation depicts the helplessness of people whereby untruth is made as saleable as truth.

It is often held by some writers that post-modernism does away with the distinction between truth and falsity. If there is no truth there cannot be a way to say what is falsehood or error. This brings in a situation where anything or everything can be true or false. In Feyeraband's words, 'anything goes'. Hence, all beliefs are equal. But, as apprehended by some, this need not lead to nihilism. It only suggests that all beliefs and truths remain at the level of probability or possibility and anyone is as true or false as any other. As David Hoy suggests, "it has a liberating effect and it only seeks to take note of the complexity of such truths and beliefs". Non acceptance of truth claims, in Derrida's view, does not bring in nihilism. It only works towards showing the impossibility of totalitarianism. The reason for this view lies in the fact that totalitarianism not only depends on its own version of truth but also aims at driving others out of court. This, of course, leads to relativisation of truth and the post-modernists must agree to its application to their own position. The stand of "No-truth" is a self-reflexive one which radicalizes rejection of all truth claims. Hence, post-modernism is haunted by the possibility of contradiction when they assert the truth that "there is no truth". They accept, in order to be consistent, that their own view is no more veracious than those of others and if they present it before others they do not claim any privileged position.

In order to understand and appreciate the main thrust of post-modernism one has to place before oneself the assumptions and achievements of modernism. Since post-modernism is, as a matter of fact, anti-modernism, it seeks to supplant all the master narratives of modernity which absolutises truth, reality and nature and seeks to replace alternative *petite* or regional narratives about all that can be lived or experienced. These narratives become polemical in relation to all the positions propped up by modernism. Almost all the founding assumptions of Western European culture are challenged. Alternative descriptions of them in all important areas like philosophy, science, politics, art, literature or social sciences open up new vistas and ways of understanding the universe without any claim to truth, objectivity and certainty. This involves multi-disciplinary effort by coalescing concepts and methods which were for long segregated in the domains of academics and practical life. The cultural epoch of modernity, based on the belief that the world is one, a unified field explicable by a single unified explanatory system, is sharply negated and jettisoned. Hence, most of the post-modernists disavow any common denominator in nature or truth which may facilitate oneness of the world or the possibility of objective thought. They often argue that human systems operate like language and are self-reflexive rather than referential systems which constitute meaning and value.

Modernism gave rise to master narratives under the rubric of Enlightenment project whose credibility post-modernism sought to question. The categories of truth, reason and social have been termed mythical by men like Lyotard (The Post-Modern Condition, University of Minnesota Presss, 1984). The view of history as a struggle for gradual liberation of humanity and progressive evolution of humane societies is dismissed as mythical and illusory. Global consumerism, the impact of information technology or the cyber cafes have destroyed the mode of human relations and social concerns. The traditional community-based culture is overtaken by superficial commonality imposed by electronic media which propagate a unified culture.

As against the totalitarian stance of powerful American and European governments which still persist with colonial approach to the non-Western societies, post-modernists seek to encourage a human condition with a genuinely free and interactive public sphere. It is needed by the individuals to have a meaningful participation in order to express themselves. But the vested interests of the neo-colonial powers have almost closed the public sphere declaring them less than civilized and non-progressive, Edward Saids' Orientalism is an honest indictment of the stereotypes which the West, especially America, have propagated and exploited to breed falsehoods and misinformation. Its political fallout has also been severely criticized by Chomsky. According to Habermas, the concept of the public sphere assumes that public dialogue and deliberation, freely engaged among individuals, can achieve an approximation of truth through an exchange of ideas (Habermas, "The Public Sphere, An Encyclopaedia Article", New German Critique, No. 3, 1974). The public sphere makes the critique of political authority possible within a democratic set-up. In his view, it would result in reconciliation of differing which may lead to some sort of general agreement, But it is felt, and rightly so, that the public sphere as an independent arena of discussion is threatened. The distinction between public and private is said to be disintegrating or is being obliterated or corrupted. Habermas holds that the role of mass media is no longer either to communicate information about political matters to the public or to facilitate activity in the public sphere. It rather deforms public debate and transforms politics into theatre and entertainment. J. Baudrillard (Simulations, N.Y. 1983) and Zygmunt Bauman ("The Left as the Counter-current of

Modernity", Zelos 1986-87) also think that it obliterates the distinction between private and public as people internalize the mass message, and take it to be real. The media, as Bauman says, "define political issues as matters of emotion and image". Hence, the mass media, which has become an inalienable part of contemporary culture, do not facilitate the functioning of a healthy public sphere separate from the private sphere. One of the factors responsible for the distortion and limitation of public sphere is the failure of representation because in social and political spheres it has not fulfilled its purpose. Every representative only serves or represents either his/her interest or merely represents and defends preconceived opinion that reflects the collective interest of those who elect him /her or arrange finances for the election. As Habermas says, representation has become "translation of interests". The legislatures have turned into fora for propaganda. The neo-Marxists as well as Habermas advocate creation of autonomous public spaces for the feasibility of intersubjective communication. These spaces should not be subordinated to the profit motive alone. But the rejection of representation by the post-modernists is equally disturbing because in any democratically organized society there is no easy alternative. Despite all the misconstruing and misuses of representation, it has to be resorted to in order not to give an easy passage to totalitarianism and fascism.

Such a way of thinking had a radical effect on ethics where anti-foundationalism and anti-logocentricity have revised the accepted theoretical paradigms and has focused attention on practical concerns involved in our notion of virtuous life. Writers like Bernard Williams, Mac Intyre, Walzer and Philipa Foot have revised the notion of ethics as a practical science. The area of virtue ethics is a reincarnation of Greek ethical wisdom. Displacing the unified way of analyzing good, value or obligation, multiple standards have been recommended.

There were certain forceful expressions of dissent concerning the prevalent mode of thinking in ethics or moral philosophy. In the twentieth century it was spearheaded by G.E.M. Anscombe in her paper "Modern Moral Philosophy" published in 1958 - Philosophy Anscombe made a plea to come out of the Judaeo-Christian framework of law and duty and to think more in terms of values and virtues which were entrenched in communal way of life. It was in fact a call to return to virtuous life and realise self-knowledge and self-understanding through practice of virtues in the way the Greek philosophers recommended. Morality grows, develops and is practiced in the polis through common goals, cooperation, agreements and differences. For Aristotle what is required is a consistent and permanent inclination towards living virtuously. So he calls virtue the habit of character. It is not in spite of desires but because of desires that man gets impetus to act in such a manner. In this process it is not theoretical reason but practical reason, or what Aristotle calls practical wisdom or phronesis which is involved in making right kind of choices. The post-modernists by and large accept the Nietzschian view that living morally is an activity of disciplined self-knowledge which leads to self recovery, self-fashioning and even self-creation.

One of the important voices in the post-modernism discourse on ethics is Michael Walzer's. For him, living ethically implies respect for varieties of values, moral standpoints or cultural "forms of life" which will always co-exist in any democratic society. This idea has obviously the support of Wittgenstein's views on language as revealing forms of life. The beliefs, values and moral priorities have relevance and justification within specific cultural communities. They may not be justified beyond such reference groups. Such an approach debunks the attempt to found morality on ideas of universal values or absolutely unconditional duty. For the post-modernists the vacuous and impracticable insistence on universal values and categorical imperatives do not help us in our day-to-day moral choices and decisions.

One of the most significant contribution towards the development of virtue ethics has been Mac Intyre's work. After *Virtue* which provides a comprehensive critique of the Enlightenment's a historical standards of rationality. Refocussing the fundamental questions of ethics on Aristotalian lines,

Mac Intyre emphasizes the notion of community virtue or tradition. He accords an important place to emotivism without accepting the usual conclusion that emotivism obliterates all distinctions between good and bad, right and wrong or one between facts and values. He believes that our moral tradition rests on virtues which are grounded in a teleological understanding of human nature. The problems of ethics are essentially centred around specific social practices and ethos which are manifest in our life. Our concept of good life which is tied to our community and local mores is nevertheless rooted in, and is coherently lived in accordance with our idea of the goal (telos) which often transcends particular practices. The telos within a particular tradition which informs and directs our "acceptance of a moral philosophy is not arbitrary and accidental. It is the outcome of various sociological factors which percolate through tradition.

The views developed in *After Virtue* suggest that the virtues we adumbrate and internalize in our conduct and habits are acquired dispositions as argued in Nichomachean Ethics. Virtues like courage, temperance or justice are acquired dispositions or habits through which we attain the good that is embedded in particular practices. These are human traits that control and guide practices which make our traditions within which our search of virtuous life acquires meaning and significance. This is what Mac Intyre calls the telos of man's life.

Another work which has furthered the post-modern involvement with virtue ethics and mistrust of the bipolar authority of utilitarianism/Kantianism is Bernard Williams' *Ethics and the Limits of Philosophy* (1985). His most significant criticism of utilitarianism is based on his notion of integrity which echoes the existentialist ideal of authenticity. Williams pleads for a richer understanding and psychology of motivation in the manner in which Anscombe had suggested a deeper relevance of philosophical psychology. Reasons for action can be varied and complex in different cases and the same reason need not stand in all cases as proper justification of action. An individual's motivation and action depend on her ideosyncracies and antecedent situation.

Hence, there are no independent moral truths which may equally justify all actions in the same manner. Such a view works against both utilitarianism and Kantian rationality which rejects any moral relevance of desires and emotions. For Williams, ethical judgements are more akin to desires and emotions than beliefs. Emotions like shame and regret come into play when we try to morally evaluate our own actions.

Finally, I will refer to one more writer who has moved from the traditional meta-ethical discourse to the Aristotelian framework. It is known to every student of ethics that Philippa Foot's writings were focused on ethical theories of emotivism and prescriptivism. From the standpoint of neo-naturalism, she criticized both these approaches specially for their failure to offer a sensible explanation concerning the relation between statements of fact and statements of value. Like Perry, Foot also accepts that our judgements and actions are effectively related through interest. And the most compelling interest for man is self-interest. Subsequently she leaves this position and focuses her attention on problems arising out of utilitarianism and consequentialism. In her latest phase, she comes to the Aristotelian paradigm and holds that ethical questions and problems are actually related to questions of virtues and vices. She also, alongwith other post-modernists, believes that practical reason is something which ordinary people do understand and exercise. Morality is something which needs a public sphere to grow and develop. For virtue ethics the idea of good life involves a practical approach which is not dependent upon theoretical foundations supplied by deontology and utilitarianism. Morality is not independent of particular interests and concerns of the moral agents. Moral rules are not more important than the sensitivity of the individuals. Human nature is not always strictly bound by self-interest or self-sacrifice. It would depend on the peculiarity of the situations in which the moral agent has to make decisions. The overriding concern for the individual is his eudaemonia which is to lead a virtuous life which requires a sound moral character. The complexity of the situations in which post-modern man lives requires difficult choices to be made without committing himself to either deontology or to utilitarianism as a matter of exclusive choice. Thus the grand narratives in moral discourse are replaced by *petite* narratives of individual moral concerns. There is an attempt to reconcile the good of the agent with demandingness of morality. Mac Intyre argues that in pure virtue ethics virtuous properties which are 'thick' in this view are only reason for performing such acts. Aristotle radicalized such an approach by saying that rationality of virtue consists in its promotion of the agents' endaemonia and since one's endaemonia consists only in practice of virtues, one has no reason to accept a non-virtuous life. Apart from a pure virtue ethics, as Williams suggests, there are other reason-constituting properties which are based on utilitarianism and Kantianism. The Socratic question "How one should live?" can even be answered sometimes by bringing a moral or non-moral considerations. It is not required to hold necessarily that self-interest is constituted entirely by being moral or that morality completely overrides self interest, Writers have taken seriously the criticism by Williams that both utilitarianism and Kantianism through their alleged impartiality and impersonality violate the integrity of moral agents. Foot has also developed such critical arguments within the bounds of virtue ethics.

Foot indeed accepts the rationality of desires and defends the view that moral reasons do depend on the desires of agents. Moral judgement, i.e., chiefly ought-judgements when ungrounded in our desires and inclinations become suspect. Even Kant had to make some concession tc this fact when he talks of respect for moral law. Respect for moral law as much as the maximization of utility needs motivation.

To conclude, the ethics of post-modernism is a total paradigm shift from theoretical and conceptual foundations of ethics to specific issues and problems involved in practice of virtues which are embedded in our traditions as well as in the geo-political situations surrounding us, i.e., our lived world.

Chapter - 12

What is Applied Ethics ?

M.P. Chaurasia

It is very difficult to define Applied Ethics at the outset of this article. Because it is full of many potentialities. This academic discipline is still under development. If we hope that it is a new moral system, then our views regarding this trend is wrong. It never tries to propound the standard of morality either of consequentialistic ethics or of non-consequential moral science. For the evaluation of human action, it borrows the moral standard from traditional ethics. The Applied Ethics has different branches: Bioethics, Business Ethics, Ethics of Discrimination, Environmental Ethics and above all Ecology, War, Population Control, etc., are the segments with which it deals. Why it is called Applied Ethics? Because it considers the strength of traditional moral standards with the help of meta-ethics that how much these moral standards are applicable in the real life-situation. In western philosophy, classical ethics was propounded by Socrates and nourished by Plato. Their views are regarded as deontological ethics. The disciple of Plato, Aristotle revised the scheme of his teacher and made certain corrections to apply ethics in life and society. Thus, teleological ethical views came into the existence. In this way, Aristotle was the first philosopher who considered the applicability of an ethical theory.

The world till nineteenth century had not many problems

regarding the human life and environment. But today we have enough obstacles in our day-to-day life, in the different spheres of human society. When life on the earth was very smooth and free from obstacles, pure deontological or idealistic ethical standards were very pleasant to hear and to read. But today life of the world has rapidly changed due to the changing mode of life style, we have several biological and other problems. These problems are compelling us to think of the alternative ways in the field of ethics. And this study is called Applied Ethics. So we may define Applied Ethics in the following manner: "Applied Ethics is a broad term which includes in itself the environmental, Ethical, legal and social implications of agricultural activities, life sciences,' business and the effect of medicine upon human life". On the basis of above definition, we can easily see the importance of Applied Ethics.

Now another question in this regard is about the nature of Applied Ethics. We have mentioned above that it is not a new discipline. It is also normative. But it is not only normative rather, to some extent, it is *descriptive, prescriptive* and also *interactive.* It is descriptive as it deals with life, body, environment and medicine. It is prescriptive because it discusses the norms of life and prescribed certain actions to lead a happy life. Its nature is interactive as it makes debate between people, groups within our society and communities about above two principles, i.e., descriptive and prescriptive.

How we can determine the descriptive and prescriptive nature of Applied Ethics? For this purpose we have to depend on meta-ethics. In this context, there are a few names that have elaborated the different theories in meta-ethics, especially emotivism of A.J. Ayer and C.L Stevenson and prescriptivism of R.M. Hare. These thinkers discuss the problem in detail and make the different ethical theories linguistically reachable. They have together discussed the nature of ethical basic concepts like good, right and also the basic ethical postulates. They make several attempts to show the impossibility of defining the ethical concepts. They believe in emotive. . . . descriptive nature of ethical terms. The primary meaning of ethical terms is emotive/prescriptive, while secondary meaning is descriptive. In the same way the content of moral judgements is primarily emotive/prescriptive and secondarily descriptive.

So far the proofs of moral judgements are concerned, meta-ethicists thinkers like Ayer is not of the view that moral judgements can be proved or supported by any means. C.L. Stevenson holds that though moral judgement cannot be proved in logical sense, some rational and other kinds of proofs are possible. R.M. Hare believes that ethical argument is possible. Now so far the applied ethics is concerned, we think, there are certain subject matters of it which are directly related to the descriptive materials. Problems allied with human life, mind, environment, business, sex, and abortions are discussed among the people of the society. So its primary nature is descriptive. Philosophers since Aristotle made emphasis to include the emotive aspect of human life in course of the ethical evaluation and applied ethics has made scope to inherit it.

Now we can easily know the subject matter of Applied Ethics. We see that twentieth century has created so many threatening harzards before the human life. Crisis of civilization that is at hand in twentyfirst century was never realized before. Who is responsible for this danger point? It is the human being and none else. There are several challenges which confront life of the earth: new scientific researches and inventions along with the discoveries. Discoveries of the wonders and beauties of nature do enhance the excitement, grandeur and richness of human and animal life, we have achieved the highest peak in the field of progress, search of truth, beauty and love. These things are the parameters of our civilization. But still we are facing evils. Wretchedness of human life seems to unfold itself in direct proportion to the advancement of science and technology. At some places, the evil genius in human nature seems to be under control of the decision making powers in society and abuses everything that can be instrumental in promoting the well-being of entire humanity.

Now-a-days science and wealth, both have become sharp weapons of exploitation and oppression of the majority by the minority. As Nelson Mandela, on the eve of Gandhi Jayanti, passes his tribute saying, " Small minorities consume while the masses starve."[1]. We do not ignore the importance of sciences but whatever, might be their achievements of past three centuries, instead of promoting the pleasure of human life, they have enhanced misery of human life by having an apathetic attitude towards humanity. Leaders of the wretched men, like Abraham Lincoln, M.K. Gandhi, M. Luther King and many others have been cut short either by monarchies, empires or other systems of our society. That system is still controlled by the minority. All these activities have put the human civilization at stake. Inequality in different field of life persists throughout the human history. It is imperatives of the day for leaders of different fields to debate the implications of new advancements in science and technology which not only empower the small minority to exploit the masses but also threatens the basic foundational values of life and the basic faith in human value. So to determine the utility and scope of Applied Ethics, it can be mentioned that whatever progress we may make in the realms of science, new inventions and discoveries, methods of production, communication, Information Technology, economic advancement, all these must enhance the quality of human life. Only needful justice can provide the quality of life. All economic growth must be reflected in distributive justice. We should try to stop the human's exploitation by human. All human beings are equal on social level, so they should have equal rights and privileges in the society. Science and technology should be served in such a way that these ends must be achieved. Whenever, we realize that science and technology have destroyed or have the potentiality to destroy the value of life on the earth, we must grant social control over them to prevent the malpractices of these evils. Ethics, Bio-science, ecology and economic growth are of excellent concern for the sake of humanity. So, all these disciplines should work together to serve the humanity because it is the overall objective of both physical and human sciences. Continuation of poverty in India, poverty of the mass of India, is as much an ethical challenge as Applied Ethics, Bio-ethics, environment and new genetics. Globalization of economic system in trade and commerce has opened the horizon of free business and made India a good world trade-centre. In India, it will marginalize the hope of the vast majority of its people. So such trend must be regarded dangerous as new genetics is capable of making poor man and woman simply means of the rich. It will be the fertile land to find out surrogate mothers in an easy way.

Our earth has enough capacity to fulfil the proper desires of all human beings, as Gandhiji holds, ". . . . a time is coming when those, who are in the mad rush today of multiplying their wants will retrace their steps and say: what have we done?" In 1948 two weeks before his death he made the prophetic statement that, "this (modern) civilization is such that one has only to be patient, and it will be self-destroyed".[2] If the inhuman practices of these days continue, our civilization will produce only diseases. The remedy of all these malpractices are self-refrainment and self-confinement. These two remedies will come through applied ethics.

We have mentioned above that the chief subject matter of the Applied Ethics is to lay down those principles and standards that deal with life problems. For this purpose Bio-Ethic[s] (a branch of Applied Ethics studies those problems and remedies together. The term "Bio-Ethics" is introduced by Van R. Potter in the book *Bio-Ethics, Bridge to the Future,* in 1970. In this book the author has laid down certain ideals that could be common ground for decision-making. He insisted the autonomy of individuals to make choices on the condition to respect the choices of others justice. In our all doings, we should avoid harming others and try to enhance more and more good.

The term 'good' has as many definitions as given by different ethical thinkers. But we may divide it into two broad categories: Deontological concept of good and teleological concept of good. Deontological concept of good does not exist in this world rather in an ideal world or above this world. Only *sanyasis* are capable of attaining that good. That ethical path is not for general people. Many academicians, even to day, support that concept of good. Ethical theories of Plato, Kant and Butler fall under this category. I do not insist that these theories have no merit. We shall scrutinize the merit of above theories for our practical purposes. The teleological concept of good has more practical orientation as it is construed that it can be attained in the world. J.S. Mill, Bentham and Moore's concept of good fall under this category.

In Applied Ethics our immediate concern is human life. Therefore, things that promote human life is good and things that hinder human life are bad. Many scholars of philosophy think good only as logically established concept. Everything of the world is made for the purpose of human beings, but the context makes the difference. So good can be thought only in the context of human beings. A thing may be in one situation good but in another context bad. Therefore, to believe in an eternal existence of good is worthless. In Applied Ethics good is used in the adjective sense, like to wear woollen cloth in winter is good. Now we can think of two senses of good: one is its intrinsic aspect and are another is extrinsic aspect. Only natural things are intrinsically good. Rivers, lakes, ponds, forests, insects, wild animals; etc, have intrinsic value because they seldom harm us. Medicines, hospitals, means of communications, etc., have extrinsic value, because sometimes they harm us. So moral implications are essentials to these things and actions related to them.

Above all, like the traditional ethics and meta-ethic good is also the fundamental concept of Applied Ethics a basic principle of this ethics. The goal of ethics is to determine good. Human life without good is hell. But here good can be considered in terms of pleasure or human intercourse or enjoyment of beauty or well-being of man and nothing else. The term good has moral and non-moral sense both. When it is used in non-human context, its sense is non-moral, e.g. good voltage or good motor car, but whenever it is used in human context, especially with human conduct, it is used in ethical sense. Another fundamental concept is "right". Right is always used to praise the human action. This term has also moral and non-moral sense. When it is used for things, it is used in non-moral sense, e.g., "right road", or "right sums". This use denotes correctness. But when we say "Rahul's action is right one" it is used in moral sense. For the usage of the word right, from my point of view, as Kant's and Ross' suggested are better than others.

Ethical Nihilism

Sometimes in the vast jungle of traditional moral standards, we become the victims of doubt, when the same action is evaluated right from one point of view, while from other point of view, it seems wrong. According to the Kantian ethical point of view, to save someone's life from sinking is right, even if the sinking person is one's enemy, but from the egoistic point of view, it is not right to save one's enemy. Nietzsche is perhaps the first thinker, who attracted our attention towards the *Ethical Nihilism*. In the preface of his book *Genealogy of Morals*, he mentions,".[3] .. in all morality, falters – finally a new demand becomes audible .... we need a critique of moral values, the value of these values themselves must be called in question ...." (p. 6) Philippa Foot argues that Nietzsche is the *supporter of aristocratic ethics* whose value was positive, while in modern age negative democratic value has prevailed over the society. According to Nietzsche, nihilism is not a doctrine but symptom of our society, which we should attack. The term nihilism has a broader and more important meaning in context of human existence. Nihilism is not only the collapse of traditional values, it is the demand for freedom from imposed value. Of course, these motives often appear together as the loss of foundation and faith in traditional values and again it is the ground for the demand for freedom from their now questionable authority.

What is the cause of this doubt? I have mentioned above that with the marching time, we have not changed our idea of an authority till date and on the basis of that mentality we evaluate every action by hard and fast rules of authoritarian ethics. But human life and action are not so simple. On the one hand, they, sometimes, break ethical norms and we watch silently because law does not permit us to intervene. On the other hand we do not see any divine punishment of wrong doing with immediate effect. Consequently we become the victims of *ethical skepticism.* We see that later or sooner, a law breaker is punished but not an unethical person. One can easily disobey the ethical imperatives and remain unperturbed. Occasionally we misuse our freedom with caring of other's interest. We do not concede the importance of a particular circumstances and try to seek more and more benefit for ourselves out of the situation. We sometimes impose our liking and disliking on other people. We expect that a person must behave according to my choices and should behave as per my own desire. In short, we hope that other people do good and I should have freedom to do wrong. This dual nature of human beings is the cause of ethical skepticism.

But fortunately *Applied Ethics is free from ethical scepticism,* as it provides scope for exception and human emotions. In it no ethical code is considered to be absolute and universal. What good you can perform in a situation, you must try to do and nothing else. Devashish Guha has also considered this problem at length and found out nearly the same conclusion. He insisted on the critical re-evaluation of certain ethical code but I think, we should not take care for difficult ethical code and only follow the easy path. I think Thomas Nagel is correct when he says, "most of the things we pursue are optional. Their value to us depends on our individual aims, projects and concerns . . . . they acquire value only because the interest we develop in them."[4]

Basic Assumptions and Postulates

In traditional ethics, personality, reason and freewill are considered the primary assumptions of morality. But in Applied Ethics, scenario is changed. All these postulates have been accepted here too. In addition to these postulates certain assumptions have been supplemented to enrich the Applied Ethics so that it can be flexible. The *first* assumption, in this regard, is to base ethics on rationality and yet it should not be devoid of emotion. Religion based moral views and intuition based morality are lacking such elements.*Secondly,* a moral theory should be as logically consistent as possible but not rigid and strict like egoism. *Thirdly,* a moral standard must have general application of all humanity and also it must contain applicability to particular individuals and situations. Bentham's utilitarianism and intuitionists theories are suffering from such defects. *Lastly,* a moral standard should be able to be taught and promulgated. From this point of view egoism has no credit, as it cannot be taught. Every tenable moral theory should have efficiency to resolve conflicts of duties and obligations among human beings.

We all know since Aristotle, that man is a rational animal. It means human personality has *two aspects*: *cognitive and affective*. Whenever we establish an ethical norm, we have to take consideration of these two aspects of human beings, so that norm can be applied to every one. But relation between reason and emotion should be balanced. Here, *'reason' does not mean 'reasoning'*. Reasoning is an *activity* that we do. It needs learning of certain processes and rules, while faculty of reason is an ability which human beings have. Reasoning is formal and logical process, while reason is simply cause that justifies our feelings or emotions, in any ethical controversy since opposite parties may have contrary attitudes towards the same ethical issue. And here we need reason to resolve the conflict, for example, we can cite the case of abortion. It has different pros and cons reasons. Opponents may say that abortion means abolition of human life, as life begins with conception, and only God has right to cease any life. Its supporters may say that women have absolute right over their bodies and rights of previous born must prevail over the right of unborn, etc. Both parties bring evidence and facts to enrich their reasons and test these bases with rational and logical arguments. They can examine all of the biological, sociological, and psychological evidence that is available concerning when human life can actually be said to begin. For the purpose of the stability of moral decision making, ethical system should be logically consistent. If an ethical system sanctions any action in particular situation, but keeps silent in another similar situation, it cannot be regarded logically consistent system. But a good moral system should not be rigid towards the logical consistency, because it will increase the unnecessary complexity and diversity that comprises human beingness. In that case we will be unable to justify extraordinary action in a typical situation. We should try to be consistent and yet allow enough flexibility so that the ethical system can remain truly applicable to the complexity and variety of human beings.

Any ethical system should attempt to help all men and it is possible too, and it is possible only when, the morality has universal applicability. If a moral system is applicable only to one person, like personal ethical egoism, then all remaining human beings are essentially excluded from the system. The system should not be based on religious postulates or any dogmatic truths, which have no conclusive evidential or rational proofs. But on the issue of universality it should never be so rigid. In that context, it will never be applicable in a particular situation with an individual. Morality never takes place in abstract rather in a concrete situation. It deals with living individual. So it should always be consistent with human beings and the particular situation. For example, a blind supporter of religious faith cannot support abortion in any situation, as it is abolition of life. But it is possible that the life of mother is at stake and her life can be saved by aborting the foetus. So, in this situation ethical norm should be loosened.

A moral system, if it applies to all persons, should be teachable and it must be able to be promulgated. From this point of view, Mill's utilitarianism and Kant's theory of morality are very suitable. Finally, a workable ethical system should be able to resolve conflicts among duties and obligations of the people, who participated in this course. For example, universal ethical egoism has not the capacity to resolve the conflict between the participants on the same issue, as it holds that everyone should always seek one's own interest. In that situation no person can be ethically blamed for his doing. For example, in a moral system, it is established that it is wrong to lie and also wrong to break promises. But it is possible that two wrongs take place at the same time in a particular situation and the moral system does not mention which wrong should be preferred to at that period then with all its merits, the moral system is worthless. From this point of view the view of W.D. Ross is fine one, as it prefers to the *prima-facie* duty in a particular situation. For example, if I have made a promise to my friend that I will save his life from his enemy. My friend has stayed at my house and his enemy, searching him has come to me. In this situation I can do only one action. Either I speak a lie or keep my promise. It is ethically worthy to keep my promise and save the life of my friend than to speak a lie because human life is more precious than telling a lie.

Basic Principles

If we glance over the history of traditional ethics, we shall find that all ethical standards have at least one basic principle. For ethical egoism the basic principle is personal inclination, for utilitarianism, interest of all concerned and for Kantian categorical imperative, performing the duty without any personal inclination and treat every human being as an end in himself, not the means for others. Here, we are concerned to find out some principles upon which all moral thinkers may agree. For this purpose we should search out some fundamental elements related to morality and human life both. From this point of view the value of life principle is the most fundamental principle for any ethical system. Because ethics has to deal with human beings living in the society. If there is no man, then there is no ethics. Therefore, the preservation and protection of human life is essential for an ethical system. It is an empirical fact that we cannot or should not talk on ethics without including the human beings. But it does not mean that people should never die or someone may not be killed or be allowed to die. The basic creed of ethics must be 'no human life, no ethical system' because it has not only a pragmatic purpose, but also justifies the morality. All religious and ethical systems condemn the human killing. But in extraordinary situation all religions provide scope of human killing, e.g., *The Bhagvad Gita, Koran and Bible.* So our first basic principle for *applied ethics is the value of life principle with exception that in an extraordinary situation human life can also be abolished in case of capital punishment or to kill a vigorous criminal who is a history sheeter.*

Principle of Goodness or Rightness

The essence of ethics is the concept of 'Good' or 'Right. We can not have ethics without mentioning Goodness or Rightness. All moral theories, this way or that way, believe in the principle of Goodness or Rightness. All ethical systems preach us to be 'good' human beings and always attempt to act rightly. We should always avoid to be bad and to do wrong. We should always try to promote goodness over badness and cause no harm or bad to others. Moral philosophers may vary concerning the nature and degree of Good and Right but they all emphasize these two concepts.

Principle of Justice

The principle of justice advises people to treat others as his own and be justful in distributing goodness and badness among the fellow beings. Only performing right and try to be good is not sufficient ground of morality. We should distribute good and bad equally to the people on the basis of their merits. During distribution, we should take care of the needs or abilities of the people. We should not be unfair in distributing good and bad among the people as George Schreiner said, "You should be logical and say that when a man stops going to church or is divorced or loses his job, he ought to be removed from the programme and somebody else who fulfils these criteria be substituted."[5]

Here it may be said that no resources can be found on the earth that can satisfy the needs of all the people. Only thing we can do can be that we may arrange more and more resources but it is next to impossible to fulfil all the needs of the people, as there are so many needs but resources available are limited. Therefore, it is difficult for a noble man to choose and to distribute justly. We cannot easily say, "let the better person live or avail as every life is precious for the sake of one's family and himself". From this point of view, I think, egalitarian way of determining justice is the most ethical, just and fair. Kantian categorical imperative treats all human beings as "ends rather than means" his justice at its core. In the same way utilitarianism in its all forms advocates the strongest concern for justice of all because it attempts to deal with happiness of all concerned.

The Principle of Truth Telling

The principle of justice is fully sufficient to explain ethical problems. But for the sake of communication between two or more than two persons in a social context, the principle of Truth Telling or Honesty is a prior condition of a moral system. No moral system can function well if its participants cannot deal with each other honestly. How other people will rely on a teacher who teaches morality if he does not speak truth? Social relationships depend on agreement and reliability and both these factors need assurance, honesty and truth telling. Mostly, religions of the world have emphasized truth telling.

The Principle of Individual Freedom

In traditional ethics, Johnson is champion of individual freedom. In recent period it is advocated by Michael Scriven. For him, this is the foremost fundamental principle of morality. Actually he defines morality in terms of "equal consideration from which all other moral principles can be developed" and if we realize in it then according to him, "People have equal rights with you in moral matters until they prove otherwise."[6] Though none will agree with Scriven, but we cannot marginalize the importance of individual freedom in the field of moral life. In short freedom is a condition of moral conduct. If we do not grant freedom how we can expect a voluntary action? And only voluntary action is the subject matter of ethical consideration. This principle means that people, being individuals with particular differences, must have the liberty to choose their own ways and means of being moral within the framework of the above mentioned four basic principles. Human beings cannot be absolutely free as they are the subjects of nature. Absolute freedom is possible only in the forest and not in a society. We can enjoy individual freedom within the limits of above basic principles. Individual freedom varies from situation to situation. In a panic situation, we cannot claim our freedom rather duty. When our nation is in danger, we postponed our rights and become anxious for our nation. When Kant says that, "treat every individual as an end and not as means", he implies the principle of human equality.

Justification of the Basic Principles

We have mentioned above that morality should be based on reason and empirical evidence. Our concept of the value of life principle has enough support in its favour by both reason and empirical evidence. This principle is prior to all principles, as without human life, no ethics is possible. Life is common for all human beings. No individual can share the life of other individuals. This means life is basic and important but not everlasting. We all must die one day, so we should not try to save life at all costs. We should not try to enhance the quantity of life rather the quality. It simply states that no life should be ended without very positive justification. Individuals have absolute right concerning their life and death. So any decision related to the individuals must be taken with the consent of the concerning individuals. In this way the value of Life Principle is nearly absolute and primary from the ethical point of view.

If we accept morality then we must accept goodness because morality is defined either in terms of goodness or rightness. Whenever we speak about a Goodman, a good life and a right action, we mean an ethical man, ethical life or moral action. In our previous paragraphs, we have made a synoptic approach regarding the concept of good. Here, again we need to repeat it. The most difficult task is to define 'good' as it varies from thinker to thinker. But there are several facts of human life that can be regarded as good because those things are shared by all. These include life, consciousness, pleasure, happiness, truth, knowledge, beauty, love, friendship, self-realization, freedom, honour, peace and security. Among these, some may deserve high ranking and some low. Some may be omitted from the list, but most people will probably include many of these. For the sake of applied ethics we should *accept many 'good'*. Because, if we accept any one of them alone as good then our moral evaluation of an action will be one-sided and not exhaustive. Human life is complex and so we must keep complexity of life in our mind during moral decision.

Can Supernatural Concept be Good?

The supernatural concept of good or non-natural concept of good is untenable because we have no conclusive proof in favour of it. Precondition of knowledge is that if we know *P* then *P* must be true. We should have enough strong proof in favour of *P* and we must believe in the truth of *P*. Secondly, knowledge that we possess can be demonstrated. If knowledge does not fulfil these criteria, it cannot be regarded as knowledge. From this point of view, we cannot have any proof for supernatural existence and we are unable to demonstrate it.

Suppose some one believes in the very existence of God and His heaven. In Hindu religion (*Mimansa*) considers heaven as the supreme good. In heaven there is a coral tree. Soul, which goes to paradise, is sent to sit under that tree. The tree has capacity to fulfil all the desires of the soul. If we accept this postulate of *Mimansa,* we have to face many problems. First of all, there must be soil, oxygen, nitrogen, calcium, phosphorus, zinc and water to grow the tree. All above chemicals are essential for the development of a tree. For all these, there must be a fertilizer factory and for factory many things will be needed. But we know that if there is soil then it is earth and not heaven. Secondly, if pure soul has gone to the heaven, then it cannot desire, as desire is the part of body and body is burnt on the earth. So such postulate is full of contradiction. So it is untenable.

Now to see the above difficulties, we should concede on the natural concept of good. Generally, people consider those things or conducts good that involve happiness and pleasure to some extent and bad or wrong those that cause pain. This concept of good is named after hedonism. Here hedonism means all forms of hedonism. But it is difficult to find out pure happiness. Pleasure always implies some amount of pain. And if we have a chance of great pleasure at the cost of slight pain, we can afford it happily. We can very easily endure the pain of operation to free ourselves from the toothache. Knowledge and power are not good in themselves, as both are abstract. They are good in actual context. Their goodness depend on their function that how they handle the situation. We do not insist on the theme that whichever thing or action satisfies us and provides pleasure is good. For example, we cannot appreciate the action of a sadist who seeks pleasure out of the fortune to others. Here I agree with W.K. Frankena who holds that "Whatever is good will also probably involve some kind or degree of excellence. What is bad in itself is so because of the presence of either pain or unhappiness or some[7] kind of defect or lack of excellence."[7] The word "excellence" denotes towards the performance of action or conduct and the situation in which such acts are performed.

Besides these characteristics of good and right some more facts can also be added. Those facts are *harmony* and *creativity* on the one hand and on the other *destruction* and *disharmony* may be considered as bad and wrong. If our actions help to bring harmony among men then they are good. But if instead of harmony they create friction among the people, they are bad. Lester A. Kirkendall has rightly remarks over this fact:

> Whenever a decision or a choice is to be made concerning behaviour, the moral decision will be the one, which works towards the creation of trust, confidence and integrity in relationships. It should increase the capacity of individuals to cooperate and enhance the sense of self-respect in the individual. Acts, which create distrust, suspicion and misunderstanding, which build barriers and destroy integrity, are immoral. They decrease the individual's sense of self-respect and rather than producing a capacity to work together. They separate people and break down the capacity for communication.[8]

We have thus sketched out the concept of good and right so far. On the basis of above discussions, we may say that good means happiness, pleasure, excellence, harmony and creativity and all of these must be justification of good.

It is an empirical fact that no person can appreciate bad and condemn good. But it is not the justification of good. For all systems of ethics the *principle of Goodness is logically prior to all other principles* just as the value of *Life Principle is empirically prior*. Without human life no *moral evaluation* is possible, in the like manner without the principle of Goodness no ethical judgement is possible.

So far as the justification of The Principle of Justice is concerned, we may say that no people can live in isolation and we all perform our actions in companion of others. So goodness must he distributed fairly among the people concerned. If we grab the entire goodness for our own sake how other individuals will lead their lives? We have condemned ethical egoism throughout our discussion. So we must grant the Principle of Justice. No human action is possible that does not produce either good or bad result. So there must be an order in distributing the good and bad among the fellow beings. Here, fair distribution simply means equal opportunity to every one. What can individual desire if he has ability, he can acquire it. Every man has not the capacity to be a doctor, but if someone has such ability, he must be provided the chance to be so. People should never be discriminated on the basis of caste, creed and culture or sex. In this way we will recognize the common equality of human beings as human beings and yet allow for individual differences in attempting to distribute goodness and badness fairly.

Truth telling is another principle, which needs justification. The term *'truth' is related to the epistemology* and there are three criteria to determine it. The relevant criteria are correspondence, coherent and pragmatic theories of truth. As we have left the supernatural concept of good, so coherent theory is meaningless for our present purpose. Here we are not concerned to discuss the metaphysical or epistemic aspects of 'truth' rather its status in ethics. At this juncture we should follow C.L. Stevenson and P.H. Nowell Smith's views. According to them, meaning of a term depends on the context in which it is used. This view is nearer to correspondence theory. In applied ethics, nothing is eternally truth and every truth is transitory. Sometimes we also follow the pragmatic aspect of truth, i.e., if one's statement functions truly in the existing situation then it is true.

From these point of view, in moral discourse, every individual in his day-to-day life states some moral content that may be sometimes descriptive and on the other occasion pure emotive. In social dealing, if every man tells a lie, what will be the situation of our society? Every individual is not M.K. Gandhi, who narrated his mistake of life in his autobiography Complete 'truth telling' is a difficult matter, because human beings are necessarily very vulnerable in the area of human relationships and they always try to protect this vulnerability. They always try to hide their truth from others. This is the truth of our modern crowded and complex civilization of twenty-first century. But instead of all these facts, the human relationships extremely need the truth telling to establish and maintain such vital and meaningful relationships. Man enters into relationships with each other with a sense of mutual trust, believing that whatever they say or do to one another will be as honest and open an expression of their thoughts and feelings as possible, we do not insist that people should never tell a lie or they should never be dishonest. To be dishonest or liar depends on the context. if there is a crucial context, people may be dishonest or liar and we should sometimes, overlook the matter but so far normal situation is concerned, we should never try to tell a lie. We should always attempt to be truthful and honest in human relationships, because, morality, in its final analysis, depends on what people say and do. We should be firm on our statement till the existing situation remains the same. For example '*A*' borrows money from '*B*' and agrees to return it within the month. When '*A*' borrowed money from '*B*' he needed it badly. But after a month, when '*B*' asks '*A*' for the money, '*A*' replies negatively. During the money-lending there was mutual sense of trust involved in the situation between the two. Now the sense of mutual trust is broken, not only for this one transaction and relationship, but also for further relationships. Therefore, since all human relationships are based on verbal and non-verbal communications and since moral relation is the most important of all human relationships, so it is absolutely essential that truth telling and honesty be regarded fundamental and basic to any ethical theory.

Justification of the Principle of Individual freedom is a necessity for a moral system, especially for two causes, the first without freedom we cannot assign responsibility to any individual. The terms reward and punishment will become meaningless, if there is no freedom to the individual concerned. In absence of freedom, praise and blame are the same. Secondly, if we do not harm others from any point of view, we must have freedom to do what we like. So the Principle of Individual Freedom is justified.

The Priority of the Basic Principles

We have discussed above the five basic principles under which any moral system can be flourished. These principles are broad enough to cover all human beings' conducts. They are near absolute but there is scope for exception. If we have strong empirical evidence and reason we can relax all these principles or any of them according to the situation. But all men are not able to evaluate the situation and provide the priority to the any one of them. For this purpose, we shall divide these principles in two broad categories; Primary Principles and Secondary Principles. Under primary principles we shall include the value of The Life Principle and The Principle of Goodness. Under secondary principles rest three will fall.

The above distinction among the basic principles is based on the logical and empirical priority. Logical priority means the path logic determines and the principles must have to follow that path. Empirical priority denotes that priority is established on the basis of evidence obtained from sense-verification.

From the ethical point of view the principle of Goodness logically comes first because, to some extent, morality is synonymous with goodness and the aim of ethics is to follow the principle of goodness. So this principle is logically prior to all other in ethics. Again, if there are no human being, then there can be no human morality. It is obvious empirical fact. So these two principles are prior to others.

The third principle is justice because in most human actions more than one person is involved, and some kind of distribution must be established there. Truth is fourth and individual freedom is the fifth.

On the basis of priority we can interchange the Principle of goodness with the value of life Principle and *vice versa*, if we have strong justification in favour of the either, otherwise not. For example, if a criminal is very dangerous for the innocent people of the society, we are morally entitled to kill him. In the same way if by our actions we do not harm others in any way, then our freedom should not be interrupted even by justice. If some adults may organize themselves and do something for their pleasure in a legal way and also do not seriously affect others in any way, no law should interfere in their actions. In the like manner, sometimes individual's freedom is interrupted by justice for the sake of society and *vice versa*. So is the case with the Principle of Truth Telling and honesty. These two ethical factors may also be interrupted by justice or individual freedom when some extraordinary situation come before us.

Moral Standard

In the vast domain of ethics there are several standards of morality. The Psychological Hedonism, Ethical Hedonism, Ethical Egoism, Altruism, Utilitarianism, Hedonistic Utilitarianism, Ideal Utilitarianism, are regarded to be teleological standards of morality, while Intuitionism, in its all forms, Duty's Ethical standards are considered to be deontological standards of morality. Every standard of morality has its merits and demerits. At the very beginning of this discussion we want to clear one thing that we shall not entertain ethical egoistic standard of morality. We shall amalgamate hedonism, ethical egoism, utilitarianism, hedonistic utilitarianism and ideal utilitarianism under one banner of teleological standard of morality. In the same way all forms of intuitionism will be brought under categorical imperative of Kant.

In this context it can be said that act utilitarianism has certain merits but its implication in actual ethical life situation is difficult, as it varies from situation to situation, and person to person. Again this standard of morality needs a high rational training to acquire the capacity to evaluate particular action in a particular situation and that is not an easy task for all men. Ethical egoism is in no way a moral theory in its any form rather a question, "why should I be moral?[9] From my point of view, there is no great difference between ethical egoism and act utilitarianism, if egoistic action is performed by a rational person. Ayn Rand has also supported this view when she holds, ". . . . the self-interests of rational human beings by virtue of their being rational, will never conflict."[10]

From this point of view rule utilitarianism, standard of morality of J.S. Mill is the best one because it is easy to memorize the rule and act accordingly. For example, if rule is made that "killing of human being is bad except in self-defence" then this rule covers all human beings in the situation concerned. According to J.S. Mill an action performed for the maximum pleasure of maximum number is right, so act accordingly, is a rule and anybody who has a firm belief in ethics can follow the rule till the extraordinary situation does not come. The only pitfall of this theory is the negligence of minority over majority.

In the same way, intuitionistic standard of morality varies from individual to individual because the same action may be intuited by one person as right while by others wrong. This standard of morality is able only to guide the individual who pursues and not for all. From this point of view, Kant's categorical imperative is better than intuitionistic standard of morality, because this theory insists on universal aspects of morality and forbids us to treat other persons as means. Every man is an end in himself and nothing else. Kantian ethics emphasizes the nature of intrinsic goodness which is the most important factor of the environmental ethics.

So, we shall follow these two standards of morality in evaluating any human being's action from the applied ethical point of view.

REFERENCES

1. *Times*, edition of Person of the Century, Dec. 31, 1999.
2. Gandhi on Modern Civilization.
3. Philippa Foot, "*Nietzsche: The Reevaluation of Value*", Nietzsche University of Notre Dame Press, 1973, p. 157
4. The view from Nowhere O.O.P.NY., 1986, p.168. In applied ethics no principles are absolute but nearly absolute. So one can relax the principle as per the context.
5. Quoted by Paul Ramsey, *The Patient as Person*, New Haven, Yale University Press, pp.246-47.
6. *Primary Philosophy*, New York, McGraw Hill, 1966 p.232.
7. *Ethics*, 2nd ed. Engel Wood Cliffs, N.J.:Prentice Hall, 1973, p. 91.
8. *Premarital Intercourse and Interpersonal Relationships*, Jullian Press, 1961, p. 6.
9. Kai Nielsen's "why should I moral?" in *Problems of Moral Philosophy*, ed. Paul W. Taylor, Dalmont, La: Dickenson, 1972, p.497.
10. *The Virtue of Selfishness,* New York, New American Library, 1964, pp. 57-67.

Section – III

ENVIRONMENT ETHICS

Chapter – 13

The Need of an Environmental Ethics

Dr. Sarita Kumari & Avinash Kumar Srivastava

Jharkhand

At the very outset I express my deep sense of gratitude to the organizers of this seminar for inviting me on this occasion and permitted me to read my paper. Since I am not an environmentalist professional nor had been a student of life science, my reactions to the problem will be somewhat different to others. Being a student of Philosophy I feel that environmental problems need some attention and awareness among the common mass in order to tackle it in a proper way. The reason is simple. Environmental problems are really social problems. They being with propel as the cause and end with people as victims . . . . It is people who create a bad environment and a bad environment brings our worst in people.[1] Hence, the reason and remedy to the environmental tragedies has to be searched in the history of civilization and human nature itself.

The history of human civilization is the history of the man's march from the lush green forest to the jungle of concrete.[2] This march was man centric wherein the human interest had the top most priority in comparison to the nature and the other species of the world. Man being the highest evolutes had the responsibility of caring and maintaining the planet Earth. But due to the gross selfish interest the exploited and mutilated the echo system to the extent that the environment has becomes grossly polluted and nature has started reactiong in terms of *Tsunami, Katrina,* earthquakes and so on. This has placed the human destiny dark, dismal and disparaging. Due to environmental degradation the planet earth is turning into an unsuitable place for human habitation. Here, a question arises what is the reason behind it? How can we repair the damage and curb our exploitative attitude towards the nature? For that there is a need of an ethics that can generate in us an eco-friendly attitude as ethics is a normative science of the conduct of human being living in the society.

Modern civilization stands in the need of a new ethics and economics that may set the human relation to the natural environment,. This will deal with man's relation to land, animals and plants that grows upon the planet earth. Here, a question arises do we not have such ethics in our tradition? Yes, we do have. The old and the prevailing ethics too deal with man's relation to nature. But the guiding principle behind it is the proverb, *homomensure;* man is the measure of all things. In the prevailing old ethics man is free to deal with the nature, as he pleases, as they do not effect others and are not subject to moral sanction. In this sense trees and other natural entities are in a goods sense and behaviour is beyond the scope of the prevailing ethics. Now as extension of the traditional morality is required in order to fill a moral void. Hence, there is a need of a new environment ethics that may evaluate the human conduct in an echo centric way. This paper aims at exploring out the possibility of a new environmental ethics.

This is, in fact, a very tough task to present even the outline of a new environmental ethics. This ethics should be radically different from the prevailing ethics. Under it even traditionally permissible conduct may be accounted morally wrong. An industrialist or a farmer who clears 75 per cent of the wood and dumps its rainfall, rocks and soil into a community creek would be held responsible for his morally wrong conduct and they will be subject to proper moral criticism. Since the old prevailing ethics in not clearly articulated or well worked out to identify the criteria of its application, there is a need of a new environmental ethics. Secondly the new ethics should be clustered in the family of the prevailing ethical system and should not differ on the core or fundamental principles together as one ethics, i.e., the Hindu, Buddhist, Jain, Christian, ethics, etc., respectively, just provide it an umberella notion covering a cluster of differing or competing systems. This give rise to two other possibilities apart from a new environmental ethics : (i) extension or modification of the prevailing ethics, and here in the ethical principles will be developed that are encompassed or latent in the old prevailing ethics; and (ii) The environmental evaluation should be incorporated or ecological problems be solved within the framework of the ethics in vogue. In this connection when we turn our eyes on human civilization and theories of ethics we find three important traditions in the west that deal with the man's relation to nature. They are the (a) despotic view, (b) the stewardship view, and (c) the co-operative view. The evaluation of all the three views will present a clear picture of the need of a new environmental ethics.

(a) The despotic : According to this view man is suspect or a tyrant. He mercilessly exploits the nature for his benefit, comfort and greed. The reason behind this is the common belief that nature is the domain of man. He is free to deal with it as per his specification desires, pleasures and whim. The entire nature and natural entities are meant for man. He is the enjoryer and nature is to be enjoyed.[4] In this background if we cast our glance at the beginning of the human civilization we find that "There is a race for dominance and control over the nature by human beings having different goals set in mind, i.e., to revealt the mystery of nature, to enhance the material accumulation, comfort and so on. It resulted in industrial revolution. The desire to accumulate wealth started systematic exploitation of the nature in terms of deforestation, land erosion, indiscriminate use of fertilizer, oozing out every ounce of the fertility of the land and turn it to a barren

chunks . . . . Not only the land even the poen sky and air have become heavily polluted.[5]

This view, at the very outset, appears to be inconsistent with an environmental ethics for two simple reasons. The first is the disastrous effect of this view, as we have already seen that the damage caused by following this principle have put the question mark over our survival as a human being, together with the survival of many endangered species and fragile eco-system.[6]

Secondly, according to this view, man is free to deal with nature as he pleases, as nature is meant for him only. On the contrary, for a environmental ethics man is not so free to do as he pleases because he simply is a member of this ecosystem and the rules of environment are equally applicable on him. Here man is not in the centre and nature is not meant for him only, he has to care and share both as per the requirement. Hence, there is no place of the despotic view in an environmental ethics.

(b) Stewardship view : According to this view man is the custodian of nature. The prime purpose of this theory is to conserve nature in order to maintain ecological balance. Modern environmentalists, in order to counterbalance the evils of deforestation, urbanization, industrialization and so on have prescribed this theory. Herein nature is protected by conserving and creating the wild life sanctuaries, parks, ponds, etc. In fact, most of the world's religions recommend these activities not only for fetching merit but also consider these morally good. This religio-ethical principle has helped conserve the nature from human encroachment. In different religions very many trees have been considered auspicious, i.e., Peepal, *Bale*, *Tulsi*, etc. and hence they are not only saved from destruction but also were saved in draughts as the followers of a few religions pour water to it and thus their life is protected. In nutshell it can be said that in stewardship view man's role towards the nature is just like farm manager he makes nature productive by his efforts though not by means that will deliberately degrade its resources.

This view is not tenable as it has the religious background. It can by no means adequately characterize anywhere when its religious background is removed. Secondly, this view implies the theory of complete interference for improving the nature for human ends; hence, it is inconsistent with environmental ethics.

(c) The co-operative view : According to this view, man should work as a perfecter of nature. Here the proper role of the man is to develop, cultivate and perfect the nature by bringing out its potentialities. In order to perfect nature, one must desist oneself from its misuse of the natural resources. It implies types of action plan : (1) need based use of the natural resources, and (2) Frugality. A brief explanation of these is needed here.

(1) It is known to all that mind is the fountainhead of all the good and bad actions,[7] we must control our greed and nurse only the need from the nature. Being its part and parcel we should work in harmony and we must care and share it. We should use its resources for the normal sustenance of our life. In this way the damage to the system will be the minimal and it will be repaired in its normal course. In this way there will be a perfect co-operation between man and the nature.

(2) *Frugality :* We should use one thing in multiple ways as well as explore the possibility of renewable sources of energy. This will help not only conserve the natural resources but also in making the nature blossom in its fullest form.

The critical evaluation of the above mentioned last two view, although depart from the despotic view and seems to be nearer to the so called "environmental ethics", but actually they are not so. The reason is simple. The population blast and the finite areas are not going to allow a man to protect nature from his exploitation and encroachment. Human efforts in this background may lead to perfecting, farming and utilizing the natural areas. But a thorough going environmental ethics may reject it because here also nature is exploited on the principle of total use. Here also natural areas are cultivated or used for human ends. If we extend somewhat illicitly, to include use for preservation, the total use principle is rendered, innocuous, at least as regards its actual effects. For example if we begin with some environmental laws that yields options, we find that it results in the life promoting obligation.

	Technical ought ifoption	*Environmental low*	*Antecedent*
1.	*You ought to recycle to preserve the environmental*	*For the life-supporting ecosystem recycle or perishes*	*if you wish human life*
2.	*You ought to recycle to reserve the ground*	*for the value supporting eco-system recycle or perish*	*if you wish of human value*
3.	*We ought to stabilize mutually to preserve the ecosystem through Mutually imposed limited growth*	*for the life-supporting ecosystem stabilizes at a finite carrying capacity or is destroyed*	*if we wish human life.*

The above three examples categorically reveal the hidden agenda that Environmental ethics and homeostasis are blended together. If we begin with the so called environmental laws we find that it yield such option that results, if translated, into a life-promoting obligation. Thus the balance of nature provides an objective, normative model which can be utilized as the ground of human values on which other values non also grow, keeping be a kid of ultimate value which is not a product of human convention or Supernatural authority. It is a natural norm where in human norms are for und objectively. This can be determined through man's ecological relation with nature.

Chapter – 14

Nature and Scope of Environmental Ethics

Dr. Shiva Bhanu Singh

The entire human civilization is passing through a phase of great crisis. We are currently heading towards a phase of environmental evolution. During mid-twentieth century and after, various philosophical and intellectual tendencies came to fore which may explain a sort of rupture or discontinuity in philosophical tradition and particularly in the ethical discourse which is our main concern. It has been a debated question in contemporary philosophy as to which beings have and which do not have a claim to be considered morally important in their own right. Modern western ethical theory has been anthropocentric or human-centred because it does not give importance to non-human beings. It does not establish any moral relations with the natural environment and non-living beings. The contemporary moralists have advocated for a new ethics, i.e., environmental ethics, that extends the range of morally considerable cases beyond human-beings and includes in it non-human beings, animals, plants and other living beings by accepting their moral worthiness and establishing their independent moral status.

The environmental ethics is mainly concerned with the question, should we value non-human being, living as well as non-living only because of their utility to human beings or they are valuable in themselves. Here we can adopt *two standpoints.*

According to one stand point, the non-human beings are morally valuable and important because they are relative to human interest. This view has been called as *narrow scope view*. The second view may be that non-human beings and entire eco-system are morally important and valuable in themselves, irrespective of any relation to human interest. This second view can be called as *wide scope view*. The supporters and propounders of this view maintain that recognition of human transcendent value in the natural environment, or the eco-system as a whole commits to the adoption of new moral principles that constitute radical departure from the mainstream moral tradition of the west.

Western attitudes to nature grew out of a blend of those of the Hebrew people as represented on the early books of the *Bible*, and the Philosophy of the ancient Greeks, particularly that of Aristotle. In contrast to some other ancient traditions for example, those of India, both the Hebrew and the Greek traditions made human beings the centre of the moral universe—indeed not merely the centre, but very often, the entirety of the morally significant features of this world. In Genesis we find Hebrew view of the special place of human beings in the divine plan, in the biblical story of creation.

And God said, "Let us make man in our image, after our likeness; and let them have dominion over the fish of the sea, and over the fowl of the air and over the earth, and over every creeping thing that creepeth upon the earth".

So God created man in his own image in the image of God created he him; male and female created he them.'

Modern Christians, concerned about the environment, attempt to explain the meaning of dominion by saying that it should be regarded not as a license to do as we will with other living things, but it must be taken as a directive to look after them on God's behalf and be answerable to God for the way in which we treat them. However above interpretation can hardly be justified. The most influential early Christian thinkers had no doubts about how man's dominion was to be understood. Referring to stories in the

New Testament, Augustine establishes man's dominion over nature by an example in which Jesus destroyed a fig tree and caused a herd of pigs to drown. Augustine clarifies that these puzzling incidents teach us that to refrain from the killing of animals and the destroying of plant is the height of superstition. Again great medieval scholastic, Thomas Acquinas, whose life work was the melding of Christian theology with the thought of Aristotle also regarded nature as a hierarchy in which those with less reasoning ability exist for the sake of more with those reasoning.

Plants exist for the sake of animals and brute beasts for the sake of man-domestic animals for his use and food, wild ones for food and other accessories of life; such as clothing and various tools.

Since nature makes nothing purposeless or in vain, it is undeniably true that she has made all animals for the sake of man.

In his own major work the Summa Theologica, Aquinas followed this passage from Aristotle almost word for word, adding that the position accords with God's command, as given in *Genesis*. While classifying various kinds of sins, Acquinas mentions sins against God ourselves or our neighbours. There is no possibility of sinning against non-human animals or against the natural world.

In 1967, Lynn White Jr. Wrote an article in *Science* on the historical roots of ecological crisis facing the west and the world. According to White, what individuals and communities do to their environment depends upon how, they see themselves in relation to nature. White maintained that the exploitative view that has generated much of the environmental crisis, particularly in Europe and North America, is a result of the teachings of Christianity, which conceives of man as superior to all God's creation and of everything else as created for man's use and enjoyment. He suggested that the only view to reduce the environmental crisis facing mankind is to reject the view that nature has no reason to exist except to serve man.

From the above analysis it is obvious that according to the dominant western tradition, the natural world exists for the benefit of human beings. God gave human beings dominion over the natural world, and God does not care how we treat it. Human beings are the only morally important members of this world. Nature itself is of no intrinsic value and the destruction of plants and animals cannot be sinful, unless by this destruction we harm human beings. However western tradition though appears harsh, does not rule out concern for the preservation of nature as long as that concern can be related to human well-being. For instance, entirely within the limits of the dominant western tradition, one could oppose nuclear power on the grounds that nuclear fuel whether in bombs or power stations is so hazardous to human life that the uranium is better left in the ground. In the same manner many arguments against pollution, the use of gases harmful to the ozone layer, the burning of fossil fuels and the destruction of forests, could be couched in terms of the harm to human health and welfare from the pollutants, or the changes to the climate that will occur as a result of the use of fossil fuels and the loss of forest. The green house effect—to take just one danger to our environment—threatens to bring about a rise in sea level that will inundate low lying coastal areas. Thus we see that even within a human centred moral framework, the preservation of our environment is a value of the greatest possible importance.

Contrary to western tradition, in Hindu tradition and religion we see a deep respect for nature and the concept of environmental harmony and conservation through its scriptures, religious codes and mythologies as narrated, in *Vedas*, *Upanishads*, great epics and *Puranas*. The Hindu *rishis* of the *vedic* and the *upanishadic* era perceived the value of maintaining a harmonious relationship between the needs of man and the spectacular diversity of the universe. They believed that nature was not only the mother that sustained their life, it was the abode of divinity. They never supported the exploitation of nature for fulfilling the selfish purpose of man. Man in Hindu culture was instructed to maintain harmony with nature and to show reverence for the presence of divinity in nature.

The principle of the sanctity of life is clearly ingrained in the Hindu religion. Only God has absolute sovereignty over all creatures including man. Thus man had no dominion over his own life or non-human life, man has not been allowed to act as a viceroy of God over the planet, nor assign degrees of relative worth to other species. The religion provides no sense of absolute superiority of man over nature. Hindu *rishis* believe that all lives, human and non-human are of equal value and all have the same right to existence.

Hindu tradition gives respect to whole natural world including the flora and fauna of the earth and creatures in the sky and under the sea. It is believed that all that exists has been created by the Supreme Being, comes from this Supreme Being and will return to the Supreme Being which is an adequate basis for the veneration of the natural world in which man finds himself. The history of human survival stands as a good example of the interdependence, cooperative living and close association which exists among the forces of human and non-human nature. Hindus accepted the whole creation as the unfolding of the supreme one into many. To them the worlds in the heaven, all the planets and stars; and the sun and the moon were created by Vishvakarman, who also made earth with its animals, birds, trees, flowers, rivers, mountains and of course, man and left them all to interact for further evolution and development. This perception of man is represented in Vedas where it is said that the earth is not only for human beings to enjoy but also for all other bipeds and quadrapeds, birds and animals and other creatures. The most important aspect of Hindu theology is the association accorded to different species with reincarnation and deities. Most importantly, it is believed that supreme being actually gets Himself incarnated in the form of various species. In Hindu religion, nature has been regarded as indispensable in the life of human beings. It has also been considered as revered bestower of good, and protector from the evils with a concept of God living in it. The sense of worship that developed among the Hindus has a background of utility and spiritfulness. Hindu society was very much conscious of the fact that flora of the country has a protective power and indiscriminate destruction would result in pollution and chaos in the society. Some of the plants and trees have been well known for their medicinal power, for their spiritual power and some as an abode of God. In *Rigveda*, tree worship was regarded as a duty of man. Cutting of tree was regarded as a punishable offence. Hindus were very much aware of pollution (*vikṛti*) and considered water as a powerful media of purification and also as a source of energy. The water in the sky, the water of rivers, water in well whose source is ocean, may all these sacred waters protect me (*Rigveda,* 7-49.2) Charak had pointed out air pollution as a cause of so many diseases. The concern for environment can be glanced from this passage— A person who is engaged in killing creatures, polluting wells, and ponds, and tanks, and destroying gardens certainly go to hell". (*Padma Purana*, *Bhoomikhanda,* 96.7-8).

From the above observation of Hindu tradition, it is obvious that Hindu culture in ancient and medieval times, provided a system of moral guidelines towards environmental preservation and conservation. Environmental ethics, as propounded by ancient Hindu scriptures and the seers, was practised not only by common man, but even by rulers and kings. In Hindu culture control and dominion over nature by human being was not accepted.

Exploitation and abuse of nature for selfish gains was regarded as unjust. Indian ancient scriptures have stressed that man and nature need to live in close harmony and plants and animals should be the objects of unlimited kindness and benevolence since they make no demand for their sustenance.

Developing an Environmental Ethic

It is very obvious that the set of ethical virtues praised and the set of ethical prohibitions adopted by the ethic of specific societies always reflect the conditions under which men live and work in order to survive. Many of the ethical standards that we accept today can be said to be universal because they are beneficial to the community in virtually any conditions in which humans live. As far as our contemporary living conditions are concerned we are facing a new threat to our survival. The proliferation of human beings coupled with the by-products of economic growth is just as capable as the old threats of wiping out our society and every other society as well. No ethic has yet developed to cope with this threat. Some ethical principles that we do have, are exactly the opposite of what we need. The fact is that ethical principles change slowly and the time we have left to develop a new environmental ethic is short. Such an ethic would regard every action that is harmful to the environment as ethically dubious and those that are unnecessarily harmful as plainly wrong. An environmental ethic would find virtue in saving and recycling resources, and vice in extravagance and unnecessary consumption. We may clarify it by the following example : From the perspective of an environmental ethic our choice of recreation is not ethically neutral. At present we see the choice between motor car racing or cycling, between water skiing or wind surfing as merely a matter of taste. Yet there is an essential difference, Motor car racing and water skiing require the consumption of fossil fuels and the discharge of carbon dioxide into the atmosphere. Cycling and wind surfing do not. Once we take the need to preserve our environment seriously, motor racing and water Skirting will no more be an acceptable form of entertainment than bear baiting is to day. A truly environmental ethic fosters consideration for the interests of all sentient creatures, including subsequent generations stretching into the far future. It is accompanied by an aesthetic of appreciation for wild places and unspoiled nature. An environmental ethic rejects the ideals of a materialist society in which success is gauged by the number of consumer goods one can accumulate. Instead it judges success in terms of the development of one's abilities and the achievement of real fulfilment and satisfaction. It promotes frugality, in so far as that is necessary for minimising pollution and ensuring that everything that can be reused is reused. Carelessly to throw out material that can be recycled is a form of vandalism or the theft of our common property in the resources of the world. Thus the various green consumer guides and books, about things we can do to save our planet-recycling what we use and buying the most environmentally friendly products available are part of the new ethic that is required.

Thus we see that the new environmental ethic will promote frugality and simple life. Simple life does not mean that environmental ethic frowns upon pleasure but that the pleasure it values do not come from conspicuous consumption. We can get pleasure from warm personal and sexual relationships, from being close to children and friends, from conversation, from sports and recreations that are in harmony with our environment instead of being harmful to it, from food that is not based on the exploitation of sentient creatures and does not cost the earth from creative activity and work of all kinds; and from appreciating the unspoiled places in the world in which we live.

It may be suggested that Hindu tradition can be of great help in transforming society from its current preoccupation with materialism and consumerism to a conserver society. Various norms, moral standards and laws can be enacted for environmental protection by moral awakening. Hindu religion can exert a unique moral leadership among its followers, particularly with respect to strengthening man's harmony with nature. We may be guided by motto "*Jeevasthea Jivyasam*" live and let live and *Kamaye dukh tapta nam praninam artanashnam*"-The aim of life is to remove the suffering of living being. In Indian approach we find in place of man opposing nature and nature opposing mankind, ontic identity between them, the identity of microcosm and macrocosm and entire creation is being governed by extraordinary moral cosmic order (*ṛta.*). In *Yajurveda* it is prayed that sky, atmosphere, earth, water and plants be peaceful. May all the-learned persons, God and *Veda* be peaceful. May peace itself be peaceful and let peace come unto me —

> *Om dyauh shantih, Antariksah shantih, Prithvi shantih, Apah shantih, Oshadhyah shantih, Brahm Shantih, Sarvam shantih, shantireva shantih, Sa Ma shantiredhi.*
>
> —*Yajurveda, 36-17.*

Hence, we can say that holistic Hindu view of life and entire indian philosophical tradition is the right way of establishing relationship between man and nature.

Chapter – 15

Environmental Ethics and Deep Ecological Consciousness

Dr. D.C. Srivastava

Environmental Ethics

Ethics is as old as Philosophy — and older. Environmental Ethics is very new. Why is this so? Because ethics is, in large part, the critical study of personal and collective responsibility toward vulnerable things—most acutely, toward persons, social institutions and human communities. Until recently, nature was believed to be too large and too permanent to be vulnerable. Now, at last, the science of ecology has shown us that this is not so. We now know that nature itself is imperilled by deliberate human action, and, reciprocally, that human beings are affected by the way they deal with nature. So now we see that our dealings with nature are matters of moral responsibility. Hence, there is environmental ethics.

"Ethics is as old as philosophy — and older."[1] Thus moral philosophy has a great deal to offer to the critical study of mankind's responsibility to nature; namely, concepts, theories, principles, and, most of all, methods of analysis.

"Environmental ethics is very new." Hence, strategies for applying moral philosophy to environmental issues and concepts are now being tested, and thus unless the student and scholar is careful, his conception of this new field and its problems might be distorted and constrained. The philosopher should be cautious if he proposes to place old wine in new bottles. Does the old wine belong in the new bottles — that is, should the concepts, theories and principles of traditional moral philosophy be applied to the environmental issues that have recently emerged, both with our industrial civilization and out of our developing ecological science and consciousness? Herein lies a point of deep division of opinion among philosophers. Some, notably William Frankena and John Passmore, believe that the challenges of the new ecological awareness and conscience call for "better" use of familiar philosophical and scientific ideas, but not a rejection or reconstruction thereof. With refinement, they contend, "the old ways" are quite good enough. Others (e.g., Aldo Leopold, John Rodman, Holmes Rolston and Paul Shepard) suggest that a revolution in philosophical thinking may be in order—in particular, a reorientation of perspective. Perhaps "counter-revolution" is a better term, in that these philosophers and ecologists are urging a reversal of Immanuel Kant's establishment of human consciousness as the centre of philosophical attention, and, in contrast to Kant, a new direction of attention and evaluation upon the external context of human life and experience.

Anthropocentrism, the view that humanity's needs and interests are of supreme and exclusive value and importance in nature, so dominates the thinking of most people in our culture that it is virtually preconscious — an unexamined presupposition of most popular reflections, feelings, and utilization policies regarding wild nature. Anthropocentrism has both a religious and a secular foundation. The religious theme is set rather explicitly in a famous verse in *Genesis* (I: 26) in which the Lord is recorded to have said: "[Let man] have dominion . . . over all the earth, and over every creeping thing that creeps on the earth". And then that famous injunction, "be fruitful and multiply and fill the earth and subdue it. . ." (*Genesis* I::28).[2]

Some historians (notably Lynn White, Jr.) have focused upon those verses as typifying the Western religious approach to humanity's place in nature. By this account, nature was created for mankind's benefit, and it is his role to be the master of nature. The Lord created the earth as a garden and habitat for human beings, who are then given little restriction regarding his use of it. Moreover, there is little acknowledgement in this tradition of the limits of mankind's capacity to wisely manage the earth exclusively for his own use.

The rationale and justification of the secular approach to anthropocentrism are somewhat different, yet they lead to essentially the same conclusion as the religious. By this account, life has recently evolved to include a self-conscious, rational, deliberative, personal species — Homo sapiens. Some species have sentient lives; that is, they are capable of feeling and, most significantly morally speaking, of feeling pain. Most species, however, are neither sentient nor conscious. That it is alive or not "matters" not a bit, say, to an insect or to a tree, and perhaps very little to a hummingbird. These species have not the mental (which is to say the neural) capacity to "care." Life matters most, if not exclusively, to the one species we know of that can contemplate the past, present and future of its own life, and act rationally and deliberatively to affect the condition of that life. Again, that singular species is, of course, the human species. Nature, according to this point of view, matters, has value, has significance, only if there is a species to whom it can have significance. It follows, then, that values in nature are almost exclusively human values. The only possible qualification to this rule would be the value of avoiding cruelty to non-human sentient species — the so called "higher animals." Except for that proviso, that sole personal and rational species, homo sapiens, has acquired with its capacities the privilege, even the right, to do with nature what it pleases. So we come, at length, to the same conclusion as that of theological anthropocentrism: nature exists for mankind's advantage and use. What counts exclusively is humanity—its aspirations, its desires, its interests—with possibly the minor qualification that, as moral agents, human beings should not be wantonly cruel to animals that have the capacity to suffer.[3]

Anthropocentrism, or "human chauvinism" as it is often called by its critics, is starkly expressed by Prof. Clare A. Gunn in the journal *Landscape Architecture*:

The only reason anything is done on this earth is for people. Did the rivers, winds, animals, rocks or dust ever consider my wishes or needs? Surely we do all our acts in an earthly environment, but I have never heard a tree, valley, mountain or flower thank me for preserving it.[4]

The anthropocentric position is supported by the interest theory of rights proposed by the contemporary philosopher, Joel Feinberg, who writes, "without awareness, expectation, belief, desire, aim and purpose, a being can have no interests; without interests, he cannot be benefited."[5]

Of course, from all this it also follows that without interests a being cannot be harmed either. It is difficult to accept Feinberg's "interest theory of rights" and at the same time reject anthropocentrism. It is difficult, but not impossible, and we shall presently encounter attempts to do just that.

Anthropocentrism has been regarded by many critics as the moral equivalent of racism, and accordingly has been dubbed with the derisive name of "speciesism." The anthropocentrist retorts that this is mere argument from analogy, and a poor one at that. After all, he notes, people of other races are, after all, people. In contrast, non-human species are not, to our knowledge, personal; that is to say, they are not self-conscious, rational, deliberative and morally responsible. Trees, insects, rocks and landscapes have no sentient lives. (Accordingly, solicitude for their feelings is not an issue in environmental ethics.) Human beings, due to their rational, deliberative consciousness, are beings apart. They are unique in their capacity to accept and be liable to moral evaluation (that is, to be morally responsible). Since only human beings can evaluate nature, they alone are entitled to treat nature strictly according to the perceived needs and purposes of their species. So the anthropocentrist will argue.

Does the anthropocentric position offer no safety or security for "sub-human" species and their habitats? Well, perhaps it does —at least for the short term. After all, we often enjoy the company of such creatures. And so long as we feel that way about them— so long, that is, as they entertain and delight us—then we may take some trouble to keep them around. But, again, we will do so on account of what they do for us. But if that is the reason we protect wild species, then their safety is hostage to our taste and modes of entertainment. But tastes and attitudes change, as do our moral fashions.

Is there a view toward nature that does not require an "aw gawsh" response, or other such simple-minded projections, that will cause us to care enough to take some trouble and expense to protect a "useless" species? Perhaps so, but anthropocentrism does not seem to be that view, for it is doubtful that the uncompromising human chauvinist will offer us much warrant for protecting a species that cannot readily be shown to be useful, entertaining, or of some other value to human beings. And so if other human values compete and conflict, say, with the integrity of some wild species habitat, the "aw gawsh" factor might readily be over-ridden and the tenure of that species on the earth may be placed in great peril.

How, then, might one answer the human chauvinist? There are several strategies for rebuttal, but many of them will have little appeal to the modern frame of mind. For example, one might attempt to defend the primitive belief in animism or perhaps pan-psychism. (This approach, after all, is not unheard of these days. Recall the book *The Secret Life of Plants*.) Both positions hold that nature is alive and sentient. Thus the animist may even believe that a cliff "objects" to being reduced to paving stones, or that a tree "objects" to being cut into cordwood. But few of us will be convinced of this unless we are shown that rocks and trees have nervous systems. Failing this, it follows that most of us will likely be disinclined to believe that rocks and trees are capable of "caring" about their fate. They have no interests in their own right.

A more promising answer to anthropocentrism might be to

attempt to dissolve the hard conceptual line that is customarily drawn between human beings and "nature," and to challenge the implicit assumption that we can somehow physically, organically, and even psychologically, detach the fate of mankind from the fate of nature. One might even challenge the notion that such a view of the man-nature relationship is productive of scientific or moral insight. (This, we will recall, was the approach of Aldo Leopold). Perhaps there is a better way of viewing the natural order and man's place in it. But in what sense "better"? An example from the history of astronomy might clarify this point.

Before the days of Copernicus it was, of course, possible to plot the positions of the planets and to forecast the occurrence of eclipses and other celestial events, even with the assumption that the earth was the centre of the solar system. But, as most students of the history of science are aware, the geocentric view required the positing of an array of complicated theoretical entities (such as "epicycles") which "adjusted" the conceptual model to permit moderately accurate predictions. For this system to "work" for it to "fit" the observed data, the theoretical scaffolding had to become quite complicated and unwieldy and was overburdened with otherwise useless ("*ad hoc*") assumptions and concepts. "Suppose instead," Copernicus asked, "we just assume that all the planets, earth included, are satellites of the sun. What then becomes of our capacity to make predictions and to the conceptual equipment required to do so? What happens is that we make better predictions and do so with but a fraction of the theoretical baggage and the computational fussing. We do not, for instance, need to assume that one insignificant speck of heavy elements (the earth) stands still while all the rest of creation moves about it. Assume further that the very concept of motion itself, and the variables that define it (namely time and space), are themselves functions of the place and circumstance of observation, then still more heretofore intractable physical problems fall within our conceptual reach and into theoretical place. The stage is then set for yet another scientific revolution. Enter Albert Einstein.

Is there analogously a better point of view regarding man's function in nature (an empirical-scientific question) and man's responsibility toward nature (a moral question) that similarly simplifies the task of the scientist and the moral philosopher, and which brings insoluble problems and paradoxes within the range of resolution? Perhaps the ecological point of view offers such a transformation of perspective. Because we shall encounter it again, a brief review might be in order.

The ecological point of view is, first of all, holistic; it focuses upon the "all-ness" of nature. The anthropocentric perspective tends to be particularistic; it focuses upon the eachness of things. To the "human chauvinist" (and perhaps especially the theologically oriented chauvinist), nature might be regarded as a museum of discrete specimens, or, to mix the metaphor, a vending machine with separate and discrete trinkets which can be had as whim and inclination require (and with an implicit understanding that there is a vendor on call, ever ready to restock the machine). Extracting an item from the machine affects no other part of the machine. The act of purchase is a discrete, disparate, isolated event. Returning to our original simile, the specimens in "museum earth" are viewed, contemplated, and perhaps admired separately and in sequence, like pearls on a string. But they remain securely in place, as the spectator leaves the museum and returns to his resident world of personal concerns and "human interests".

As we have noted earlier, the ecologist does not view things this way. Rather than tallying up each part to sum up an aggregate collection, the ecologist understands that a view of the whole illuminates his knowledge of the parts. Species have a function, a niche, in the life community. Particular organisms are not specimens in museum earth, they are conduits of energy, nutrients and information. We cannot, says the ecologist, know what an organism is, or what a species is, unless we know, additionally, what it does. Knowledge of the organism does not end with the outer membrane. The whole informs the part. Unity in system, and equilibrium and stability in and through complexity and diversity — these are the themes and principles of the ecological point of view.

By examining the whole, we discover functions of the whole

that are basic to ecological science: that diversity enhances stability, that established systems tend toward equilibrium, that life communities are complex cybernetic systems with negative feedback mechanisms, tending to restore stability following externally caused disruptions. Both ecological and molecular biology reveal, in macro and micro perspective, unimaginable degrees of complexity and suggest, beyond the shores of our knowledge, an unfathomable sea of fact, hypothesis, data, theory, law, function, diversity, structure that are and will forever be beyond our understanding and control. The biologist well knows that he is dealing with an order of nature that can encode, in the microscopic space of a cell nucleus, more information than is contained in an encyclopedia. He is privileged to study the structure of life communities and organisms that have evolved over billions of years and through infinitude of discrete "experiments" of selective evolution.[6]

Both the biologist and the philosopher appreciate that it is practically and logically impossible to comprehend all that there is to know, even generally and abstractly, about life communities. It is practically impossible because there is simply too much to be known. Furthermore, biotic omniscience is logically impossible for the simple but interesting reason that we, the knower, are parts of the (imperfectly) known. Thus our very knowledge of the life community, and our consequent activity in that community, alters that community. We can no more encompass all knowledge of ecology than we can catch our own shadow or stand at the end of the rainbow. And if we cannot fully understand, then it follows that we cannot completely manage and control. Thus Aldo Leopold is characteristically perceptive when he writes:

> . . . the conqueror role is eventually self-defeating. Why? Because it is implicit in such a role that the conqueror knows, ex cathedra, just what makes the community clock tick, and just what and who is valuable, and what and who is worthless, in community life. It always turns out that he knows neither, and this is why his conquests eventually defeat themselves.

The ordinary citizen today assumes that science knows what makes the community clock tick; the scientist is equally sure that he does not. He knows that the biotic mechanism is so complex that its workings may never be fully understood.[7]

Knowing this, the life scientist is generally both epistemologically humble and technologically conservative. He is understandably reluctant to reach blindly into the life machine and blithely pull out and discard random parts. In Leopold's splendid phrase, the ecologist is disinclined to remodel the Alhambra with a steamshovel.

I write here of the science of ecology; specifically, of the mode of knowledge characteristic of that science, of the structure that the science displays as the ecologist gathers, interprets, and integrates his data, as he defines and clarifies his concepts, and as he formulates his laws, principles and theories. But how do we move from a scientific to a moral point of view? We move with great caution and difficulty, for here we encounter perhaps the most formidable problem of contemporary critical ethics (meta-ethics); namely, the question of the logical bearing of facts upon values. We have surveyed some of these problems in our Introduction to Environmental Ethics (included here) and will return to them throughout this course.

Deep Ecological Consciousness

Deep ecology is based on a new perception of reality that has profound implications not only for science and philosophy but also for business, politics, health care, education and everyday life. Deep ecology was coined by the Norwegian philosopher, Arne Naess in early 70's. It was coined in Scandinavia as a result of the discussion between Naess and his colleague, Sigmund Kvaloy. Both of them shared a passion for the Great Himalayas. On a visit to the Himalayas, they became impressed with aspects of 'Sherpa Culture' particularly when they found that their Sherpa guides regarded certain mountains as sacred and accordingly would not venture onto them. Naess decided to formulate a position which extended the reverence he and the Sherpas felt for mountains to other natural things in general.

The "shallow ecology movement", as Naess calls it, is the "fight against pollution and resource depletion", the central objective of which is "the health and affluence of people in the developed countries." The "deep ecology movement" in contrast endorses "biospheric egalitarianism", the view that all things are alike in having value in their own right, independent of their usefulness to human purposes. The deep ecologist respects this intrinsic value, taking care for example, when walking on the mountain side not to cause unnecessary damage to the plants. Furthermore, deep ecology also endorses what Naess calls "the relational, total-field image", understanding organisms (human or otherwise) as "knots" in the biopheric net, the identities of which are defined in terms of their ecological relations to each other. Naess maintains that the "deep" satisfaction that we receive from close partnership with other forms of life in nature contributes significantly to our life quality. As developed by Naess and others, the position also focuses on the possibility of the "identification" of the human ego with nature. The idea is briefly that by identifying with nature we can enlarge the boundaries of the self. Self-respect thus extends beyond the boundaries of my skin. My larger — ecological Self — (the capital 'S' emphasizes that I am an individual some of whose parts are found outside of my skin), according to Naess, deserves respect as well. And to respect and to care for myself is also to respect and to care for the natural environment with which I identify myself. 'Self-realization', in other words, is the reconnection of the shrivelled human individual with the wider natural environment.

Historical Context

Environmental Ethics, a field of Applied Ethics is concerned with those issues that arise when human beings interact with the natural environment. It not only seeks to evaluate past and present attitudes and practices, but aims to offer guidance as to how people

ought to think about, and conduct, their relationship with the natural environment; for example, environmental ethicists debate whether the natural environment is simply an exploitable resource for human interests, or whether it has significance independent of any use that might be made of it, a value that ought to constrain certain practices.

While there is little doubt that environmental matters occupy an important place in present-day public concern, historically this was not always the case. Some commentators have suggested that the historical roots of current environmental problems are to be found in the Judaeo-Christian tradition, which, as in *Genesis*, appears to confer upon humanity dominion over nature. In repudiating this interpretation of biblical scriptures, however, others have found in the Judaeo-Christian tradition of stewardship the basis of a new ethic of caring for nature. It is only since the late 1800s that there has been a developing interest in the conservation of the natural environment.

The common ancestry of all life explained by the Darwinian theory of evolution offered scientific encouragement to the view of life as an interdependent whole. It was only in the twentieth century, however, that calls were made for the extension of ethical concern to include all life on Earth. Studies in the 1960s and 1970s of the destruction of the natural environment resulting from pollution, logging and clearance of the rainforests, and the excessive use of pesticides, and fears that natural resources, such as fossil fuels, were being rapidly depleted, intensified calls for a re-evaluation of human attitudes towards, and interactions with, the natural environment. Occasionally, apocalyptic visions of humanity acting as its own executioner by creating a world inhospitable to life gave impetus and urgency to the field of environmental ethics.

Among environmental ethicists there is debate about what should be the object of moral concern. In an article of 1973, the Norwegian philosopher Arne Naess sought to distinguish between "deep" and "shallow" ecologies; whereas "shallow" approaches to environmental problems are anthropocentric, in that they are concerned only with the detrimental impact of the problems on human well-being, and promote conservation only with a view to securing the maintenance of natural resources for continued human consumption, "deep" environmental ethicists propose that the natural environment, or at least parts of it, are worthy of protection because they have an independent value regardless of their usefulness to humanity.

Environmental ethicists have sought to show that moral standing is not restricted to human beings by arguing, for example, as Peter Singer and Tom Regan do, that non-human sentient animals have a morally significant interest in not suffering, comparable with that of human beings. The British philosopher Robin Attfield finds independent value in the capacity of all life to thrive in its own fashion; while others argue that it is not individual animals but species, or ecosystems that are deserving of moral attention.

It is worth noting that the nature of many of the concerns of environmental ethics—for example, nuclear energy generation, the consequences of which may extend far into the future—means that the temporal extent of its reasoning goes far beyond that of traditional concerns, making it necessary to theorize about not only the interests of the present generation but also those of future generations of both human beings and non-human species. In recent years environmental ethicists have increasingly recognized the need to combine concern for the natural environment with concern for economic and social justice, particularly in developing countries.

In recent times, i.e., in the year 2002 a very thought provoking and illuminating book has been produced by Fritjof Capra, the famous physicist of our contemporary time. This book, entitled *The Web of Life: A New Scientific Understanding of Living Systems,* is very important from the point of view of deep ecology and it is very relevant for the present discussion. I, therefore, would like to highlight some of the important tenets of this book.

This book concentrates on biological aspects of Capra's ongoing thesis of the interconnection of the earth with all its inhabitants. Here he refers to a "new paradigm that may be called a holistic worldview, seeing the world as an integrated whole rather than a dissociated collection of parts. It may also be called an ecological view, if the term 'ecological' is used in a much broader sense than usual". Distinguishing between "shallow" and "deep" ecology, he describes shallow ecology as "human-centred". It views humans as above or outside of nature, as the source of all value, and ascribes only instrumental or "use" value to nature. "Deep ecology, on the other hand, does not separate humanity from nature: It sees the world not as a collection of isolated objects, but as a network of phenomena that are fundamentally interconnected and interdependent". It recognizes that all living beings have intrinsic value and views mankind "as just one particular strand in the web of life". Moreover, "Ultimately, deep ecological awareness is spiritual or religious awareness".

Capra goes on to assert that: By calling the emerging new vision of reality "ecological" in the sense of deep ecology, we emphasize that life is at its very centre. This is an important point for science, because in the old paradigm physics has been the model and source of metaphors for all other sciences. "All philosophy is like a tree", wrote Descartes. "The roots are metaphysics, the trunk is physics, and the branches are all the other sciences".

Deep ecology has overcome this Cartesian metaphor.... physics has now lost its role as the science providing the most fundamental description of reality. However, this is still not generally recognized today. . . . Today the paradigm shift in science, at its deepest level, implies a shift from physics to the life sciences.

Spectacular discoveries in astrophysics and the theories of some physicists suggesting the universality of consciousness would seem to counterpoise Capra's remarks. Moreover, there should not be competition between the various scientific disciplines. While the life sciences are certainly important, the physical sciences — and also non-scientific fields — have as much to contribute to human understanding.

Capra examines the views of scientists such as Maturana, Varela, Lovelock, others. He considers various living systems—including rain forests and the human body with its cells—that scientists have tended to view as mere "mechanisms". But can we have an organism without an organizer of some kind to place function and collaboration within a larger picture? Each component should itself be considered as an organism. Nor can it be proved that an organism composed of many elements is the product of a chance assembly of units of a variety of kinds.

One implication of this book is nothing less than the overthrow of Descartes' dictum that mind is synonymous with reasoning. Capra asserts that in the emerging theory of living systems mind is not a thing, but a process. It is cognition, the process of knowing, and is identified with the process of life itself. Thus, a bacterium, or a plant, has no brain but has a mind. The simplest organisms are capable of perception and thus of cognition. They do not see, but they nevertheless perceive changes in their environment—differences between light and shadow, hot and cold, higher and lower concentrations of some chemical, and the like.

The reactions Capra lists suggest an innate awareness to be found in all the children of nature whatever their stage of evolution.

Another approach to life and its processes worth consideration is that of Hindu thinkers millennia ago. They looked upon life (*jiva*) as an omnipresent universal expressed in particular units. They also recognized "essence of mind" as a universal, calling it *mahat*. They called the human manifestation of this universal mind *manas*, and held that the development of the human mind was the expression of its innate potential as an increasingly perfected aspect of universal mind.

From the observations of Capra one can arrive at the conclusion that the whole question of values is crucial to deep ecology. Whereas the old paradigm is based on anthropocentric (humancentred) values, deep ecology is grounded in eco-centric (earth-centric) values. It is a world view that acknowledges the inherent value of non-human life. All living beings are members of ecological communities bound together in a network of interdependencies. When this deep ecological perception becomes part of our daily awareness, a radically new system of ethics emerges.

Such a deep ecological ethics is urgently needed today and specially in science, since most of what scientists do is not life-furthering and life preserving but life-destroying. With physicists designing weapons systems that threatens to wipe out life on the planet, with chemists contaminating the global environment, with biologists releasing new and unknown types of micro-organisms without knowing the consequences, with psychologists and other scientists torturing animals in the name of scientific progress–with all these activities going on, it seems most urgent to introduce 'eco-ethical' standards into science.

It is generally not recognized that values are not peripheral to science and technology but constitute the very basis and driving force. During the scientific revolution in the seventeenth century, values were separated from facts, and ever since that time we have tended to believe that scientific facts are independent of what we do and are, therefore, independent of our values. In reality, scientific facts emerges out of an entire constellation of human perception, values and actions—in one word, out of a paradigm—from which they cannot be separated. Although much of the detailed research may not depend explicitly on the scientist's value system, the larger paradigm within which this research is pursued will never be value-free. Scientists, therefore, are responsible for their research not only intellectually but also morally.

Within the context of deep ecology, the view that values are inherent in all living nature is grounded in the deep ecological, or spiritual, experience that nature and self are one. This expansion of the self all the way to the identification with nature is the grounding of deep ecology, as Naess clearly recognizes. For Naess, this togetherness or unity with nature is a matter of what he calls "the great Self". This concept of great Self is highly reminiscent of classical Indian philosophical visions of the ultimate unity of everything. Whether in *Samkhya*, Buddhism, or *Advaita Vedanta*, the cosmocentric vision is intended to shape our place in reality, and to regulate our conduct not with an exclusivist principle of human autonomy, but in tune with the cosmic order.

I would like to conclude the discussion with the alarming remarks and the pronouncement made by the well known British Philosopher, Bertrand Russell. In his Lloyd Robert lecture given at the Royal Society of London, on November 29, 1949, Bertrand Russell said :

> *". . . . we are in the middle of a race between human skill as to means and human folly as to ends. Given sufficient folly as to ends, every increase in the skill required to achieve them is to the bad. The human race has survived hitherto owing to ignorance and incompetence; but given knowledge and competence combined with folly, there can be no certainty of survival. Knowledge is power, but it is power for evil just as much as for good. It follows that, unless men increase in wisdom as much as in knowledge, increase of knowledge will be increase in sorrow."*

In my own interpretation of this passage, there are two pairs of ideas conveying the central message. The first is the idea of "human skills as to means" paired with the idea of human knowledge; the second is "human folly as to ends" paired with the idea of lack of human wisdom. The central message is, of course, means and ends that characterize human civilization. We employ our skills to devise various means for various purposes, and the purposes define the ends of our continued existence. Evidently it is the means-ends nexus that determines human survival.

Russell is focusing on the human means-ends nexus in the present condition of humanity, with a prudential consideration of the prospect of human survival given the logic of that nexus. And the logic of means-ends nexus is quite clearly stated: "knowledge and competence combined with folly" (where folly is reflection of lack of wisdom) would make human survival doubtful. Increase in knowledge without a corresponding increase in wisdom is said to be inversely proportional to happiness.

By "means" Russell, of course, refers to the entire instrumental human set-up created by means of scientific-technological skill. Western technological culture has had a pervasive effect on the present human condition. The entire human situation is technologically structured, and that structure is designed apparently to make the condition of human survival more comfortable than earlier. This, in a very general sense, is the end. Human knowledge and competence are deployed in facilitating what is reckoned as human flourishing.

There may be the suspicion that unless human knowledge and competence are applied to the technology manipulation and control of the natural surrounding of humanity, humanity's survival strength may diminish in the face of adverse natural forces. There may be some truth in this suspicion. But a great deal depends on how judiciously we apply the technical skill at our disposal to our natural surrounding. It is obvious, from Russell's remark, that humanity is liable to folly, or lack of wisdom. For the human mind is capable of exercising knowledge or intelligence in a manner divorced from wisdom. When the natural surrounding is exploited by knowledge divorced from wisdom, the resultant condition is one of sorrow.

One might say, using Russell's phraseology, that this awareness of environmentalism or eco-friendliness is a belated awareness of environmental wisdom. Environmental wisdom or deep ecological perspective of environment is necessary for our proper negotiation with the environment in our inevitable interdependence with it. Environmental ethics would, therefore, have to come to terms with this ecological perspective or wisdom.

REFERENCES

1. Naess, Arne,"Identification, Oneness, Wholeness and Self-Realization" in Benson, John, (2000) (ed.), *Environmental Ethics*, Routledge, London, pp. 241-256.

2. Srivastava, Dinesh Chandra,"Environmental Ethics: To What Extent Does It Go Beyond Human-centred Ethics?" in Srivastava, D.C.(2005), *Readings in Environmental Ethics: Multidisciplinary Perspectives*, Rawat, Jaipur, pp. 81-88;
3. Capra, Fritjof (2002) *The Web of Life: A New Scientific Understanding of Living Systems*, Flamingo, p. 6.
4. *Ibid*, p. 7.
5. *Ibid*, p. 12-13.
6. *Ibid*, p. 174-175.
7. Naess, Arne (1973),"The Shallow and the Deep, Long Range Ecology Movement", *Inquiry*, Vol. 16, pp. 95-100.

Chapter – 16

The Need of Ecosophy in Technocratic Society

Dr. Sanjay Kumar Shukla

I

Man has shown himself capable of the knowledge to give him certain mastery over environment. The danger to man in the future comes not from nature, but from man himself. John Passmore in his *Man's Responsibility for Nature,* argues that the Old Testament (*Genesis* in particular) not only confers on man, dominion over nature, but also leaves open the possibility for an attitude of absolute despotism towards nature on the part of mankind.[1] Man must let go his technological and material narcissism because there cannot be real, responsible and effective environmental ethics in a world "dominated by technological mentality and crass materialism". Only by creating a workable environmental ethics and world conservation strategy can there be a chance for human survival. The reason for destruction of environment in the name of development lies in the mistaken separation of man from nature as Arundhati Roy has rightly pointed out that "nature needs to be saved from the humans for the humans"[2] What is needed today is to remind ourselves that nature cannot be destroyed without ultimately mankind being destroyed itself. Centuries of rapacious exploitation of the environment have finally caught up with us, and a radically changed attitude towards nature is now not a question of spiritual merit but of sheer survival. Betrand Russell has beautifully depicted the present alarming situation that knowledge and competence combined with folly (lack of wisdom) would make human survival doubtful. Increase in knowledge without a corresponding increase in wisdom is said to be inversely proportional to happiness. It can be stated in this fashion that when the natural surrounding is exploited by knowledge divorced from wisdom, the resultant condition is one of sorrow and repentence. That the most intelligent species on the earth lives such an eco-unfriendly life is a glaring example of human folly. Environmental wisdom is necessary for our proper negotiation with the environment in our inevitable intercourse with it and this has given birth to different models of environmental ethics. The ecosophy (ecological Wisdom) will come as a rescue for present environmental crisis.

II

The dominant Western tradition, influenced by the mainstream Christianity, assumes that the natural would exists for the benefit of human beings. Morality begins and ends with human beings. Nature being devoid of intrinsic worth or value, the destruction of any part of nature is not sinful, if by such destruction we do not harm other human beings. Objects of nature merely exist for the use of human beings and are valued because they serve as instruments for the satisfaction of human needs and desires. This can be termed as anthropocentric or human centric environmental ethics which presupposes man's superiority over nature, on the ground that man is the only rational being. The hypothesis that animals do not even possess feelings and consciousness, shaped the ethical perspective of humans in such a way that non-humans are kept apart from moral considerations.[3] The instrumental value we ascribe to other things is indicative of the selfishness of human beings. Thus the anthropocentric model provides utilitarian approach to nature, which lacks the virtue of respecting nature for its own sake. The Baconian and Cartesian doctrine glorifies humans as the conqueror of nature. They can manipulate and improve upon these natural surroundings, demonstrating that they are superior to non-humans. This view should not be supported if we want to preserve the nature. This natural process is something that is beyond the control of any species. This assumption provides a cosmic vision that promotes the thinking that humans are not the controlling authority of natural happenings and will give different picture to nature-human relationship. The sense of sharing will be strengthened only if we (the humans) accept that we are part of the integral whole.

III

Ecocentric model of environmental ethics is the holistic theory according to which the whole ecosystem comprising both the biotic and abiotic parts of nature deserves moral worth. The American philosopher, Aldo Leopold, favoured eco-centrism, an ethics dealing with the man's relation to the land and to the animals and plants. He virtually changes the role of *Homo Sapiens* from the conqueror of the land community to its preserver. His 'land ethic' prescribes "a thing is right when it tends to preserve the integrity, stability and beauty of the biotic community. It is wrong when it tends to otherwise". The holistic "land ethics" and "deep ecology ethics" represent eco-centrism in environmental ethics. Arne Naess, the Norwegian philosopher, wrote influential article entitled "The Shallow and the Deep Long Range Ecology Movement." He made an important distinction between "Shallow" and "Deep" strands in the ecology movement as the former is limited to the traditional moral framework while the latter is radical in its outlook. Shallow ecology wants to protect and preserve the nature if it serves the interest of the human beings meaning thereby it has anthropocentric traits based on utilitarian maxim. Deep ecology directs us to preserve the integrity of biosphere for its own sake, irrespective of possible benefits to humans alone that might follow from so doing.[4] It believes in biospheric egalitarianism. All biotic communities, including the abiotic nature, have right to live and blossom. The attempt to deny the fact of interdependence and the subsequent efforts to dominate nature resulted into our self-estrangement. Eco-centrism uphold the principles of diversity and symbiosis. Diversity increases the level of survival, thereby enhances novelty and richness of life-forms. "Live and Let Live" is the contention of ecology, rather than "Either You or Me".

Arne Naess and George Sessions have formulated several principles for a deep ecology ethics—

1. The well-being and flourishing of human and non-human living on earth have value in themselves. These values are independent of usefulness of non-human world for human purposes.
2. Richness and diversity of life-forms contribute to the realization of these values and are also values in themselves.
3. Humans have no right to reduce this richness and diversity except to satisfy vital needs.[5] Richard Sylvan and Van Plum Wood also extended their concern beyond living things, including in it an obligation not to jeopardize well being of natural objects without good reason. Hence, deep ecology advocates our essential oneness with nature, where to be one with nature means to become part of "great self" — where the great self symbolizes what Naess calls "the living earth". This is evidently a cosmo centric vision of our place in reality as espoused by traditional Indian philosophy. Warwick Fox linked deep ecology with transpersonal psychology through the idea of identification with the non-human world and the notion of expanded self that is capable of moving beyond.

IV

The eco-centrism maintains that all eco-system and species have equal right to live and blossom, and we have to acknowledge it. If this is admitted, then the harmful bacteria and virus causing disease and death and humans have to be considered as equal.

But such a total egalitarianism is wrong, and not only that it goes against the *modus operandi* of nature. Human should be given some sort of priority in value distribution, as morality is a matter of choice and it is in fitness of things to consider that humans are the evaluator and creator of value. K.A. Parker has rightly remarked, "Blind anthropocentrism has deplorable consequences for the non-human world, but a blindly misanthropic eco-centrism is no less deplorable."[6] Undoubtedly, human chauvinism is condemnable, but we should at least acknowledge human experience as the measure of all things. Hence, as long as the valuer is a human being, it is impossible for being radically non-anthropocentric in environmental matters. Human valuers must give priority to the basic needs of non-humans over the non-basic, trival human needs. We are supposed to strike a balance between anthropocentrism and eco-centrism. For an acceptable version of eco-centrism, we have to put emphasis not only on the thesis of intrinsic value, but also on a form of human self-realization, which springs out of ecological consciousness. The ideal of self-realization is best exhibited in *Bhagvad Gitā* as "He whose self is harmonized by *yoga* sees the self abiding in all beings and all beings in self; everywhere he sees the same" (*Sarvabhūtasthamātmanam Sarvabhūtani Cātmani / Ik'ate Yogayuktātma Sarvatra Samdarūana !!).*

This attitude of protectiveness, based on the identification with the nature, marks the shift from an ethic of duty, grounded in the recognition of the intrinsic worth of nature, to an ethic of care. Hence, it can be stated in the conclusive manner that the attitude of conquering nature has to be given up as a debunked ideology of Western culture. We need a paradigm shift from "victor-vanquished" model to the Buberian 'I–Thou' paradigm. What we need today is a sort of ecosophy, which in the words of Naess, "can provide a single motivating force for all the activities and movements aimed at saving the planet from human exploitation and domination".

V

The desire to preserve the environment led to a world view that regards the universe as a unified system, all of whose parts are connected and interdependent. Reacting against the homogenizing centralizing tendencies of modern society and its technology, many people have looked to ecology as a rationale for the promotion of decentralized, selfsufficient and pluralistic forms of politics and social structures. Schumacher has linked the concept of decentralisation to environmentally sound form of "appropriate" technology based on renewable sources and smaller scale. Devall and Dasmann are among the ecologists who have promoted this concept in biological terms. Thus they relate the idea of cultural pluralism to the principle of ecological diversity and stability.[7]

Our preferred worldview hinges upon the following two fundamental ethics—

(i) *The Ecological Ethics* — If an individual identifies with the whole of nature and perceives that he is one with the planet, he is naturally drawn to an ethic which relates his own self interest to that of fellow humans and to all planetary life. Such an ecological ethics recognizes limitations on available resources and calls on our species to act in partnership with nature in protecting the complex life support systems of the planet.

(ii) *The Self Realisation Ethics*—This ethics affirms that the proper end of all experience is the further growth in individual and collective awareness. Such an ethics is supported by human potential movements (psychosynthesis and humanistic psychology), and it is found at the core of almost all religious philosophies. Self realization provides the most satisfying answer to alienation and anomie.

What is needed is perfect blending of these two ethics. The ecological ethics affirms that human life is inextricably linked horizontally to its physical and social environment. We also require a self realization ethics that links humanity vertically to the transcendental or spiritual dimensions. It is value of caring which is central to self realization ethics. In caring, I experience the other as having potentialities and the need to grow. Hence, it is the materialistic outlook which is responsible for environmental degradation while spiritualism nurtures the ideal values of love, pity and sacrifice and visualizes the spirit of companionship between man and nature.

REFERENCES

1. Passamore, John, *Man's Responsibility* for *Nature,* pp. 26-27.
2. Roy, Arundhati, *The Greater Common Good,* p. 12.
3. Srivastava, D.C., *Readings in Environmental Ethics,* p. 49.
4. Singer, Peter, *Practical Ethics,* p. 280.
5. *Ibid,* pp. 280-81.
6. Parker, K.A., "*Pragmatism and Environmental Thought*" in Light, Andrew and Katz, Eric (edited), *Environmental Pragmatism,* p. 33.
7. Devall, Bill, *Natural Resources,* Journal 20, No. 2, p. 312.

Chapter – 17

Ecological Ethics : Indian Metaphysical and Ethical Viewpoint

Dr. Kakoli Basak

At present the whole world is going through an ecological crisis which has raised serious concerns about :

- Loss of forests, especially rainforests that contain a large variety of plants and animals.
- The threat of extinction to one-fourth of all the species on earth by the year 2020.
- Annual discharge of 3500 metric tonnes of carbon dioxide and 600 tonnes of carbon monoxide into the atmosphere as a result of combustion, motor vehicle and exhausts.
- Increase of human population daily by a quarter of a million.

We find that the two main causes for environmental degradation are:

1. Overuse and exploitation of natural resources.
2. Pollution of environment.

We further see that the ever increasing population is the root cause of over-exploitation of natural resources and environmental degradation. This points to the fact that the traditional anthropocentric approach towards nature and its components is responsible for the present ecological crisis. This approach regards development as an increase in the facilities of human convenience and completely ignores the other forms of life, thus causing an ecological imbalance. So, we must learn to minimize our role in disturbing the balance of nature.

The present scenario may be changed by adopting ecological ethics which can change this anthropocentric view-point and develop the sense of moral responsibility in us for future progress of the world.

There is also a need to redefine development. Ecological ethics aims at sustainable development, i.e., development which has stability, continuity and tenability. There may be no loss or decrease in the process of development. It is said, *"Sustainable development which meets the necessities of the present time without making any compromise with the needs of the coming generations"*[1]. It is well-balanced in which there is no place for loss or decrease. In the process of physical development we should see that if any loss is made in any part of nature, the loss must be compensated in some way. Ecological balance is to be maintained, failing which punishments may be given by Nature.

The Unsuitability of the Western Approach

In the West, there are three broad traditions of ethics:

(1) Virtue ethics (starts with Aristotle) is concerned with developing Some virtues in oneself which leads to *'eudemonia'* (happiness to promote well-being of all). Rational activities of man can control his senses thus achieving the goal, according to Aristotle.

(2) Deontological ethics of which Kantian ethics is an example which makes guidelines for behaviour or duties. According to this theory rules of morality should be practiced not for getting any pragmatic end but should

be followed unconditionally. The Kantian philosophy treats man as an end and not as a means. In the present context we can extend the idea to include all living beings like animals and trees as the thought behind the Kantian philosophy makes every being equal from the point of view of morality.

(3) The third tradition is of teleological ethics which refers to some non-moral end in reference to which an action is to be judged. Utilitarianism founded by Bentham and developed by J.S. Mill is an example of this kind. According to this view the highest good is the greatest happiness for the greatest number. *"Greatest happiness for greatest number"* may be understood as development of all beings.

But, we find that all three are concerned exclusively with human beings and their inter-relationship and thus these are inadequate to serve as an ethics which may properly guide us in the present ecological crisis.

Development of Western Ecological Ethics

In the Western anthropocentric view Nature and its components are not attributed to any intrinsic value *(value of their own)*, only instrumental value (means for attaining some valuable things) of them is accepted. So, ecological ethics started and developed through its various phases for making changes in the present value system. The anthropocentrism was replaced by ecocentrism which again had three various forms:

1. Shallow Ecology which is the *"fight against pollution and resource depletion"*. According to Naes, human beings constitute the sole value in it.
2. Intermediate Ecology according to which natural items have some intrinsic value, but whenever they conflict with human interest, the latter is given more importance.

3. Deep Ecology (developed in Scandinavia by Naes) takes different forms, all of which are ecocentric. It holds the view that all living beings are alike in having value of their own, and that *the "ecological community forms the ethical community"*. The position also came to focus on the possibility of the identification of the human ego with nature. In Stan Rowe's, *"Deep ecology platform"*, it is believed that the well-being and flourishing of the living earth and its many organic and inorganic parts have value in themselves. It also believes that richness and diversity of the earth's eco-systems contribute to the realization of these values and these are also value in themselves. Human beings have no right to reduce this diversity.

Indian Ethics

Compared to this present Western view of Ecological ethics we can see that the Indian Ethics is based on its metaphysical viewpoints has a great possibility to serve as a suitable Ecological Ethic. This chapter also suggests that broader value of Indian tradition might contribute in this effort.

Metaphysical Basis of Indian Moral System

Indian moral system has a metaphysical basis. It is also based on a spiritual outlook with regards to the universe. *"It is not autonomous like in the west. Here it is believed that if there is no metaphysical foundation for ethics it would be shallow and rootless."*[2] This foundation gives it deeper meaning and seriousness. Man acts according to his beliefs. So, Dr. Radhakrishnan says, *"As we think the ultimate reality to be so, we behave. Vision and action go together"*[3].

The classical Indian ethical thought is nominative and practical. So, Indian philosophy is often described as "way of life, not merely a way of thought"[4] .In Indian metaphysics a holistic viewpoint is adapted for the Nature or the World so, morality is not only related to the human world but extends to the whole world. Indian ethical thought guides us to act for the welfare and development of the universe. Man is regarded as a part of the nature community. Every component and part is attributed equal importance as God has created them all.

At present, Nature is conceived as an all-comprehensive unity where complexity and bio-diversity is regarded as the basis of ecological balance. The ancient saints of our country had the knowledge of the internal relationship between Nature, its components, and all living beings. The ecological balance can be maintained in the best way when this harmony among all beings is preserved. The three basic aspects of human personality related to body, life and mind are deeply connected to the environment.

In Indian thought right from the age of the *Upanishads*, emphasis has been laid on self-perfection or self-realization. Due to his ignorance, man thinks himself to be his *'narrow self'*, but in his essence he is one and identical with the cosmic self *(viswa atma)*. This realization of the unity of the self with the whole universe makes man responsible for the preservation of every element of nature.

> *"Reality, which is one has three phases—* 'Sat', *i.e., things are or exist, all animate and inanimate things relate us through the relationship of common existence. The second is* 'Chit', *i.e., we know the unity of all things; and the third is* 'ananda' *or ecstasy. When our consciousness realizes all things as spiritually one with it, it gives us joy. So, for us, the highest purpose of this world is not merely living in it, knowing it and making use of it, but realizing our own self in it through expansion of sympathy — not alienating ourselves from it and dominating it, but comprehending and uniting it with ourselves in perfect union."*[5]

Again, according to the *Vedas* there is an order or law governing the whole cosmos. This is called *'ṛta'*, which stands for order which includes within it the ritual, the natural and the moral order all at the same time. This law makes our feeling of unity with the whole world more firm.

According to some of the modern thinkers like Tagore, Gandhi, Vivekananda, the liberation is conceived as realizing the universal self within the individual self and it is to be attained by moral actions. When one extends one's consciousness to reach the universal consciousness one also develops the feeling of participation with everything that is going on in the universe.

Some metaphysical concepts of Buddhism may form ground for ecological ethics. In Buddhism, the need for arousing the universal consciousness in oneself has been given importance. *"This universal consciousness postulates the unity of microcosm and macrocosm."*[6] To reach this level of consciousness, it is necessary to develop *"Bodhichitta"*. The aim of attaining *"Bodhichitta"* is the welfare of the whole cosmos.

The principle of emptiness *(shunyata)* of Buddhism denies the inherent existence of things and phenomena. A thing exists only through dependence on others. Nothing exists permanently. As human activities are the causes of extinction of many species in the world. We must not forget that this theory rings an alarm for the failure of humanity as well. Again, the principle of interdependence of all entities shows the complexity of the inter-relation of all things and beings on the earth. So, from this we can say that this diversity and complexity is essential for the maintenance of the ecological balance. So we see, *"though 'nirvana' is the highest good, it is realized through universal goodwill and love (maitri)"*[7] in Buddhism.

In Jainism we find that the goal of life is considered to be the attainment of the *'siddhaloka'*, a world where all the liberated souls live eternally in bliss. However, the path to reach this *'loka'* entails great care regarding how one lives in relationship to all other beings that surround us. "The world view of the Jainas may be characterized as a bio-cosmology. Due to their perception of *'livingness'* of the world, the Jainas have an affinity for the ideals of the environmental movement."[8]

Indian Ethical Thoughts

Apparently Indian ethics as a whole may be characterized as teleological considering that liberation or *"'moksha' is regarded by almost all the views as the highest goal of life and morality or 'dharma' as the means to it. But conduciveness to 'moksha' is not the criterion of any virtuous or moral action"*.[9] Moral actions are those which are in accordance with the laws of the *shastras* or will of God. So, according to Dr. K.N. Tiwary, *"In a way the whole Indian ethical system is deontological. Moral duties are to be practiced as they are prescribed by the Vedas or shastras. Virtues are to be inculcated not for getting anything in return but simply because one must be virtuous."*[10] As there is no intimate relationship between virtues and duties so the term '*dharma*' is used to denote both. Virtues are to be inculcated and duties are to be performed for serving ones own end of attaining salvation as well as for contributing to the progress of the whole world. So, morality has two kinds of values—

1. Intrinsic value, i.e., to practice virtue and follow moral law has its own value.
2. Instrumental value, i.e., morality leads to worldly progress or *'abhyuday'* and liberation or *'moksha'*.

In contemporary Western thought Nature and its components are said to be treated in a friendly manner from the pragmatic point of view. Nature and its components like air, water, the sun, trees, animals, etc., are valuable as they have instrumental value for the welfare of mankind. Though, in *'Deep Green Theory'* they are granted intrinsic value, but the difference between the man and the rest natural elements are always maintained. Man is attributed the highest place in the Creation. But in Indian ethical thought social duty *(dharma)* is expanded to include the ecological community, as each and every component of nature has its importance from the point of view of existence. So, natural forces are worshipped here to show respect to them. It is said *"Mata bhumih putroham prithivya"*[11]. This means that the earth is regarded as mother.

In Indian philosophy a very important ethically significant distinction is made between the good *(sreyah)* and the pleasant *(preyah)*, the desirable and the desired. *'Preyah'* is usually desired, but the desired is not desirable. This distinction arouses a moral consciousness in man. The message is given that man's aim is not simply to enjoy the things of the world but to live a life of certain virtues and to perform duties towards the world. One should regulate and control his basic instincts. The present ecological crisis may be solved by the guidance of the *Upanishads* dictum, as we know that it may be desired to use and exploit the Nature for our benefit but we should be guided by our reason and conscience which attributes equal value to all for harmonious co-existence.

It is conceived,

> *"that the whole creation is like a sacrifice (yajna) made by the Supreme Creator. He creates the cosmos just to "give" himself. The feeling of "sacrifice" is to be perceived everywhere in nature."*[12]

The rivers, the forests, air, fire, trees, animals give us help us and without their help man cannot live. Man is the greatest creation of the creative process as he has sensibility and intelligence. He also possesses a high level of conscience in him. So, he cannot hold the highest position in the creative order if he does not give importance to the act of *"sacrifice"* and is not ready to "give *himself*". Being the best among all creation, it is his moral duty to sacrifice his *"narrow self"* to keep the world-order progressive. When our thinking process is limited to our narrow self, we may use natural resources without making any effort for conservation of these properties. But this will act as a hindrance to sustainable development. So, Nature, as a whole, is to be protected with this sense of sacrifice with the awakening of the conscience. It is said in the *Upanishad*:

> *"Ishavasyam idam sarvam yat kincha jagatyam jagat.*
> *Tena tyaktena bhunjitha ma gridham, kasyasvit dhanam."*[13]

Know all that moves in this moving world as enveloped by God, and find enjoyment through renunciation, not through greed of possession.

The *'law of karma'* which is a basic postulate of the moral effort or practice in the Indian context says that all our activities, words and ideas form the condition of our existence in future. So, the law convinces man to accept responsibility for the present as well as for the future condition. With reference to this law, we can understand the man's daily activities shape his life in the future or in a broader sense nurture the development of mankind, and help the global ecological situation.

As our past and present actions are responsible for the present ecological crisis, therefore, our thoughtful actions only can change the picture. Our actions are guided by our thoughts, so, thought is the creator of the whole universe. Therefore, in Indian tradition the emphasis is laid on purity of heart *(chittashuddhi)* as only in a pure heart good thoughts automatically arise. Hence, *"greater emphasis is laid on virtue of individual purity than on the social virtues"*[14] As it is believed that one who is pure in mind will always be harmonious with the well-being of all. This purity of mind may be awakened by one's realization of unity with the cosmic self.

We see, *"the term* 'dharma' *as used in Indian philosophical and ethical tradition is very broad and comprehensive."*[15] *"It is variously translated as Religion, Virtue, and Duty. Sometimes it stands for Nature or the intrinsic quality, sometimes for civil and moral law, justice, virtue, merit, duty and morality."*[16]

The *Vedas* has various texts and rituals that extol the earth *(bhu)*, the atmosphere *(bhuvan)* and the sky *(sva)*, and detailed account has also been given about what should be our duties to the dwellers of these planes. Men are asked not to harm the three planes but enrich these.[17] Our duty is to free these from pollution.[18]

As the air, water and earth are divine in Nature, it is man's duty or *'dharma'* to *'yajnas'* to make this pollution free. The fire of the *'yajnas'* purifies the atmosphere.

The Vows and Virtues

At the core of the Jaina and Buddha's faith lie five vows that dictate man's life. These five vows of non-violence *(ahimsa)* truthfulness *(satya)* not stealing *(asteya)*, sexual restraint *(brahmacharya)* and non-possession *(aparigraha)* are given importance in Hindu tradition too. These five constitute the *'yamas'* of Hindu tradition, the *'Panchamahavrata'* of the Jaina tradition and *'panchasila'* of the Buddha tradition. The vows are to be practiced to minimize harm to all living beings.

About the first vow, *'ahimsa'*, it can be said that it was born in the foundation of Indian culture and belongs to all directions of Indian thought. *'Ahimsa'* refers not only to overt non-killing of living beings but also to non-harming or non-injuring any creature in any way. In Buddhism and Jainism, special stress has been given to this vow. In the Jaina view, man is asked not to hurt in any way any living being— an animal or even an insect.[19] In Buddhism, it is said, *"Let one refrain even from hurting any creature, both that are strong and those that tremble in the world."*[20] In a positive sense it means traits of love, kindness, etc. So, *"We should pervade the whole world with love, pity, sympathy and equanimity."*[21] To develop a feeling of unity and intimacy with all beings and natural components is possible by awakening the feeling of friendship *(maitri)*, compassion *(karuna)* and love as described in Indian thought.

'Ahimsa' and *'satya'* are given the highest place among the virtues in the epic of *Mahabharata*. Truth should be in harmony with righteousness and devout of injury, harshness, cruelty and oppression of all creatures. A truthful person can see the interdependence of every being and interrelatedness of everything. Such a person will not be the cause of suffering to any other.

The vow of non-stealing which means not to take anything from anyone without taking his permission may be reinterpreted in the ecological context. It means that if we take anything from Nature for our use, we must compensate it in some way.

The concept of *'non-possession'* or *'aparigraha'* means non-attachment to worldly objects. Due to our attachment to worldly objects we want to possess more and more by exploiting natural resources. To avoid this and minimize our personal needs the virtue of contentment (*santosa*), is to be practiced. In Jainism and Buddhism importance is given on taking only that much which is necessary *(parimita parigraha).*

As we have seen that the ever increasing population is the root cause of the present ecological crisis, the vow of celibacy or *'brahmacharya'* may guide people to control passion. Sexual restraint might help to minimize population growth.

Therefore, one has to practice to control one's senses *(indriyanigraha)* so that one may follow these vows. The virtues like respect *(shraddha)* to all, friendship *(maitri)* compassion *(karuna)* are emphasized in the *Vedas*. Duties like *'dana'* which include plantation of trees to make dwelling places for animals are to be performed. In Buddhism it is said, one should abstain from purposeless sin which include thoughtless action like breaking the branch of a tree.

In Hindu ethics there are concepts of *'rina'* and *'panchamahayajna'*. It is said that as man takes the help of his parents, natural elements, and different members of the society in his life, it is his duty to show gratitude and respect to all of them. Generally there are descriptions of three kinds of *'rina'* which are (i) *'deva rina'*, (ii) *'rishi rina'*, and (iii) *'pitri rina'*.[22] In *'deva rina'* the five divine elements of the world *(earth, water, fire, air, ether)* by whose grace human life is possible on the earth are required to be respected and preserved.

Again man's duty for all living and non-living beings is shown in the concept of *'panchmahayajna'*. In the *Upanishads* and *Brahmana granthas*, *Samhitas*, five kinds of *yajnas* – *'deva'*, *'brahma'*, *'pitri'*, *'bhuta'*, *'nṛi'* are described. Man becomes free from the debts *('rina')* by performing these *'yajnas'*. In *'deva yajna'* gratitude is shown to the divine powers or natural forces, in *'bhutayajna'* one is asked to provide food to lower animals from his own share. It gives the message of practicing virtues like reverence, tolerance, compassion for the welfare of the whole world.

Lastly, to answer the questions like why should we be moral and do justice to all we can say, following the Indian tradition, that it is our very nature or *'dharma'* to be virtuous. It is our duty to work actively and superlatively for the maintenance of the world order, and ecology.

Contemporary theories regarding 'ecology' which are appreciated all over the world suggest change in the ecological policies to include the non-human world, Indian traditional ecological ethics may guide us in this so that we do not regard ourselves as masters but citizens in the life community. At present much emphasis is laid on the responsibility towards the environment. This responsibility implies, (1) knowledge, (2) choice and (3) value significance. Here we may say that the holistic approach of Indian Philosophy towards the world can help us in developing a better understanding our environment whereas Indian ethical views can guide us to make proper choices through a proper appreciation of value significance.

REFERENCES

1. World Commission for Environment and Development Report 1987, p. 8.
2. Dr. K.N. Tiwary, — *Classical Indian Ethical Thought*, Motilal Banarsidas, p.10.
3. Dr. S. Radhakrishnan, *Eastern Religion Western Thought*, Oxford. p. 80.
4. M. Hiriyana, *Outlines of Indian Philosophy*. p.29.
5. *R.N. Tagore*, 'The Religion of the Forest' in *Creative Unity*, Macmillan Press Company, p.49.
6. *Jainism Buddhism and Ecology* — available at ecological ethics-http/eco.gn.apc.org.
7. J.N.Sinha, *Indian Philosophy* (Vol. 2), Motilal Banarsidas. p.241.

8. Christopher Key Chapple, Jainism & Ecology available at http/ online.sfsu, edu.
9. K.N.Tiwari, *Classical Indian Ethical Thought*, p.75.
10. *Ibid.*, p.76
11. *Atharva Veda* (12-2.12)
12. R.N. Tagore, *Creative Unity*, p.32
13. *Ishavasyo Upanisad*
14. Mackenzie, *Hindu Ethics*, Oriental Book Reprint Corporation, New Delhi, p.38.
15. K.V. Rangaswamy Aiyar, *Some Aspects of the Hindu View of Life*.
16. *Yajur Veda,* 13/18, 15/64.
17. *Atharva Veda*, 12/1/12.
18. "*Savve pana savve bhutah savve jiva savve satta na hantavva na ajjabetavva*".
19. *Dhammika Sutta*, p.393.
20. *Madhusudana Sutta*, II-8-11.
21. *Rinanitrinya pakritya mana moksha niveshyate*, *Manusmriti,* 6/35
22. *Shatapath Brahman,* 11/5/6/7

NOTES

Patrick Curry, *On Ecological Ethics*.- http/eco.gn.apc.org.
Ronald Epstein, http/online.sfsu, edu

Chapter – 18

The Role of World Religions in Environmental Crisis

Dr. Sucheta Shukla

I

Modern Science, ostensibly under the influence of Hebrew and Greek traditions, is based upon the Cartesian dualism of mind and matter, which led to the development of anthropocentric ethics. The growth of science, rather than emphasizing the rational powers of man, has vastly extended the means of exploitation of man and nature by him. With the success in the advancement of scientific knowledge, man developed an arrogant attitude to conquer the nature, leading to environmental degradation and ecological imbalance. Human beings, in order to secure and promote their existence, growth and comforts, have been resorting to indiscriminate exploitation on plants and animals. Nevertheless, there has been the belated realisation that, for the existence of human species and promotion of human welfare, the existence of flora and fauna is indispensable.

World religions can play an important role in resolving the environmental crisis because they are capable of evoking a positive awareness towards the nature. In creating such an awareness, religion helps in realizing that there are limits to our control over the animate and inanimate world, and that our arrogance and manipulative power over nature can backfire. It is religion that says that a man's life cannot be measured by material possessions, and that the ends of human life go beyond consumption. Any religion provides at least three fundamental strengths to help man remain sane in a technological society.

1. It protects an individual's existence from the depersonalizing tendencies of the techno-industrial society.
2. It forces man to recognize human fallibility, helping us to realize our follies of the past and offering opportunity to rectify them.
3. It is our religion that gives restraint, humility and liberation from self-centredness.[1]

II

The religious beliefs of Semitic religions and scientific strides have provided enormous material comforts to human beings but we should not feel any hesitation in conferring that they have brought human existence on the brink of disaster. It is from historical point of view we find that man is fashioned according to his own faith and belief. The notion of alienation can be traced back to the *Bible* where it is stated that "then God said let us make men in our own image, in our likeness, and let them rule over the fish or the sea and bird, or air or livestock, over the earth and over all the creatures that move along the ground" (*Genesis,* 1.26). This statement provides us licence to exploit nature in every fashion. The historian Lynn White has criticised Judeo-Christian attitude towards the environment. He argues that the dualism of spirit and matter lies at the root of our contemporary environmental problems. Christian cosmology is based on the notion of *creatio ex nihilo,* created out of nothing. This doctrine teaches that God created the whole cosmos with all animate and inanimate beings out of nothing . It secularises nature and when nature is secularised, it becomes easy for human beings to objectify nature and control it. White accuses Christianity of being most anthropocentric (man-centred) religion the world has ever seen. He believed that man has been given dominion over all of God's creation and Christianity made it possible for man to exploit the nature. Protestant theology interpreted the doctrine of creation in such a way as to establish an absolute distinction between God and creation. The dichotomy between God and the world logically implies secularisation of nature and thereby rendering justificatory mechanism to dominate and exploit the nature by human beings. Contemporary theologians argue for stewardship in place of domination theme. "The Lord God took the man and put him in the Garden of Eden to work it and take care of it." (*Genesis*, 2.15). Both these motifs in the final analysis objectify nature for anthropocentric ends. The only difference with the stewardship theme is that man is placed at the centre of nature, while with the domination theme man is above nature. Christian theologians are now willing to consider a unity theme as a basis of human world relationship.[2] Unlike the domination and stewardship theme, which survive on the distinction between human beings and nature, the unity theme affirms the co-substantiality of both human being and the world.

III

The ancient Indian spiritual traditions conceive man as part of nature, linked by indissoluble spiritual and psychological bonds. It is obvious that the Hindu *rishis* of the *Vedic* and the *Upanisadic* era perceived harmonious relationship between the needs of man and spectacular diversity of the universe. They did not subscribe to the prevailing Western worldview that true nature of man was esentially to dominate and control nature by all possible means. It is noteworthy that man in *Vedic* age treats himself as a part of nature. It is said that the whole world is a creation of sacrifice undergone by cosmic *Puruṣa.* It may be further noted that the relation of man with rivers in *Vedic* time was that of a worshipper and the worshipped. *Mahābhārat* is a war between the divine and the demon (*Daivi Sampat* and *Āsuri Sampat*). Divine forces are unselfish and fostering equilibrium and harmony in the universe, while demonic forces are selfish and tending to spread disequilibrium and disharmony in the universe. Man is called to develop the *Daivi Sampat* which respects all existent beings alike and which advocates the utilization of resources of nature with a sense of gratitude and humility. The motto of our daily prayer is that let me coexist peacefully with all these beings and let me not sin against anyone of these—

Mā Vighnam Mā Ca Me Pāpam Mā Ca Me Paripanthinah/
Dhruyo Jayo Me Nityam Syāt Paratra Ca Shubgatih//

Yajña in its cosmic setting and the concept of *Loksamgraha* also point to the same ideal. Preservation of ecological balance in nature is good for all beings. The ecological awareness can be very beautifully located in *Manusmṛti* as we learn that man should protect the moveable and immovable components of environment for taking into consideration their usefulness for human health and welfare. The earth is not a natural object but a loving mother who sustains all beings. He, therefore, prays to the mother earth every morning because he regards himself guilty of touching his mother with the feet—

Samudravasane Devi Parvatstanmandale/
Vishnupatni Namastubhyam Pādsparśam Ksamasva Meiv//

The Indian approach exhibiting relation between them recommends coherence with natural order by psycho-physical transformation (*Mano-daihika Rūpāntarana*) in human beings in place of producing changes in natural order and environment. In Hindu *Dharma* we find in place of man opposing nature and nature opposing mankind, ontic identity between them, the identity of microcosm and macrocosm and entire universe is being governed by extraordinary moral cosmic order (*ṛta*). In Yajurveda it is prayed that sky, atmosphere, earth, water and plants be peaceful. May all the learned persons, God and *Veda* be peaceful. May peace itself be peaceful and let peace comes unto me.

> *Om Dyauh Śāntih, Antariksạh Śāntih, Prithvi Śāntih, Apah Śāntih, Oshadhyah Śāntih, Brahm Śāntih, Sarvam Śāntih, Śantireva Śāntih, Samā Śāntiredhi*
>
> (*Yajurveda* 36-17).

The sole aim of life in materialistic culture is to enjoy all the transitory sensual pleasure of the world and is the root cause of greed, misery and disharmony in the world. Hinduism, on the other hand, believes in the doctrine of live and let live (*Jeavastha Jivyasam*) and the aim of life is to remove the suffering of living beings. (*Kāmaye dukha taptānam prāninām ārtināśanam*). The principle of the sanctity of life is clearly ingrained in Hindu religion. Only God has absolute sovereignty over all the creatures including man and, therefore, man cannot act as a viceroy of God over the planet, nor assign degress of relative worth to other species. It provides no sense of absolute superiority of man over nature. It is considered in Hindu belief that all that exists has been created by the supreme, which is an adequate basis for the veneration of the natural world in which man finds himself.[3] The most important aspect of Hindu theology is the association accorded to different species with reincarnation and deities. It is believed that Supreme Being has actually got Himself incarnated in the forms of various species. The justification for animal worship is to be found in the incarnation doctrine. The sense of nature worship that developed among the Hindus has a background of utility and spiritfulness. Some of the plants and trees have been well known for their medicinal power, for their spiritual power, and some as an abode of God. Hindu society has been much aware of the fact that flora of the country has a protective power and indiscriminate destruction would result in pollution and chaos of society.

Hindu culture does not accord a superior status to human beings over their natural surroundings. Hence, its traditional attitudes towards the ecosystem has been kind and respectful. Charak had written extensively about pollution (*vikṛti*) and warned about the side effects of seasons, foul air and polluted water. "A person who is engaged in killing creatures, polluting wells, and ponds, and tanks, and destroying gardens, certainly goes to hell" (Padma Purāna, Bhoomi Khanda (96.7-8). Hinduism does not subscribe to the Western World-view that man's role on the earth was to exploit nature for his selfish purpose. Man in Hindu culture, was instructed to maintain harmony with nature and show reverence for the presence of divinity in it. Hence, Hindu religion (including other religions of India) can be of great help in transforming society from its current preoccupation with materialism and consumerism to a conserver society.

IV

The essence of Islamic tradition is that the entire universe is God's creation. The word Islam has the dual meaning of submission and peace. Mankind is special, a very particular creation of *Allah.* It is only when we submit to the will of God (Allah) can we find peace, peace with in us as an individuals, peace between man and man, and peace between man and nature. Mankind's role on earth is that of viceregent or trustee of God (*khalifa)* and therefore, cannot be master of this earth. The *khalifa* is answerable for his/ her actions, for the way in which he/she uses or abuses the trust of God. He will render an account of how he treated the trust of Allah on the day of Reckoning. The notion that describes the accountability of the *khalifa* is *akharh.* The Central concept of Islam is the unity of God (*tawheed*). *Allah* is Unity; and His Unity is also reflected in the unity of man and nature. His trustees are responsible for maintaining the unity of His creation, the integrity of the Earth, its flora and fauna, its wild life and natural environment. So unity (*tawheed)*, trusteeship (*khalifa*) and accountability (*akharh)* , the three central concepts of Islam, are also the pillars of the environmental ethics of Islam. Islam is very practical world-view. The notions of *tawheed* and *khalifa* have been translated into practical injunctions in the *Shariah*. In *Shariah* we have *haram* zones, inviolate areas within which development is prohibited to protect natural resources, and *hima*, reserves established solely for the conservation of wild life and forests, which bears testimony to environmental legislation of Islam. Hence Islamic environmental ethics are not limited to metaphysical notions, it provides a practical guide as well.[4] The teaching of mercy is an essential part of the faith of Islam. The *Quran* essentially stresses the mercy of *Allah* to man, and man is thus taught to show love and kindness to his fellow.[5] It also states "*Allah* does not approve of (ecological) disturbance." The activities of destroying agriculture and bio-culture have clearly been defined in Islam as "*Fasad*" which is not permitted by Him. It is the duty of all Muslims to respect the God-Given environment, and to this end, Islam dictates responsible and proper management of resources. Today when we are exploiting natural resources unjudiciously and moving towards chaos, such understanding must be developed by re-establishing the cultural and religious values in society.

V

Sikhism teaches us to have respect for God's creation. God does not confer absolute power on man to control and dominate nature. The human race is not an alien species foisted upon this planet to dominate and exploit it, but rather an integral part of nature itself linked to the rest of creation by indissoluble bonds. Sikhism conceives man's relationship with the environment as both physical and spiritual. The creator gave shape to nature from five elements, which means a state in which the five basic elements are in perfect equilibrium and harmony. Whenever the balance is in disequilibrium it leads to abnormalities in nature. Since everything belongs to God, mankind has only a guardianship over God's creation, not outright ownership. Hence, Sikhism expects men to develop a respectful and fearful attitude towards ecology and the environment. It is only then a full development of nature and man possible.

Buddhism has accepted the equal sanctity of human beings by explaining that since there is no distinction by origin among trees, shrubs, insects, reptiles and birds, there should be no superiority or inferiority by birth among all species including human beings. All objects of this world are fruits of *karma*. The eight fold path taught by Buddha stresses right livelihood (*samma ajiva)* which means abstaining from a livelihood that brings harm to other beings. It has preached about humanity, universal love and abstaining from harming fellow beings. Hinduism, Buddhism and Jainism have always preached the need to lessen one's cravings. Desires are the root cause of suffering (*tanham dukkhasa sambhavani)*. We all know it well that motive behind the exploitation of nature is selfish worldly desires. Why we are disinclined to listen to ancestors and follow the path trodden by them for humanity? It is because of our greed and blindness, and have kept aloof from following the four noble truth (*Ārya Satya*). It is now the time, as propagated in *Majjhima-Nikāya*, to develop right conduct, right understanding and right aspiration if we are to arrest the growing environmental damage and promote a sense of protection, goodwill and harmony.

Jainism can be very useful practical guide for environmental preservation, irrespective of the fact that one is follower of Jainism or not. It provides ecological imperatives to entire humanity. Right faith, right knowledge and right conduct all the three together constitute the path to emancipation (*Samyag Darśana* — Jñāna — Cāritāni—Moksa Māргah—Tattvārtha— ādhigama-sutra, 1.1). It has laid great stress on non-violence (*ahimsa*). Desisting from injury is observed by control of speech, control of thought, regulation of movement, care in taking and placing things, and examining food and drink. Similarly speaking out of passion what is not commendable is falsehood or words that lead to injury constitute falsehood. Stealing is taking out of passion anything that is not given . It follows that, activity actuated by impure thought, is stealing, whether external objects, are taken or not. Infatuation out of passion is attachment to possessions. Even in the absence of external things, he who thinks "this is mine" is an infatuated persons . The universal vows of non-injury and limited possession preached by Jain preceptors can be great help in resolving the environmental crisis.

Hence, it can be safely concluded that world religions can provide a foundation for moral guidance towards environmental preservation and conservation. Environmental ethics can be integrated into a new universal concept for this purposes. A belief based on the partnership-cum-stewardship ethic which stands for holding of the land (including trees, rivers and other species) in trust for God and for the general benefit of mankind should be considered. Man is simply the trustee of the universe. Therefore, as a trustee, he is authorized to use natural resources, but has no divine power of control over nature and its element. World religions can play a very crucial role in harmonising us with nature which will be a landmark in the path of eco-balance and environmental preservation.

REFERENCES

1. Barbour, Ian G., *Technology, Environmental and Human Values,* pp. 76-78.
2. *Ibid,* pp. 14-15.
3. Morgan, K.W., *The Religion of the Hindus,* p. 102.
4. Dwivedi, O.P., *World Religions and the Environment,* p. 332.
5. Hussain, A., *Spirit of Islam,* p. 12.

Chapter – 19

A Philosophical Vision of Environment

Dr. Mritunjay Kumar

It is the need of the hour to reflect on the theme of Applied Philosophy with special reference to Environmental Ethics. No longer speculative Philosophy attracts students or brings up anything fruitful to the present day society. Therefore, some serious efforts have been made to associate it with various branches of science. As a result, Philosophy, today, has acquired some new dimensions, i.e., Bio-ethics and Environment Ethics. Environment Ethics, indeed, has picked up the momentum. World thinkers of all hues are making desperate efforts to study ecology and associate it with Moral Philosophy.

While dealing with environment one comes across the term "ecology" and "eco-systems"—which are connected with environment. Ecology is concerned with the relationships between plants and animals (including man) and the environment in which they live. As the term ecosystem indicates 'eco' meaning thereby environment and 'system' implying an interacting inter-dependent complex. Thus ecosystem may be defined as any unit which includes all the organisms (i.e., communities) in a given area, interacting with the physical environment resulting in the flow of energy and biotic diversity as well as material cycle.[1]

There are two types of ecosystem, Natural and Artificial. Natural ecosystem operates independently without any major interferences by man. On the basis of various kinds of habitats, natural ecosystem may be further subdivided into terrestrial type (e.g., grassland, desert, forest, etc.) and aquatic including freshwater (ponds, rivers, etc.) and marine (sea, estuary, etc.) ecosystems.

Artificial ecosystem is man-made. In it natural balance is disturbed by addition of energy and planned manipulation. Cultivation of crops represents man-made ecosystem.[2]

Biosphere or ecosphere is an important dimension of environment. It is an atmospheric layer of 5 to 20 km from earth surface which contains all life forms. Thus the biosphere is that part of earth in which life exists.[3] Biosphere may be divided into parabiosphere and eubiosphere. The former has difficult environmental conditions for life. It includes higher altitude, the Polar Regions, deepest ocean, extreme desert; volcanic areas, etc. Eubiosphere has good environmental conditions for life, i.e., land, air and water. Nature has so designed the living beings along with non-living objects that disturbing any aspect of it may result into ecological imbalances. Man today has dealt a severe blow to nature. Destruction of flora and fauna, pollution of all forms, depleting ozone-layer, contamination of river and sea-water-all are the instances of ecological hazards which are of conspicuous philosophical concern. We are also aware of green-house effect. Excessive amount of CO_2 obstructs Sun's radiation into open sky from earth's surface, thus causing intense heat.

After a brief discussion on the basis of environment we may evaluate it from the perspective of philosophical study.

The all-pervading space contains our earth, moon, sun, stars, planets and the like. Our *Vedic* philosophy believes that movement in celestial body is caused by a cosmic-divine principle *"Rita"*. On our earth the wind blows, springs and river flow, vegetation grow, seasons change— all due to this cosmic rule. Several demi-Gods follow the dictates of *Rita*. It also disciplines our moral conducts.

The principal of *Rita* proves that environments and natural global systems do have intrinsic moral values independent of any human interference. Even when the human civilization did not come into existence, nature and its values remained and it will continue to exist even though there is no human being on this planet.

There is still a narrow vision in this regard which considers that human beings have attached values to nature. We know that western ethics had been human-centred and only very recently it started looking beyond the set limit. It now accepts that nature and her myriad components are subject to ethical consideration. But it hardly believes in the intrinsic values of nature.

Here our concern is to evaluate values of nature from Indian standpoint which is predominantly spirituality and religious. Indian mode of spiritual is all-enveloping and all-accommodating. It inspires us to inculcate a feeling of oneness, universal friendliness and love for all life on this planet. As a rational-self endowed with freedom of will, man has got special responsibilities towards Nature. Human beings are supposed to honour nature as Mother-Nature and earth as Mother-earth since these are but gifts of God, the Supreme Creator.

God has created the nature and hidden himself into it. He now smiles through the beauty of Nature. Whatsoever is good beautiful and truthful in nature there is God behind it. So let us care for nature. If we care for nature, nature will care for us. This is a corollary of the famous dictum, *Dharmo radshti raksitah.* What is required is not the attitude of consumerism and reckless use of material resources, domination over and exploitation of nature, but responsible use, equitable distribution and preservation of the splendours of nature[4]. Following the attitude of *yoga-ksema* towards the nature we should love, honour and preserve it.

It is the need of the hour that Ethics should define the conducts and roles of human beings in respect of nature and her myriad components so as to make all life worthy and blissful. There is a need to formulate a charter of environmental conduct and create environmental awareness in human begins through proper and adequate education[5]. But Ethics should also incorporate the holistic spirit of Indian philosophy.

A holistic spirit towards nature will give us an insight to look upon her as source of divine bliss. The sweet breezes, ever-flowing streams of the dense forests, ranges of beautiful hills and mountains, twittering of birds, flowing rivers, oceans, varieties of fruits, crops and the likes are but the rare gifts of nature. It reflects love, harmony and bliss, as if the characteristics of Supreme Creator were being expressed. Whatsoever is good, beautiful, mysterious and awe-inspiring in the nature, there is Supreme Divinity. Amidst laps of nature our philosophy and culture found their origins. Since time immemorial forests in India have been the centre of religious and spiritual practices.

We know our sages dwelt in forest and practiced spiritual austerity. They realized the supreme truth in the jungle and preached it to the entire world. Our *gurukul* system existed in the forests where Indian students used to spend their early days in learning under the guidance of a "*Guru*". Those were the natural surroundings which led the foundations for would-be citizens. Since our sages lived in the forest, they naturally attached great importance to trees. Beneath a tree was the correct place for a disciple to receive spiritual instruction from a "*guru*". The tree is the symbol of patience and tolerance. The sages carefully studied and recorded the herbal and medicinal properties of the forest. The tradition of valuing tree was passed on into Indian culture and led to a subtle ecological relationship between human communities and the forest communities of trees, plants and animals. The basis of this relationship was the recognition of the rights of the trees, forest-dwelling animals and plants to a life of their own, free from exploitation by human. Human society depended on the forest for survival and prosperity and, therefore, they had to protect it. Furthermore the forest was a place of peace and harmony with God where the spiritual goals of life could be pursued by the forest sages[6].

In fact, the bond between Indian people and tree is very strong. Also Indian consciousness is full of trees and forest. Hindu scriptures like *Ramayana* and *Mahabharata* present a rich and vivid description of forest. Load Rama spent fourteen years in jungle amidst natural surroundings. The picture of dense forests –monkeys, bears, the holy *Ganga*, clouds, rains, oceans, etc., moved around this great personality. Again we record Krishna as a student and adolescent spending his life in forest. '*Vrindavan*' still exists to remind His love for nature. The *Yamuna* river is still there but no longer pure.

It is said that during ancient period there were three categories of forest in India. One was *shrivan* the forest which provided prosperity. Then there was *tapovan*, where one could contemplate as the sages did and practiced austerity to seek after truth. The third was *mahavana*—the great natural forest where all species of life find shelter[7].

Shrivan was considered the property of villager and hence it was maintained by *panchayat*. No village would be complete without its corresponding woodlands in and around its houses. The *shrivan* could be the form of groves. Many such groves would be looked after by temples, having been given to the temples in the distant past and kept up by it for countless generations. Such sacred groves with temples still survive in places today as a reminder of the old system.

The second category of forest was *tapovan,* the *karmabhumi* of sages. This type of forest was natural and untended. It used to be full of wild animals living together in great harmony by virtue of spiritual atmosphere prevailing over the region. People respected the home and hearth of sages and never tried to cause any damage to it. Forest department of today would simply dream of ensuring the safety of forest by force of law. From this profoundly natural setting emerged the *Vedic* teachings of *Upanishads* such as the *Brihad—Aranyaka*, which means "The teaching which began in the forest". Our great epics were written in *tapovan.*

The third category of forest being *mahavana* was a purely natural dense forest. Such forests were in abundance in India covering a large tract of lands.

Presently, India has lost much of the natural forest. Government agency has done precious little to safeguard and preserve this rare gift of nature. One can witness that hills and mountains of India do not have thick forest and varieties of wild animals. Most of them wear a deserted look. Till date we do not have adequate green covers over our land to maintain ecological balances.

Ecological hazards arising out of deforestation are horrible. Scientists say that deforested lands in the long run become desert. It is because such deforested lands do not attract rain-clouds and on the other hand, mercury in such area often shoots up to bring intense heat. Water-table slides down. When fertility of the land is gone and water is scarce, population will have all sorts of hardships for survival.

In Himachal Pradesh denudation of forests are causing land-sliding problems. If the forest cover from the mountain-ranges is removed, soil-erosion and flooding of the down regions take place quite regularly. Actually, the forests over the mountains retain 90 per cent of the rain-water and release it over the days and weeks to streams and rivers during dry season. The forest thus acts as a soaking device and plays a vital role in the hydrological cycle. It has been estimated that in India 60,000 million tonnes of top soil is carried away annually by rain water from the deforested areas. The washed away top soil silts river beds and reservoirs to reduce their holding capacity and flood in surrounding areas as natural calamity [8].

Our big townships need some green spots to keep the pollution in check. It is believed that an acre of forest absorbs 4 tonnes of carbonic acid gas and recycles 8 tonnes of oxygen into environment.

These are some facts and figures about forests. It is high time we realized the importance of flora and fauna. Indians will have to return to the age-old spiritual wisdom to have an inner urge of protecting nature her splendour. Science can give us knowledge about the working of nature but love for nature can be learnt through philosophy. Philosophising nature can give us a spiritual insight to understand and love nature. One can appreciate the philosophical vision towards nature in the poems of some great English poets. The great English poet Robert Frost once got so bewitched by the beauty of nature that he stopped his horse in the middle of forest. To quote him,

"My little horse must think it queer,
To stop without a farm house near,
Between the woods and frozen lakes,
The darkest evening of the year.
The woods are lovely dark and deep,
But I have promises to keep,
And miles to go before I sleep,
And miles to go before I sleep"

REFERENCES

1. Singh, S.P., *An Introduction to Animal Ecology*, P.G, Rastogi, Publication, Meerut, 1992.
2. *Ibid.*, p. 96.
3. Shukla, R.C.& Chandel, P.C., *Plant Ecology*, p. 5,S.Chand & Company Ltd. New Delhi, 1998
4. Prof Bhatt, S. R., D U., *Presidential Address at IPC 77th Session*, Udaipur, P. 19.
5. *Ibid.*
6. Prime Ranchar, *Hinduism* and *Ecology, Seeds of Truth,* p. 10, Moti Lal Banarasi Das, Delhi, 1994.
7. *Ibid.* P. 10
8. Shukla, R.C. & Chandel, P.C., *Plant Ecology* , p. 287.

Chapter – 20

Do Trees have Right of their Own ? A Buddhist Reply

Avinash Kumar Srivastava

Buddhism expects human beings to live as "Man–In Nature", in contradiction to "Man *versus* Nature."[1] For Buddha earth is the home for all living beings whether it is man, animal or vegetation. Hence, every one has equal right to live peacefully. This is the only world to live in and any act of ours to mutilate should be an offence. Hence, to fell trees or any act of deforestation is an offence. Such is the unwritten moral code of Buddhism, no one can escape from the consequences of good or evil deeds.[2] In fact Buddhism strictly believes in the law of *karma*. In its abstract form, the doctrine states, "That being this, this comes to be; from arising that, this arises; that being absent this is not; from the cessation of that this ceases to be.[3] Hence, if trees are fell for any one's selfish end, one has to face its consequences. Buddha has categorically said that felling trees or destroying the plants is a *Pacittiya*.[4] This can very well be interpreted that any act of causing harm to a tree or felling it is a cognizable offence. Nature takes cognizance to it. This evil act is reviewed in the court of the cosmic law and proper punishment is given to the mankind for their acts of deforestation in form of ecological imbalance and its disastrous results.

It is thoroughly unwise to think that trees are rightless as they are incapable to speak and they cannot institute a case or take a legal action. But it is not the case, the natural objects in general and trees in particular can communicate their wants (needs) in unambiguous terms. One can judge with more certainty and meaningfully whether and when my lawn, farm or plants need water. They express very explicitly through a certain dryness of blades and soil as immediately obvious to the touch or by appearance of blade spots, yellowing and lack of springiness after being walked on. They tell the farmer their demand in a very strong language and the farmers do meet their demands. Failing in it they are liable to punishment in terms of poor harvesting and famine due to drought. Hence it is imperative of the man to understand the language of plants, take cognizance of it and try to meet the demand of trees as they too are the right holders because they fulfil the first criterion.

Secondly, Buddha did not discriminate between man, animal, plants and trees. His loving kindness showered forth on each and every thing and being of the world whether it is man or tree. For Him all biotic beings including trees and men have the same origin and are made up of common elements, *i.e. rupa* and *arupa dhatus*. They all have common basic characteristics of form, warmness, and consciousness.[5] Hence, they all must have equal rights. The only difference between man and the tree is that the total personality of man is composed of *Pancaaskandha, i.e., rupa* (corporeality), *vedana* (feeling), *sanna* (perception), *Samkhara* (disposition), and *vinnana* (consciousness)[6] where as trees are *composed* of three *skandha* only, they are *rupa, vedana* and *vinnana skandha*. Hence, plants and trees are qualitatively inferior to human beings. However, they may be put under the category of foetus, infants and senile old man for all the legal and practical purposes, which are decidedly inferior to normal grown up man. Since plants, trees and men have common origin and are composed of the same elements, *rupa* and *arupa dhatus*, plants and trees cannot be denied of their natural or legal rights. Another point that needs to be made clear is that man is qualitatively superior to plants and trees, hence, it is the responsibility of man to recognize and protect their rights, have good relations with them and plead or lodge a complain in the court of law, if their rights are encroached. This is how trees will be considered as a substantial right holder in legal sense of the term. This is the reason that Buddha has personified the trees as He calls them *vanaspati*, the lord of the forest.[7] This can be interpreted as a person in the legal sense of the term, that holds genuine right.

Whether in granting the Relief the Law Court takes into account the Injury caused to the Trees or Not?

The answer is apparently negative. Though the law provides protection to trees owned by individuals but trees at its own are denied rights in the second sense of the term, as it is not possible to decide the merit of the case as is done in the case of an individual who is competent and willing to establish it. It is a fact that we want to maintain balance, but any such balance that adjusts the economic interest can be done in the case of an identifiable human. For example, if any plant or tree of anyone garden is cut or destroyed then, as per general rule no one has any right to destroy other's property, the court will appoint commissioner to enquire into the damage caused by the culprit. Although rules vary from place to place and one is suing for an equitable injunction or for damage. What they all have in common is some sort of balancing. Thus here the plaintiff's grievance is meant for a mere private or personal inconvenience. But what about the trees that are ownerless? How can inquiry be made and on whose request? Since the tree itself lost sight in a quantitative compromise between two conflicting interest, hence the matter for judicial cognizance does not arise on its own standing.

Let us evaluate the second condition under which trees are denied rights. In fact, for adjudicating the merits of the present controversy a good case can be made for considering the injury to the trees or forests in their own right. The court issues an injunction in law suits wherein harm is caused to the communal trees and strike some sort of economic hardship on the human being who causes such injuries. But such injunctions are sought through the guardians, trustees or the department concerned as senile human being, minor or foetus is represented in the court of law. "By doing so we in effect make the natural object, through its guardian, a jural entity competent to gather up these fragmented and otherwise unrepresented damage claims, and press them before court even where, for legal or practical reasons, they are not going to be pressed by traditional class action plaintiffs."[8] This is in fact a homocentric way to view a guardian of trees or natural objects similar to the guardians of unborn generations, infants, senile old man, etc.

But in doing so, two things have to be kept in mind – (1) The forest department is an adequate guardian only with respect to National Parks, forests and plantation made by the department. Its guardianship does not include either the trees of local public land or on private lands. (2) The forest department itself is charged with several institutional goals that it may not do justice with the particular cases. In such circumstances the court appoint guardian outside the institution as protector of communal trees within the existing legal structure. But their statutory powers are limited and often unclear. In such circumstance the injury may not be calculated properly. Here a question may arise, why do we want the trees to be judged indirectly as a lost profit to someone else? Why not the trees are important in damage calculation? By making the tree or the forest themselves the focus of these damages the legal system can effectively take proof upon and confront the wood cutter with more representative measures of the damage he caused. Here again a question arises how will the cost of damage be calculated? The answer is with the reference of fair market value of the tree. But what about the lost environmental values that are priceless? In that case one possible way can be of the instance of human injury. When a man is injured in an accident with an automobile the medical expense is imposed on the responsible party. And if the man succumbs to the injury the amount equivalent to ten years of his salary is paid to his legal heir or family members as compensation. In the same way the comparable expense to the tree or forest is the cost of the injury. If the illegal deforestation is done for a personal gain such damage computation will be made with regard to environmental loss. In doing so, one is fully aware that it is fully normative judgement, such as pain and suffering, wherein rule of society is taken into consideration while valuing the damage rather the market value. Such normative estimate will never be wrong, though it may ignore the immediate human interest. The estimate of damage should be our experience in environmental matters that tell us categorically that our activities have caused a long range damage that we are able to appreciate at the outset. The conjectural damage calculation in all events of injury to the trees or forest would be of more interest from the socio-psychic point of view.

During Buddha's time such complications, like damage calculation of nature or natural entities did not occur. The reason is simple that the damage caused to the nature was so meagre that nature could sustain it and it was also repaired in the natural process. But it is again a fact that Buddha was aware of human encroachment hence he preached to extend loving kindness towards plants and trees. He expressed compassionate and non-violent attitude for vegetable kingdom that provides us with all necessities of life. In *Petavatthu,* it is categorically said we should not break even the branch of a tree that gives us food and shelter.[9] He has prescribed several rules that prohibit monks and lay men from causing harm to it. In *Vinaya Pitaka,* it is said that "One must not urinate, spit or saliva on green grass."[10] In *Sutta-nipata* it is said one should throw waste food materials on green grass.[11] *Digha Nikaya* under the heading of *Mjjhima Sila* Buddha has categorically asked not to cause harm or destroy seeds, seedling, plants or trees. Not only that, He has also asked not to cut the branches of a tree even for sapling purposes.[12] Very many references are available that expresses the sense of protection of plants against human encroachment. He imposes restraint on human being from violating the rights of trees. He wanted to nip this offence in the bud itself and maintain balance in the environment.

In order to compensate damage to the plant life, some rituals have also been developed in Buddhist countries like Sri Lanka, Thailand, and Japan, etc. The Buddhists pay respect to *Bodhi Tree* by pouring water unto the foot of the tree. In the time of drought trees were kept alive by this practical ritual.[13] The sole purpose of all these of Buddha and rituals performed by the Buddhists is not only to protect the vegetable, kingdom from human encroachment but also to meet their redressal and maintain balance in a simple religious way instead of legal complications. This also hints that trees have right to live in the eyes of the Buddha and Buddhism.

The Relief must run for the Benefit of the Right Holder

Trees do not fulfil the third condition in strict sense of the term; hence, the common law makes the trees right-less. Now a question arises, who becomes beneficiary of a favourable judgement? Obviously trees are not. It is the individual who gets this benefit and this makes a considerable difference. It is not the tree that counts in its own right. Let me explain this. If we speak of ascertaining the legal damage to the natural object we mean here the "total damage", i.e., in the sense of making it a whole. It includes various factors. If a forest is destroyed the damage will include the cost of reseeding, repairing watersheds, restacking wild life, destruction of trees—the sort of cost the forest department calculates after a fire. Now what is important to note here is that in our present legal system even if the plaintiff, i.e., the forest department or a guardian wins the suit for damage no money goes to the benefit of trees or the forest itself to repair its damage. Even if the damage is paid by the offender this will be far less than the actual damage caused to the woods. This penalty is again not so much as to force the destroyer to desist, for example it can be imagined that a wood cutter whose wrongful activities cause damage to the forest of worth of rupees one lacks annually. But the aggregate of all the damage calculated by the court in the said suit is only Rs.2,00, 000. Here the wood cutter is in gain. Now he would pay off the damage and continue to fell the trees for his benefit. Secondly, even if an injunction is issued by the court against the wood cutter at the behest of the plaintiff, there is nothing to stop the plaintiff from selling out the trees, *i e.,* agreeing to dissolve or to make injunction inoperative at some price. This is in fact a contract between the guardian and the offender and not between the wood cutter and the forest. What I want to make clear here is that the common law as it affects in normal human case is not exactly the same as law affecting the environmental objects. Again there is a difference between the National forest or the communal trees on the one hand and trees as owned by the individuals on the other, *i.e.,* the trees on the suburbanite's lawn and the trees on road side. Here one thing is very much clear that none of the natural objects including trees whether it is public property or private one, whether standing in the common place or situated in any individual's land, do not fulfil the third criteria of a right holder. Hence' they do not have standing of their own right. Their unique damage do not count in determining the outcome, they are not beneficiary of awards. Trees have traditionally been regarded by the common law as "objects for men to conquer and use". The measure that are being taken to conserve them are meant to conserve for us and for our future generations. In other words, it is good for the greatest good for the greater number of human beings.

In the light of above discussion, it seems proper to make trees the beneficiary of their own injury settlement claims and thereby include them in the club of right holder as per the third criterion is concerned. By doing so the interest of the private litigants, not to enforce the right of the natural entity by selling them out in their conspired negotiation among themselves, will be frustrated. Thus it will enable the trees for being a party to injunctive settlement for any sort of injury caused by the offenders. And more important thing is that in this way they will become a beneficiary of money award too. But the question is who will receive the money? Obviously it is a human being who is either the owner or the guardian of the trees. Now there may be a question mark on making the balance of injury to the trees. In such a situation if court decides not to enjoin the wood cutter to the extent of Rs.1,00,000 annually than the owner and the trees of the forest both be awarded damage. The portion of the forest could be put in the trust fund which will be operated by the guardians or owners. Not only that the criminal fine (slapped on the wood cutter) should be sent to the same fund instead of general treasury. From this fund the cost of filing the suit, advocate fee, guardians remuneration, etc., should be remitted. And above all this fund should be utilized to maintain and preserve the forest, standing of the trees on communal land as well as for reforestation. This will amount to make the trees, the environment or natural entities legal right holders.

Often it is argued that deforestation is made to meet the human needs such as cultivation, constructing houses, etc. Trees are cut for fire-wood, furniture and to meet other essential human needs without which development is not possible. When we have to choose between two alternatives, i.e., feeding the hungry and providing the shelter to the houseless mass on the one hand and conserving the nature (forest, trees, etc.) on the other, obviously one will choose the first one. This is a pure and simple ethical issue that puts environmentalists or the conservation lists of nature on the defensive. But Buddha is very much clear in this connection. In *Singala Sutta,* he has categorically said "A house holder should accumulate wealth like a honey bee that collectsnectar from a flower without hurting or causing harm to it."[14] Hence, nature has to be utilized in the same way.

It is a well known fact that Indian philosophy believes that nature (world) is a continuous theatre in which things, beings and species (eventually man) are destined to enter and exit. During the coexistence of man and the trees (environment) each has to compromise for the good of the both. Some example of deforestation or felling the trees may probably be inevitable for some time. But this should occur in those instances where the social need of a tribal or habitable land or wood and wood product is so high that enables the person encroaching the right of the trees to cover all homocentric costs plus estimated cost of environment *per se*. This money should be deposited in the trust fund. Secondly, the trust fund should be a corpus of preserving money which can be utilized for repairing the damage portion of the orchard or forest or environment, if becomes technologically feasible.[15] Such funds may also be utilized for financing the research and development of the environment and forest or trees in particular.

In this background if we cast glance over the *Tripitakas* we find that although there is no reference of any system wherein provisions are made that relief of an injury must run to benefit the trees. However instructions are very much clear about mode of maintaining balance with respect to the injury caused to the plants and trees in an indirect way. Buddha has given a clear cut instruction to the lay devotees for plantation, construction of parks and pleasure grooves as he was aware of the fact that man for his need and greed causes injury to the nature and the natural entities. He keeps felling the trees to meet his ends. Since he was not in position to enforce rules or acts for legal compensation, he declared such acts are pious from religious and ethical point of view. These are great deeds and fetch much spiritual merit.[16] According to the Buddhist legend even Buddha is said to have reached this position as a result of construction of parks, pleasure grooves, ponds, wells, roads as well as conserving and protecting the trees and making plantation in his previous life.[17]

So far as the question of trusteeship is concerned Buddhism believes that "human do not own the land rather are its protectors. The creation is intended for the benefit of all equally— even birds, the trees and the humans.[18] The nature do not belong to humans alone, the individual is just an enjoyer and in that sense Buddhism is humanism par excellence.[19] It is the duty of human beings to care it as they share it. Since man makes use of the trees and plants for his personal benefit, it is his duty to spend some portion of his earning for the benefit of these natural entities. Buddha has categorically said that "man should divide his earned wealth into four equal portions. Two portions should be used for him and household works, one portion should be spent for life's friendly things (i.e. trees, plants and the other natural entities) and one portion should be kept reserved for crisis management."[20] This has got a radical similarity with the above mentioned modern thought of Christopher D. Stone who has suggested for a creation of trust fund, a corpus of preserving money that has to be utilized for guardian, advocate and court fees as well as for the maintenance of forest, orchard or standing of trees on communal land.[21]

It is a brute fact, that Buddha was neither a ruler nor his preaching were meant to guide the rulers of his time with regard to the matters of crime and punishment. He was a human healer. To utilize His instructions in formation of laws, rules and acts is although very difficult but not impossible. Because a perpetual work is in progress. It is evanescent, dynamic, productive, tantalizing and bottom up. It has emerged out of customs, rituals and the rules of the tribe. It has used the materials, for its formation, from the religion, ethics and philosophy. The sacred texts and the preaching of the great seers had been the source book for formulating the acts. That is why the law of the land varies from culture to culture, place to place and time to time. It has also the climatic effect. Ethics, religion and philosophy of the land do influence it. It can be said that law is a rhetorical activity that can only be properly appreciated in its historical and political context. Custom tradition and transformation are locked in a mutually reinforcing but thoroughly contingent embrace. Like life law too is an organic process (i.e., events are product of localized causes). It is not a miraculous one (i.e., events are the result of some grand plane or intervention). This is the reason that laws of different countries have taken into account their sacred scriptures in their formation. For example, The Muslim Law has utilized *Quran* as its immediate source. The Hindu Law has translated *Mitaksara* and *Dayabhaga* rules of Hindu tradition. If we give a perusal of criminal law of any country it will reveal that religious moral code of conducts have taken the shape of rules, laws and penal acts. For example, violation of *ahimsa, satya, asatya, brahmacarya* and *aparigraha* have been considered punishable in the eyes of law, and there are acts relating to them. The religious directives have converted into the principles and acts of the constitutions. In the same way if Buddha's teachings be interpreted, analyzed, utilized and applied in the environmental cases, laws regarding right of trees may emerge. Though such laws are taking shape or have been enacted in several countries of the world. Hence, there is a possibility to frame out environmental laws from the antiquity of Buddhist religion and ethics that may provide protection to trees as their right.

REFERENCES

1. *Encyclopaedia of Buddhism: A World Faith, Buddhism and Environment*, IV, A.P.H. Publication House, p. vii. (Preface).
2. Neither in the sky nor in the midst of the sea, nor by interring into the cleft of the mountains. There is no place known in the whole world, where a man can escape from the consequences of his evil deeds. *Dhammapada*, verse no. 127
3. *Imasmin sati idam hoti, imassa uppada idam upajjhati.*
   Imasmin asati idam na hoti, imassa nirodha idam nirujjhati.
   —Samayutta Nikaya, II 28
4. *Vinaya Pitaka*, Bhikkhu Patimokkha,No. 11; Bhikkhuni Patimokkha, No. 47
5. *Digha Nikaya,Maha Stipatthana Sutta*. Quoted in "Threads of Environmentalism in Early Buddhism"by Avinash Kumar Srivastava, published in Buddhist Ethics some Modern Perspective, 57
6. *Ibid.*
7. *Samayutta Nikaya*, IV 302
8. Christopher D. Stone, *Southern California Law Review*, 45, 1972, pp. 450-501.
9. *Petavatthu*, II, 3, 9.
10. *Vinaya* II, 205-6
11. *Hi tvam brahmana ! tam payasam appaharite va chaddehi, appanake*

udake opilapesi. Suttanipat, Kasibhartdwaj Sutta 83, Motilal Banarasidas Delhi 2nd edition, reprint 1995, P.20

12. Where as some recluse and brahmins. . . . continue abdicate to the injury of seedlings and growing plants whether propagated from roots or cutting or joints or budding or seeds, Gotama, the recluse, hold aloof from such injury to seedling and growing plants. Digha Nikaya I , 11; Dialogues of Buddha I, p.7-8 . Translaeted by Rhys Devids, Low Price Publication, Delhi, 2001.
13. "The Island of Temples and Tanks", by A.T. Ariyaratne and Joanna Macy, Published in "Buddhism and Ecology". Edited by Martine Batchleor and Kerry Brown, Motilal Banarasidas, First Indian Edition, 1994, p. 80.
14. Bhoge sanhaemanassa, bhamarasseva iriyato/. Bhoga sannicayam yanti, vammiko vupaciyati // Digha Nikaya, ///, 188. It is also called Sigalovada Sutta.
15. Christopher D. Stone, Southern California Law Review, No. 45, pp. 450-501.
16. *Amaropa vanaropa ye jana setukaraka/*
    Papam ca udpanam ca, ye dadanti upassay
    Dhammattha silasampanna , te jana saggagamino//
    —Samyutta Nikaya, I, Vanaropana Sutta, 33.
17. *Jataka* I 199.
18. Encyclopaedia of Buddhism, Vol. IV, p. 37 *Op. cit.*
19. *Ibid.*
20. *Evam bhoge samahatva, almtto kule gini/*
    Catudha vibhaje bhoge, savemittani ganthati//
    Ekena bhoge bhunnjeyya, dvihi kammam payajaya /
    Catultham ca nidhapeyya, apdasu bhavissti //
    —Digha Nikaya III, 188.
21. *Southern California Review,* No. 45, 1972, pp. 450-501.

Chapter – 21

Built-in-Environment : An Integral Part of Environmental Ethics

Pratima Ganguli & Dr. Mritunjay Kumar

Generally we find two types of environments around us; one being built environment and another being natural or wild environment. Wild environment consists of flora and fauna, rivers, oceans, hills, mountains and the like, made by nature, whereas built environment, means man-made environment, such as township and the like. In ancient times, there was only one kind of ecosystem, the natural ecosystem. But with the expansion of human civilization, the situation completely changed. Several artificial ecosystems (created by man) cropped up. Man changed the faces of the earth and brought alteration into climate. The human created environment (built-in-environment) did not follow the laws of nature and, therefore, proved detrimental to human existence. Until eco-awareness dawned on him, man thought that all natural resources were meant for his own benefit, and so, he went on felling trees and destroying forests, getting the grassland overgrazed, reclaiming land by filling marshes and seacoasts for building factories, houses, parks, clubs, schools, shopping complexes and so on. Ecological systems themselves were considered of no intrinsic value apart from their economic utilization.

Long-term environmental implications were completely overlooked in favour of short-term gains. And the results are here for all to see.

1. Roger J.H. King[1]

In this regard, a comparison between the natural and man-made ecosystem will help us a lot to further our study of built or domesticated environment which are as follows:[1]

	Natural Ecosystems *(Forests, grasslands, marshes, ponds, etc.)*	***Man-made Ecosystems*** *(Factories, houses, institutions, clubs, etc.)*
1.	Utilise and also store solar energy	Utilise fossil-fuel and nuclear energy
2.	Produce O_2 and consume CO_2	Consume O_2 and Produce CO_2
3.	Produce food by organic synthesis	Produce only chemical degradation; can't accomplish organic synthesis.
4.	Filter and detoxify pollutants and waste products	Produce waste products which may be toxic
5.	Are self-sustaining and self-maintaining	Not self-sustaining and self-maintaining
6.	Not noisy	More often noisy
7.	Present a delightful sight in undisturbed state.	Present an unsightly appearance if not properly engineered or maintained.
8.	Make the soil rich	Make soil poor
9.	Store and purify water	Consume and pollute water
10.	Provide habitats for wild life	Destroy wildlife habitats.

After a brief comparison between the two different types of environments we will discuss the relevance of built or domesticated environment as an integral part of Environmental Ethics.

Environmental Ethics takes into account only wild or natural environment and leaves the build environment uncared. Here in this chapter we would like to make a case for the relevance of the built environment to Environmental Ethics.

Philosophers are concerned with how humanly engineered systems have degraded wild environments and threatened non-human species, but they have paid less attention to the built, artifactual, or domesticated environment in which humans actually live.

There are several reasons for thinking that Environmental Ethics should take a closer look at built environment.

The most significant of these is that if we are to contribute to articulating the outlines of an environmentally responsible culture, we must be prepared to address the problems faced by people in the places they inhabit. If the people's abodes are in good conditions and in a fine social set-up they will be attracted by eco-philosophical movement to contribute to the well being of ecology. Unfortunately, we have so far not realized this fact that degraded urban, suburban and rural environments are obstacles to the development of an environmental conscience. In addition, they are objective constraints on our efforts to minimize waste and pollution and to enjoy a harmonious and integrated human existence in the natural world. Built environments influence our attitudes towards ecology. Also a lot depends how we envision the built environment in consonance with environmental aspirations. Such a task calls for *philosophical attention* as strongly as our more typical concerns with non-human value and the health and integrity of wild ecosystems.

Here we are laying down certain perspectives from which we can draw support for the argument that an environmental ethics of the built environmental is an integral part of Environmental Ethics in general.

First, the built environment reflects who we are and what our stand should be towards the natural world? People belonging to an environmentally responsible culture are supposed to have better vision towards safeguarding ecosystem and understanding its importance. Environmentally responsible culture can be termed as "eco-culture".

"Eco-culture" is one in which a sound system of education based on ecological values is easily available to all and sundry, and where the children are trained to follow eco-friendly practices right from the beginning and where even technologies are eco-friendly. It must also include researches on bio-diversity in higher education. Of course, the people of such culture are never a deprived lot. The traits of the people of eco-culture are that they are supposed to have deep concern and care for ecosystem. On the contrary, people belonging to deprived section of society will least bother to conserve nature. Particularly, in third world countries where the society is torn by caste conflict and communal disturbances, and where there is serious law and order problems, people cannot inculcate a culture favourable to ecological concern. It is but natural if people's life is not secured and they spend days to meet their basic needs for survival, they are not supposed to honour ecological ideas. There are some States in India where there is serious law and order problem, where the employees do not get their salary and where the education has gone haywire, children work outside as an earning member of family. Such society will never take interest in environment matter, which is quite obvious.

Here it is noticeable that Environmental Ethics takes into account the socio-economic aspect of rural and urban dwellers. In this regard, it may not be out of place to mention the scenario of slum-dwellers which develop mostly at the outskirts of big cities. Since last few decades population grew manifold and rural society no longer was able to sustain and ensure better life. Earlier villages used to be economically self-dependent but in due course caste-conflict and Naxal activities destroyed the socio-economic set-up of village life. As a result young villagers (particularly from Bihar) migrated to big cities in search of livelihood. They were employed as labourers in some factories, stalls and other such institutions. It is these labourers who settled in slums at the outskirts of city. Presently, slums in big cities are growing fast. They live in the most unhygienic condition. Now, Government and administration want to remove all these slums to ensure a better environment for the city middle class people.

Here we see such social issues as major constraints in realizing the objectives of Environmental Ethics. We are but sure that slum-dwellers will never bother for 'clean and green city'. Therefore, Government will have to frame some serious policy regarding their relocation and raising their standard of living by ensuring health-care, sanitation and education. The primary and most important thing is to ensure socio-economic development in rural areas. We will have to hit at the root cause of migration from villages. Once we provide basic facilities and administration to villagers including health care and education at their door-step, some ray of hope may be traced. After all why should the villagers migrate to the town and city, if their social issues are settled amicably (education may play a key role) and if they taste the flavour of economic development. This requires sincere, honest and dedicated efforts by the authority and Govenment. machinery coupled with cooperation by villagers. The task indeed is tough but we will have to improve the conditions of villagers and slum-dwellers simultaneously in order to realize the objectives of "*clean and green India*". It is because hunger, illiteracy and poverty cannot entertain environment values. Only economically better off and educated people can be inspired to learn and practice, eco-culture. So this aspect of built environment is immensely important for Environmental Ethics.

Thus, ethical arguments that favour protecting wilderness and wild species must be accompanied by an ethical analysis that addresses the question of how humanbeings as they are currently situated can construct for themselves a home space that will reflect and sustain an ecological informed world-view.

Human relationships to both wild and domesticated landscapes are relevant to achieve the goals of environmental ethics. We may argue that it is unproductive to ignore the environmental contexts in which people live and then expect that these people will turn out to support environmentally responsible aspirations and practices. Arguments in favour of preserving and protecting natural ecosystems and processes must be consistent with moral, social, political and personal commitments that guide people's expectations and understanding of themselves and their world.[1]

In particular, concern for the fate of wild nature must be

integrated into a broader moral context of concern for the site of human habitation, the problem of justice in human social life, and the future of individual and community self-development. It appears that a sound setting of society is conducive to entertain the ideas of conservation of wilderness. Sound setting of society indicates beautiful township pervaded with many greenpockets, wide lea, residential areas free from congestion and pollution. This casts an impact upon the consciousncss of citizens to aspire for more natural beauty.

Built Environment as External Constraint

We know that built environment stands in a dynamic relationship with human self-understanding. Now this domesticated or built environment influences our motivation, imagination and commitment towards ecology. Here we take technology as a case-study. Built environment uses and relies heavily on technology. Technology has given us automobiles, NTPC, nuclear power, industry, high buildings, overpasses, etc. It is true that all these fruits of technology provide us comforts, power, free movements, wealth and the like but work simultaneously as great constraints to ecological safeguards.

Automobile contribute to pollution. But pollution by NTPC is quite dangerous to ecology. It pollutes the surroundings in such a manner which alters the climate. The mercury shoots up. Emissions of NTPC drive away the rain-cloud. Slowly the wide regions around the NTPC convert into arid zones.

Nuclear power generation creates all the problems of waste disposal, safety and surveillance. In this way, nuclear power, hydroelectric dams, high-rise buildings, synthetic or exotic materials, poorly designed spaces, all limit our ability to reinterpret the natural environment more responsibly, and thus constrain our hopes for a sustainable human relationship to nature.

Let us now took for a strategy to overcome this problem. *David Macauley*, a noted eco-philosopher, articulates a principle of greening the built environment in order to breach the walls that keep out wild nature and insulate the built environment from the wild. We are aware of the fact that contemporary cityscapes not only degrade local ecosystems by waste materials and pollution but they also minimize human contact with the diversity of non-human nature. So the strategy should consider focusing all attention to green the cityscapes and beautify it by planting more trees and plants. We should select certain important areas of town that fall between the artifactual and natural extremes: beaches, swamps, footpaths, bogs, overgrown lots, riverbanks and levees, gardens, meadows, orchards, rooftops and the like. We have so far overlooked such *transitional regions* in ecological discussion.

Practical work of such nature has already been taken up in some towns — like rooftop gardening, gardening in cities, use of wetlands to purify sewage, rebuilding of riverbanks and industrial areas.

In addition to the cultivation of natural areas within the city, we need to understand the metaphorical usefulness of *this concept of the margin between the built and the wild.*

The concept attracts the human fancy to explore more avenues to associate itself with wild nature and entertain love and awe for ecosystem of nature. *Once the principle of greening gets clicked it will cast a profound impact on our psyche to perceive through the build medium to connect with a wild nature beyond.*

The argument in this chapter has sought to show why the character of built environment is significant to Environmental Ethics and our concern for wilderness. There is much empirical work to be done to develop the practices of green architecture and city planning. We may work on the following principles:

> The built environment should make nature a visible, palpable presence in daily human experience.

This principle calls for the construction of a built environment that makes nature's presence visible. Such a result may be accomplished by making accessible natural areas within the built environment; such as waterways, woodlands and urban gardens. We should design built structures in such a way so as to interact more sensitively with existing environmental conditions.

The visibility of nature is essential if the built environment, the locus of human inhabitation, is to contribute to, as well as reflect, a world-view quite conforming to world nature. The assumption here is to benefit the citizens psychologically and physically from an environment in which natural processes and ecosystems are integrated.

The built environment should manifest in its construction and technologies, an understanding of the finiteness of energy, materials and the capacity of the environment to absorb waste.

This principle takes into consideration the ecological approach to "design and architecture". In the ecological approach to design, the designer must be concerned not only with the extent and range of human use of ecosystem and the earth's resources in the designed system, but also with the way wherein the elements are absorbed, stored, assembled, used and finally disposed of or reintroduced into the biosphere.

From the above analysis we come to realize that environmental problems in urban areas are deeply associated with socio-economic structure and level of people's awareness towards environmental values. This also includes town-planning, administrative aspect and surrounding landscapes.

Sometimes it appears that city people themselves are responsible for having built up a hellish living condition. For example, they do not allow gap between two residential houses, leave no room for rain-water harvesting, even open the drains of the roads, throw garbage anywhere, enjoy walking on roads full of ditches and rubbish things and practice other eco-destructive activities. However, through some sort of mutual understanding and contributions they together would have kept their surroundings neat, clean and green. At least, they can unitedly fight for 'clean environment' which is essential as a *right to live with decorum and decency*. It is totally against the basic human right that city people are forced to live in a hellish environment which even animals (like pigs, street dogs) may abhor. Are they waiting for some Mahatma who will come and ensure them clean environment with all the basic amenities? If so, then wait for Mahatma.

So far district administration and Municipal Corporation are concerned, they are known for their apathetic attitude towards people welfare programme, be it road, sewage system, management of wastes, supply of safe drinking water and the likes. District administrations sometimes come into action only under political influence or tremendous public pressure (provided enlightened people hold agitation for some noble cause). As regards Municipal Corporation, it is always fund-starved and, therefore, do not pay even regular salary to its staff. How can we expect such agency (as the case being in most of the towns in Bihar) to improve built-in-environment of urban areas?

Political parties mostly do not look beyond the next election. Also, when by raking up few communal, caste and religious issues, they get enough votes, then, why should they bother for environmental values? To our great dismay, people even do not demand a better living condition, better education or development, partly because of illiteracy and poverty and to some extent political compulsion (only concerned to short-term gain), they love to remain ignorant of environmental values, (probably because ignorance is a bliss). They do not understand the intricacies as how the city life depends on the surrounding landscapes. Let us now focus on this aspect.

According to the experts *cities are regarded as parasites upon the surrounding landscapes*. They not only import food but also water often and export sewage, solid waste, CO_2, SO_2, etc. If the cities were cut off from their surrounding environment, they would soon perish from starvation, thirst, asphyxiation and accumulation of waste-products. In exchange for these life-supporting things, cities provide great many economic, cultural and educational benefits such as jobs, housing, transport, factories, centres of learning, of entertainment, etc. So the relationship between cities and landscapes is vital in both directions, but it is particularly important to remember that as cities expand, landscapes vanish and former, therefore, cannot sustain themselves. A limit on expansion of cities must, therefore, be laid down before it is too late.

In addition to this vital issue, the one very important issue is availability of safe-drinking water. Deep boring machines over the years have been pumping out underground water without any precautionary measures which include rain water harvesting scopes in the form of ponds, wells, etc. The concrete structures of city hardly allow rain water to penetrate deep into the earth, and also ponds and wells are not made. The surrounding landscapes should have adequate number of ponds to make up for loss of underground water, and having a river beside the city is equally good. But we know that landscapes are shrinking, waning and getting defiled considerably which used to be the last glimpse of wild nature for city people.

In order to substantiate our stand on landscape we are citing here the example of New York city. The experts tell that the city's water has always enjoyed good reputation due to '*Catskill Mountains*' natural purification system. But when mountains' natural green cover was damaged, the quality of water degraded and it was no longer drinkable by late 1990s. Authority planned to build a huge purification plant whose cost was over eight billion dollars exclusive of system operating cost. The price was so staggering that the city eventually decided to restore the 'Catskill Mountains' degraded environment at a cost of only one billion dollars. This corrected and restored the natural hydrological cycle. The event clearly gives us a lesson to preserve our ecosystem and the conditions that enable our planet to sustain all lives. This also forewarns us to remember that ecosystem wants something in return in order to benefit humanity for long.[3]

About Eco-Friendly Concrete Structure

'Built-in-environment' being an integral aspect of Environmental Ethics awes one into close proximity to nature. It teaches us to derive comfort and energy from nature instead of humanly designed devices. Houses built to tap maximum air and energy from nature are quite compatible to this objective. Let us now focus on the 'model house' which is not only airy, spacious and full of greenery, in the front but also receives optimum solar energy during winter. The concept is not a complicated technology.

If the house windows are southward and well-designed, the much of the heat needed during winter will naturally be provided. Double-glazed glass on the southern wall serves as a passive solar energy collection system.

Solar heat can be trapped even more efficiently by the use of various types of solar collectors. One type of collector consists of a coil of copper pipe attached to a blackened metal base. The whole assembly is covered by a transparent layer of glass or plastic. The operating principle is not complicated. Sunlight travels through the glass and is absorbed by the blackened surface. Metal conductors heat readily, so the water in the pipe gets hot. The glass traps the heat within the collectors so it does not easily escape back into the atmosphere.

Hot water produced in this fashion can be pumped through the radiators to heat a building. A heating system of this type is called active solar heat because hot water is actively pumped and regulated by motors and thermostats.

We want here to suggest that we should leave room for free flow of natural light, air, etc., while designing and constructing concrete structure in the urban areas. A neat and clean house exposed to the nature is good for human health and development of all-round personality. Built-in-environment, therefore, should deeply interact with nature. A dark, dirty and congested house, on the other hand, casts a negative impact on the growth of human personality and health. Our children, particularly (the would-becitizens of the nation) if exposed to filthy and congested surrounding, may end up as persons having feeble personality with narrow vision and encrypted attitude. Therefore, every effort regarding laying down new human settlement and even in already built-settlement (if any scope left for remodelling) should necessarily incorporate environmental concerns.

We can redesign and make amends (if possible) in the built-in-environment of urban areas in such a manner so as to combine greenery, wide open space along with concrete structures. In this regard we can consider the following steps:

1. Urban houses should have reasonable space for gardening and water-harvesting.
2. There should be reasonable space between two houses.
3. The houses should be well ventilated, airy, spacious and surrounded by greenery.
4. There should be smooth and effective sewage system and garbage management agency in city.
5. In the heart of town (as far as practicable) there should be a park-cum-garden with wide open space surrounded by cluster of trees. This will provide city dwellers an opportunity to see something natural (although developed by men) and have better pastimes. This may help arousing environmental consciousness into them which is the objective of environmental ethics.
6. Roads should be wide and well-built with green-walling.
7. There should be enough ponds and wells in the surrounding landscapes of town. Also the landscapes should be adequate and full of greenery. We know that ecologically rich landscapes sustain city life through various ways.
8. Social Forestry and Municipal Corporation should be made accountable and effective so as to achieve the objective of '*green and clean the city*'.

9. Eco-consciousness should be aroused in the people and particularly in the new generations.
10. Historical places and ecologically rich areas of city (if any) should be developed in the tune of eco-tourism. Eco-tourism takes into account the aspirations of local people besides developing the sites with lots of greenery and fresh water facilities.

Critical Estimation

In this chapter we tried to make a strong case for built-in-environment as being the major concern of Environmental Ethics. It is because this area has long been ignored by environmentalists where human beings spend most of their time and do their major activities. It is, therefore, quite important to go for thorough analysis of domesticated environment in the perspective of the ideals and objectives of Environmental Ethics. With an approach of interdisciplinary, Environmental Ethics just cannot afford to overlook this aspect of human existence which plays a key role in shaping human vision and attitude towards conservation values. The more eco-friendly and eco-designed the domesticated environment is, the more there is possibility of expansion of environmental culture among the masses dwelling in such environment. It, of course, needs a sound education system with socio-eco orientation and an efficient administration dedicated earnestly to the task of 'cleaning and greening' city and rural areas as well.

On the contrary, people living in stark poverty amidst filthy and vitiated environment will naturally refuse to entertain any such idea pertaining to environmental values. It is because their life begins and ends in struggle for survival. Therefore, any measure to preserve and restore environment will fail to produce any result in respect of deprived section.

Here at this juncture, built-in-environment takes into consideration the socio-economic aspect of different strata of human existence. For example, there are millions of people in India who either live in slum or have no roof over their heads and who struggle hard to earn their bread. Further, there are millions of orphan children who have lost both or either of their parents in some ethnic and naxal violence or caste war. These children work as labourers in some hotels, houses, footpath, automobile centre and other institutions. In case of female children the situation is very tough since they are subject to all sorts of exploitation and finally end up as sex-workers in some brothels. The affluent sections of society just exploit and chew up the helpless innocent children and throw them out in the street. Further, there are great number of beggars in India who are more organized in metropolises. We also have huge troops of unemployed youths. In addition to this, there are millions of tribal and nomads whose resources of living have been denuded and destroyed in Indian natural woodlands. As a consequence, they became landless labourers and urban migratory who settled in slum areas of big cities. To these people, ecosystem matters a little. In this way, there is first of all an urgent need to sort out the socio-economic problems in order to realize the ideals and objectives of Environmental Ethics. It is because for poor and struggling people the problem of environment is insignificant. So built-in-environment is deeply associated with human socio-economic and political set-up.

As regards political set-up in India, it is no longer value-based. Every political party in India wants to ride to the crest by exploiting caste, communal and religious weakness of Indians. Due to bad political decisions our socio-economic development suffers a lot and our environment continues to degrade. Only healthy political practices dedicated to the task of social services can improve our built-in-environment and help inculcating environmental culture in public.

Apart from socio-political aspect, *eco-tourism* contitutes an *integral* part of built-in-environment. "Eco-tourism" probably is a bridge between wild and domesticated environment, also a window opening to the beauty of natural world. Generally, ecologically rich areas are further developed, designed and improved in the larger interest of tourism. It is considered *responsible tourism* since it takes into account the aspirations of local people and development of the entire surroundings adjacent to the tourist point in a sustainable manner. The advantage of eco-tourism is characterized by its role of providing aesthetic pleasure to the people by exposing them to the humanly designed nature and enticing them to make a "return to the Nature" and derive peace and bliss from her. This is considered one of the most effective way of bringing environmental consciousness among people and putting into practice the objectives of Environmental Ethics.

Apart from tourism, social forestry programmes of Forest and Environment Department can play a key role in improving built-in-environment particularly in urban areas. Unfortunately, this department, too, has been rendered dysfunctional in Bihar mainly because of paucity of fund and Government's apathetic attitude. Even already well-established Jai Prakash Garden (established by Forest Department, Government of Bihar in the heart of town or elsewhere) is being neglected and disfigured to a great extent. It is indeed very shocking to notice people's indifferent attitude to such type of green spot in the town. Rather, they could have forced administration and the government. to maintain the garden-cum-park which is considered the 'lung of the town'. The importance of green spot in the town increases manifold in the absence of ecologically rich landscapes in the surroundings of town. What we want to emphasize here is, people's role in improving built-in-environment in urban areas. Their combined efforts can change the scenario to a great extent.

However, it is true that deprived section of the urban society Cannot take interest in environmental matter. But what about prosperous and affluent people who have enough to eat and spare and even indulge in various types of luxuries? Unfortunately, it has always been noticed that they harm the environment most. They raise huge apartments and buildings without following any environmental norms. No place or lawn in the front, encroachment on roads, no room for rain-water harvesting, or kitchen gardening, opening of the drains on roads, throwing garbage on the roads, etc., are the most common sight of the majority of the towns in Bihar and Jharkhand. The heart of the matter is that a little bit of people's efforts and co-operation of the Government. agency could help in overcoming such shortcomings. At least people can keep their own surrounding neat and clean and also plant some trees as far as practicable. But the big tragedy with people is that they take to streets for petty political reasons, not for better domesticated environment which includes basic amenities with clean green environment. 'Big rally' in the name of caste and community attracts them whereas any noble cause fails to find any positive response on their part. It is said that poor educational policy and lack of political awareness are responsible for this sordid state of affairs. Even though this is true, the task indeed is related to social habits, conducts and attitudes which have to be enlightened in due course. A true concern for environment and a right understanding about its intricacies will help a lot in restoring the environmental values. However, it is very difficult and challenging task to bring a change in the outlook and attitude of people in respect of our ecosystem. It also requires some strict measures combined with education and reviving ancient wisdom of Hindu culture.

In the sequence of the analysis of the ingredients of built-in-environment, one of the most formidable tasks is to check the pollution of all kinds. Our big industries, NTPC and transport system pollute the air, water and soil in such a manner that the entire atmosphere is vitiated. This is a big challenge before domesticated environment which requires adopting eco-friendly technologies and having least dependence on fossil fuels in order to obtain an optimum level of pollution free surroundings. In this way, we urgently need to develop and get access to such technologies which create minimum pollution and involve least exploitation of natural resources. For example, our requirement of energy can be obtained from air and sun. Hydrogen power and solar energy are modern day requirement which can help us to run our vehicles and light our houses and streets with zero pollution. Unfortunately, we are yet to frame a policy which cares for our environment and encourages the use of eco-friendly technologies.

From the above analysis we can understand the objectives and challenges of domesticated environment which can be presented here in nutshell:

1. Built-in-environment necessarily incorporates the spirit of Environmental Ethics which includes the ideal of "clean and green environment".
2. It takes into account the different social strata of human existence. For example, condition of slum-dwellers, child labour and others.
3. It analyses the socio-economic and political aspects in respect of built-in-environment. It wants to improve the social life and political scenario in the country for a better and congenial atmosphere.
4. It looks upon eco-tourism as means to obtain the objectives of Environmental Ethics in rural-urban areas.
5. It wants to use eco-friendly technologies to improve built-in-environment.

In this way, built-in-environment rightly deserves to be a major concern and an interesting area of inquiry of Environmental Ethics.

REFERENCES

1. Environmental Ethics, 20 (2) (2002): 115-131. Department. of Phil, University of Maine, Orano, MEO4469, King has published on ecocentrism, ecofeminism, the ethics of hunting, and the role of narrative in Env. Ethics. His primary research interests are environmental ethics and American Pragmatism.
2. Roger J.H.King, "Narative, Imagination, and the Search for

Intelligibility in Environmental Ethics, Ethics and Environment, 4 (1999): 23-38

3. N.L. Narasaiah – Biodiversity and Environment Delhi Publishing House, New Delhi 2004, p. 15

NOTE

Asthana, D.K. Meera. Asthana, *Environment (Problems and Solutions)*, S. Chand & Company Ltd., New Delhi.

Attfield, Robin and Belsey, Andrew (ed.) *Philosophy and the Natural Environment*, Cambridge University Press, 1994 By Dr. Pratima Ganguli (Prof.) and Dr. Mritunjay Kumar (Lecturer), P.G. Deptt. Of Philosophy, T.M. Bhagalpur University, Bhagalpur.

Black, Paul. (ed.) *Environments and Historical Change*, Kalyani Publication, New Delhi, 2002.

Chatterji and others, (ed.) *Environment and Health in Developing Countries,* A.P.H. Publishing Corporation, New Delhi, 1998.

Chatterji, Manas; Mohan Hunasinghe and Robin Ganguly, (ed.), *Environment & Health in Developing Countries*, A.P.H. Publishing, New Delhi, 1998.

James, George A. (ed), *Ethical Perspectives on Environmental Issues in India*, A.P.H. Publishing Corporation Darya Ganj, New Delhi, 1999.

Narasaiah, M.L, *Biodiversity and Environment*, Discovery Publishing House, New Delhi, 2004.

Srivastava, K.P., *An Introduction to Environmental Study,* Kalyani Publishing, Ludhiana, 2002.

Subbarao, S. *Ethics of Ecology and Environment*, Rajat Publications, New Delhi, 2001

Turk, Jonathan, *Introduction to Environmental Studies*, Saunders College, Publishing, Philadelphia, New York, 1985

द्विवेदी पं० रमेश पर्यावरण वस्तु, डायमंड पाकेट बुक्स (प्रा०) लि०, नई दिल्ली, 1996।

Chapter – 22

Ecosophy : An Overview

M.P. Chaurasia

The term Ecosophy is a combination of '*eco*' and '*sohia*' like the term philosophy which also is a combination of two words *philos* + *sophia*. Philosophy means 'love of wisdom' similarly ecosophy means love of ecology. It is love of or *eco ecolone*. One who loves eco system is an ecosopher. The relation between ecosophy and ecology is very intimate. Sometimes it is called Ecophilosophy. The subject matter of ecosophy is to lay down those principles that will help us to restore our ecosystem once again or maintain the eco-balance. God has created the world with its things and beings. Rest things, which God has not created, are created by man and environmental pollution or ecological imbalance is one of them.

Philosophers since 1570 have criticised very bitterly the approaches of modern philosophers towards natural world. Descartes, for example, emphasised substance and ignored matter. Consequently animal world was ignored by the thinkers and this view increased the exploitation of animals in our society. During modern period the centre of study was human value. Now-a-days ethical study includes in its domain not only human values but also ecological values. This study is called *ecocentric values* and so it is designated as *ecosophy* or *ecophilosophy*. Its purpose is to make a comprehensive and deep inquiry into value of natural world and the animal kingdom. Arne Naess defines ecosophy in the following manner. "By an ecosophy I mean a philosophy of ecological harmony or equilibrium. As a wisdom, it is openly normative, it contains both norms, rules, postulates, value priority and hypotheses concerning the state of affairs in our universe (see A. Drengson and Y. Jnoue, 1995, p. 8). The mission of ecosophy is to explore a diversity of perspectives on human-nature contexts and interrelationship. It fosters deeper and more harmonious relationship between place, self, community and the natural world.

Ecosophy joined hands with ecological movement and its established motto is to develop respect for Nature and the inherent worth of other beings. We are living in diverse cultures. Every culture has its own method and technique to protect and preserve natural world. For this purpose, it requires the study of cross culture analysis of grass roots social-political movements. It studies the total human situation in present context. In its deep ecological movement, it recognises the inherent value of all other living beings, and of the inherent worth of diversity of all kinds. This awareness is used to shape environmental policies and actions. Those who work for social changes based on this recognition are motivated by love of Nature as well as love for humans. They recognise that we cannot go on with industrial culture's business as usual. We must make fundamental changes in basic values and practices or we will destroy the diversity and beauty of the world, and its ability to support diverse human cultures.

What unites the diverse cultures is a long-range vision of what is necessary to protect the integrity of the Earth's ecological communities and values. Supporters of the principles have a diversity of ultimate beliefs. "Ultimate beliefs", here refers to their own basic metaphysical, personal and religious grounds for their values, actions and support for the deep ecology movement. Different people and cultures have different mythologies and stories that can help us to solve our crises of environment.

From this point of view, Gandhian non-violence, Mahayana Buddhism and Spinozistic pantheism are the best philosophical and religious principles to which we can adhere to save the ecological equilibrium. In the domain of philosophy much emphasis has been laid down on self realisation for all beings. This self realisation does not mean only individual's ego self but the larger ecological self. This has affinities with Mahayana Buddhism and Gandhian non-violence. We have to extend our identification to realise that higher self. Everybody can develop his own ecosophy in the vast domain of Nature. The only thing to do is to adopt the norms either of religious faith or of ethical value. The main approach road is to extend our senses of identification to a larger sense of self. Humans naturally have this capacity as we find in the faiths like Hinduism, Islamism, Christianity, Buddhist or any other forms of religious faith. We have the capacity to connect with a much larger sense of self, transcending ego, by extending our sense of identification beyond the usual narrow focus on ego to a wider sphere of relationships. It is not difficult for us to identify with other living beings. We can actually practice or cultivate this capacity. One way is to practice this by extending our self their rough 'care' and 'affection'. We can also explore this larger self in a variety of other ways.

There are many forms of self-realisation norm. Alan Drengdon and Warwick Fox emphasise the view that the extension of self and the idea of the ecological self overlaps in many ways in transpersonal psychology[1]. Sometimes Fox calls these self-realisation types of ecosophies transpersonal ecologies. In the same way Fox Matthew calls it Creation Technology which is transpersonal ecology in the form of Christian philosophy and practice that finds the Christ principle of power of love revealed on the ongoing creation of the world. It is this that we should have reverence. This opens us to the expansive sense of self. A Mahayana Buddhist who is concerned for the deliverance of all sentient beings, can easily support the deep ecology movement principles. Some other thinkers have supported this view in the forms of eco-feminists and social-ecologists.

Some thinkers have alleged that in this view, more emphasis has been laid down on ecosophical movement, consequently it has increased the apathetic attitudes towards human beings. But such allegation is superfluous, because this principle sees the inherent worth of all beings, including humans. This movement deplores antihuman statements and action. How it can be antihuman? Ecosophers are the supporters of Gandhian non-violence in word and deed, then how can they be anti-humanists? Another criticism is advanced by some thinkers; that more emphasis on ecological equilibrium is nothing but anthropocentrism. But such allegation is also mischievous, because we defend our loved ones or are moved more by human suffering than the suffering of other beings, we are acting as descendants, parents, friends, lovers, etc. Everybody who is a lover of ecosophy must be consistent with such feelings. What is inconsistent is refusing to recognise the inherent worth of other beings, to the extent that one is willing to allow unmerciful exploitation and destruction of life forms purely for human convenience and profit. Such criticism is superfluous because it does not give importance to other being's life as the part of human life. Our human self in the deepest sense cannot be separated from the Earth from which we have grown. We cannot lead our life in isolation from our ecological system.

When we explore that we are the part and parcel of earth's life, then our affinities with other beings belongs to the part of human life. It provides the intrinsic value of all beings, including humans. Ecosophy is committed to respect the inherent intrinsic value of humans and other beings. This leads to action that try to minimise our own impacts on ecological communities and other human cultures. Everywhere ecosophy advocates positive steps for the humans and other beings both and try to stop negative attitude and action towards other beings. As mentioned by Hawken "that it uses bottom up initiatives, diverse leaders", and back and forth slay between workers and leaders.[2]

If we accept the principle of deep ecosophy, this naturally involves commitment to respect the intrinsic values of richness and diversity. This in turn leads to a critique of industrial society. This critique cuts across cultural boundaries. It is presented from both within and outside of industrial societies. It is partly from such a critique that support for indigenous cultures arises within modern societies. The creed of this criticism goes like this : Industrial culture represents itself as the only acceptable model for progress and development. However, application of this model and its financial and technological systems to all areas of the planet results in distraction of habitat, extinction of species, and destruction of indigenous culture. The biodiversity crisis is about loss of critical species, populations, and processes that perform necessary biological functions and it is also about loss of multitudes of other values which are good in themselves and depend on preservation of natural diversity and wild evolutionary process. Industrial society is a mono-culture in agriculture and forestry, and in every other way. Its development models construe the Earth as only raw material to be used to satisfy consumption and production to meet not only vital needs, but inflated desires whose satisfaction requires more and more consumption. Its mono cultures destroy cultural and biological diversity, both of which are good in themselves and critical to our survival and flourishing. The older industrial development models are now superseded by the ecological approaches.

Instead of accepting the industrial development model, we should prefer to follow the principles of deep ecology because that lead us to study the ecosophies of aboriginal and indigenous people so as to learn from them values and practices that can help us to dwell wisely in neighbouring places. We also can learn from the wisdom of our places and the many beings who inhabit them. At the same time, the ecocentric values implied by ecosophy lead us to recognize that all human cultures have a mutual interest in perceiving Earth and its diversity continue for our sake, for its own sake (in early Buddhist terminology) and because we love it. Most people among us want to flourish and realise themselves in harmony with other beings, because they observe presence of divine force in every thing and being of the world. It is the task of the day to develop a technique to work for the common interests which enable us to serve other cultures, creatures and beings in a harmonious way.

In western thoughts, ecosophy is developing under the shadow of *Christian ecotheology* which is based on a reverential spirit for creation. The ferment of this with the new ecocentric paradigms – influenced by field ecology and leading edge science has led writers like Tomas Berry.[3] To begin fashioning a 'new story' as a basis for Western initiatives in creating an ecologically wise and harmonious society. But people like me, who do not have faith in divine force, will never follow the above mythical theory. Then what is the alternative solution? Solution is to follow intrinsic value.

In Applied Ethics we can assimilate all the moral theories into two broad categories, i.e., Teleological Standard of Morality and Deontological Standard of Morality. The champion of Teleologist theory of morality is J.S. Mill and his utilitarianism and the pioneer of Deontologist theory of morality is Kant and his rigourism. According to the consequentialists view, action pertaining to the pleasure of maximum people is good and bad if, in the same proportion it results into pain. As Elliot remarks, "Consequentialism instructs us to behave in some way or another with respect to these values, for example, different varieties of consequentialism might tell us to maximise value, to minimise disvalue, to increase value, to reduce disvalue, to maintain value to, even, to reduce value."[4] The last version of the reference is endorsed only by those who seek to promote the bad at the cost of the good. In the same way traditional consequentialism state that an action is obligatory if, in comparison to other actions, it maximises the expected quality of intrinsic value.[5]

Now, from this point of view pleasure or happiness is the intrinsic value according to consequentialisms. Every action that increases pleasure, is intrinsically valuable and bad if it increases pain. Actions that are not directly liable to produce intrinsic value can also be good if they promote or be instrument in increasing the intrinsic value. From this point of view natural world has an intrinsic value itself and an instrument to promote intrinsic value. Consider, for a while, the extensive modifications to natural environment that human activity has caused and continued to cause. Many of these modifications such as the building up of green house gases, the depletion of the ozone layer, deforestation, land degradation, the elimination of species, pollution of atmosphere, rivers, oceans and global warming, threaten the well-being of presently existing and future humans and other beings. One who is the lover of ecology must beware of adverse impacts on human well-being and lament the destruction of ecological equilibrium, which have important economic, scientific, medical and aesthetic uses.[6] Sometimes it is urged that human well-being is more subtly dependent on the integrity of the natural environment than is suggested by a list of extrinsic value. Human can flourish only in the close contact of nature. So nature have undoubtedly an intrinsic value. Therefore, it is obligatory to act so as to increase intrinsic value. In this way, consequentialisms, in all their forms, support the policy that preserves and restores ecological equilibrium.[7] Restoring ecological equilibrium will be one way of increasing intrinsic value.

Deontological Stand

Deontologists claim that certain kind of action are obligatory, permissible, impermissible in virtue of specific properties of the action an agent performs or could perform.[8] According to this view it might be claimed that since some objects have intrinsic value, it is obligatory not to destroy them. The making of this theory is: do not destroy things that have intrinsic value. The rivers, mountains, lakes, trees, tigers and other animals never harm us. They are valuable for us. These things only give us and take nothing from us. So, these things have intrinsic value. We should never assess the loss of these things in terms of only intrinsic value which is associated with their destructions. On the other side the wrongness of an act can be established by realising the fact that it is an act of destroying something of intrinsic value. We are not ethically entitled to destroy a thing of lesser value in order to protect a thing of greater material value. According to deontologist ecosophers environmental vandalism and despoliation of ecological equilibrium will be wrong for additional seasons also. For example, such despoliation would wrongfully injure and kill non-humans and wrongfully impose costs and burdens on humans.

So, it is obligatory to perform acts which restore value lost in violation. This obligation is a binding force not only for those who themselves were active participants in the despoliation but also for those who have benefited from it. It is not out of context to advise that present humans have an obligation to restore value lost earlier and value lost at present through the destructive acts of other or their species, irrespective of whether they themselves have benefited from such acts.

Thomas Hill in his book, *Ideals of Human Excellence and Preserving the Natural Environment* maintains the view that those who engage in ecological in equilibrium display a defect of character that needs to be condemned in terms of standard of human excellence. John Passmore has rightly observed that "if humans think that nature exists only as something to be used and something also to be enjoyed, then such notions as Vandalism and Philistinism would be applicable to human relationships with the natural environment"[9]. So we can conclude as an ecosopher that only humans can be objects of ingratitude. Unless one is ignorant, one should understand that we owe our existence and well-being to natural processes.[10] We are not and should not be a vandalist, though an atheist, so we should love nature and ecological equilibrium only then we may be called ecosophers in true sense.

REFERENCES

1. [Fox Warwick, 1990. *Towards a Transpersonal Ecology*, Boston and Drengson, Alan, *The Practice of Technology: Exploring Technology, Ecophilosophy and Spiritual Disciplines for vital links*, 1995, Albany, Suny Press].
2. [Hawken, 1993, 1999. The Ecology of Commerce : A Deceleration of Sustainability, New York, Harper Collins].
3. Dream of the Earth, San Francisco, Sierra Books]
4. Rober, Elliot, *Faking Nature*, Pro pp. 42-43 1978.
5. J.O'Neil, Ecology, Policy and Politics. Human Well-being and the Natural World, pp. 20-22 1993.
6. O'Neill, *op.Cit*, pp. 23-25.
7. Ellion, *op. cit*, p. 46.
8. Elliot, *op.Cit*, p. 50.
9. *Attitude to Nature*, p. 263.
10. Elliot, *op. cit*, p. 58.

Chapter – 23

Environmental Ethics and Indian Culture

Professor Nirbhai Singh

1. Introductory

This chapter purports to focus attention on Bioethics and Indian culture, values and their relevance in the contemporary scenario. In the age of science and technology, search for global peace and justice seems to be a wild goose chase. Clouds of terrorism are hovering over our heads. Humanity is burning in the cauldron of violence and religious fanaticism and bigotry. The volcanic eruption of atomic bomb may usher in dooms day at any moment. Human beings may perish and God will have to restart the process of creation *de novo*. Oswald Spengler in his classical work *The Decline of The West* envisages that science and technology cannot yield any spiritual healing to the moral and spiritual needs of humanity.

Environmental ethics or Bioethics is an abortive attempt for healing the ailing humans. Both are illegitimate byproducts of modern technology and science. In the modern philosophical debates and seminars bioethics dominates. Science and technology have given birth to many incurable diseases. For example, cancer is incurable till today. It has distorted the Greek concept of *euthanasia* as mercy killing. In the original sense, it was used for heroic death. Modern medical science has taken a lame excuse for finishing the cancerous patient with an injection who may die peacefully. From ethical standpoint, it is immoral. Euthanasia was the key concept of the heroic societies. In the *Ramayana* and the *Mahabharata* heroic life was the anchor of *dharma* (righteous deed). The heroes of the epics are symbols of *dharma*. It was adopted by Islam and Sikhism for expounding the concept of martyrdom, supreme sacrifice for the cause of truth. Similarly, many other cultural values of India have been destroyed. Aboriginal culture of the tribal people is crushed. Indigenous art of the tribal people is withering away due to technological waves.

In fact, the new technologies give such a power of intervention on man himself and environment, which was never seen before. It is based on a reflection on the risks of man's self-destruction due to a biotechnological delusion of omnipotence. Bioethical centres have multiplied throughout the world, taking up different positions but almost everywhere pointing out new hopes for a better future. We can thank new bio-medical technologies along with risks.

In this era of post-modernity human destiny is in the melting volcanic pot of material values. Western materialistic outlook of science and technology has a satanic impact in all walks of life. In spite of these malignant influences, there are some redeeming rays of hope, which may help humanity in bridging the yawning gulf of survival and annihilation. No doubt, the Western civilization has imposed materialistic outlook on our lifestyle, but it could not dominate the essential Indian spiritual culture. I can concede this much that in our day-to-day interpersonal relations, we have evinced materialistic attitude towards the world and others but the collective psyche of the common folks of India is still tied up with its hoary spiritual culture.

Contemporary environmental ethics has focused on criticizing the anthropocentric and instrumental value theories of humanism, which develop around modern Western philosophy and upon securing non-anthropocentric viewpoints based upon the truth that both human beings and nature have equal values of life.

Indian philosophy and Confucianism have monistic viewpoint about the relationship between man and nature, existence and values, subject and object. It is an endeavour to overcome the dichotomy between fact and value, subject and object. Values do not endow to the object. Nothing is intrinsically added to the objective facts at all. Values are human creation. God is an anthropocentric value. He is incessantly transformed into non-anthropocentric formless Being (*nirankara*). Values also transcend anthropocentric aspect and culminate in non-anthropocentric monism.

Value creation carries out through self-cultivation. Thus, philosophy of self-cultivation is the meeting point of Indian philosophy and Confucianism. Monistic philosophy is the natural outcome of self-cultivation. In the Western philosophy reason is the main source of knowledge, while in Confucianism and Indian philosophy moral nature (*dharma*) serves as the source for the sublimation of life as the unification of human nature and existence. Reason posits a dichotomy of the subject and the object whereas self-cultivation dissolves it. In short, self-cultivation actualizes the value of *ren* (humanity) by overcoming the material desires. (*sannyasa*). Thus, Indian philosophy and Confucianism are inclusive humanism free from anthropocentricism.

2. Uniqueness of Indian Culture

What is Spirituality? The uniqueness of Indian spirituality is that it gives scientific spiritual discipline of yoga (yoking to the Numinous), which is the basis of different schools of thought in Indian philosophy. The *Gita* is the key of Indian spiritual philosophy and culture, which is its practical dimension and the Samkhya system, is its theoretical base. Both put together constitute perfect voluntarist philosophy of life. Spiritual discipline (*sadhana*) concentrates on *rarefaction* of consciousness through different stages of yoga. It is transformation of the self from the empirical self to the eternal self without dissolving man's 'personal identity'. It is transformation from *natura naturata* to *natura naturans.* In other words, the *jiva* is transmuted into *atman.* The empirical gross self is transformed into the subtle self—"self-consciousness" (*viveka buddhi*). Thus, our concept of spirituality does not negate the empirical world; rather embraces it.

Spirituality does not have any ontic being like the Platonic ideas. It is a lived experience of consciousness. When consciousness is rarefied, it culminates in self-consciousness. In the mystic terminology of Sufism, it is ascent (*miraj*) of consciousness towards approximation to the supreme Reality. The highest state of transcendence is ecstasy. The mystic is at once in a state of eternity and temporality. In the medieval terminology of the saints and the *gurus* it is called *sahaj.*

It needs strenuous training and discipline for taming the mind. Indian culture emphasizes on cultivation of consciousness. Control of mind (*mana*) is the essence of Indian culture. *Sadhana* (spiritual discipline) is a means for it. Guru Nanak in one of his hymns in "*The Japuji*" avers, "He who conquers his mind (consciousness), achieves victory over the worldly seductions". From Guru Nanak to Guru Gobind Singh 'martial culture' was developed. The Gurus exploited heroic and tribal spirit of the Indian heritage. It represents the spirit of the Indian culture. Material things are only means for creating heroic culture. It is cultivation of the self from within. Taming of the nature with material tools is civilization. In nutshell, freedom and culture are interchangeable terms.

A sharp contrast between Indian and Western standpoints is the subjectivist inward individual's autonomy as the supreme moral criterion *vis-á-vis* utilitarianism, contractualism, anarchism, and behaviourism. In this case, the Western fundamental reference is the concept of person, as the unique and irreproducible dualism of body and spirit. In the Indian culture, both body and spirit are reducible through self-cultivation to monism of the cosmic consciousness controlled by the cosmic law (*rita*). The study of human person, the meaning of life, and his specific nature is the basis of bioethics. Hence, the Western and Indian culture are poles apart.

Uniqueness of Indian culture lies in the fact that it does not advocate possessiveness of property and power. The Western culture is antipodes to it. It is science and technology oriented. Wealth or money is a part of power. It corrupts human mind. The menace of global terrorism is the necessary outcome of it. Use of power for selfish purposes is to be avoided. We are facing this crisis in day-to-day life. Indian culture advocates sense of disinterested attitude towards both wealth and power, and pleads for distanced involvement in the societal relations. This is meaning of *nishkama karma* of *The Gita* and *subha karma* of Guru Gobind Singh.

It is to be cultivated by deschooling and reschooling. The former process is emptying the mind of dead and morbid beliefs and concepts, which are acquired from the parents and other fellow beings. The latter is a process of indoctrinating new beliefs, ideas, ideologies, etc. The saints and the *gurus* played this significant role. Culture is cultivation of the self from within and taming of the nature with material tools is civilization.

Cultivation of mind is self-taming through education, which aims at freeing the self from the fetters of the worldly seductions. Freedom and culture are interchangeable terms. *Moksha* and *nirvana* connote emancipation of the self from attachment with the world. At the transcendental level, one enjoys eternal freedom. Paulo Freire talks of education and freedom in society. He ventilated his ideas in his works, *Cultural Action for Freedom* and *Pedagogy of the Oppressed.*[1] These are *par excellent works* on education and culture. Decolonization opens gates for true liberation of methods of learning pedagogy— deschooling and reschooling. Freire repeatedly emphasizes to imbibe the capacity for transcending what is merely given and purely determined. Man's ultimate goal of action is to realize in praxis. Radical indoctrination of mind through education transforms or revolutionizes the existing social order. This is carried out through language, education and practical action.

The dominance of material values, in the age of science and technology, is the beginning of the annihilation of humanity.

Matter has the potent quality of attraction whereas the spiritual values lay emphasis on ascent of the mind from the tentacles and seductions of the mundane world. Material values relegate spiritual values to the periphery. Hence, the present crisis of globalization technology *vis-á-vis* cultures and civilizations or of the East and the West has come to the fore. Science and industry have caused havoc and immense misery to humanity. They cannot yield peace and harmony in the world. Sufferings of human beings are increasing day and night. Humanity is being dragged towards annihilation. Indian spiritual values and culture are the only redeeming hopes of humanity.

The age of science and technology is the beginning of the end of humanity. Science and industry have caused immense misery to humanity. It is just a mirage (*mriga trishna*). From the point of view culture, there is nothing good or desirable about scientific knowledge. We are living on the hope that every cloud has a positive aspect. Need of the hour is revival of Indian cultural values in practical life. It is unfortunate that people are doggedly falling into trap of the scientists.

The Material progression is delusive. The idea of great civilizational progress is a delusion, along with the hope that the truth will be known in the future. No doubt, science is good to a limited extent. Beyond certain limits, it is injurious for humanity. It has taught us how to fly in the skies, dive deep into the oceanic waters, but it has not taught us how to live peacefully on the earth along with other human beings.

In the light of the above given global gloomy and dismal picture of the world, it will be pertinent to discourse Indian culture and values (*dharma*) which survived through the ages. It is a historical fact that Egypt, Sumaria, Greece, Persia and other fountainheads of civilizations perished, but Indian civilization survived through the epoch of history. This credit goes to the spiritual values of Indian culture which are treasured in the traditions, ethos, the *Vedas*, *Puranas*, *Upanishads*, the *Gita*, Buddhist literature, the Epics (The *Ramayana*, the *Mahabharata*, etc.), and in the medieval *Bhakti* literature). Then a question arises:

what is the spirit of the culture? It is not concerned with the progression of civilization. It surrounds the civilization. The spirit of civilization lies in its unity and continuity.

It is true that wisdom of India is found in the scriptures and oral traditions, but we have wasted time in garnering chaff instead of grain. The scriptures are the *Vedas*, but we have wasted time binding the manuscripts. The central linchpin of the sacred scriptures is "life" which the scriptures, the epics and the traditions emphasize, but we have spent time in concealing the ciphers in them with exegetical expositions and explanations, which remain at superficial level.

3. What is Culture?

I am trying to explore philosophical dimensions of the Indian culture and values that emphasize its dynamic and heroic nature that mirrors the essence of Indian philosophy. Since time immemorial, Indian culture passed through vicissitudes of social progression and retrogression, but it retained its *sui generic* identity. The medieval period was the decline of the Indian culture. India lost her cultural glory and spiritual values. Material and temporal values overshadowed its spiritual values. The Islamic culture overshadowed our culture and values in all walks of life.

The ancient and the medieval epochs are interlinked because culture and civilization are continuous processes and are the outcome of the primitive culture-forms to the civilized society. They need conceptual interlacing into a unity for having a holistic perspective on the Indian culture. The medieval India was dismal for want of religious fervour and human values. In the medieval India, religion played vital role in carrying forward past cultural heritage. Our culture was partially diminished owing to alien invasions. The medieval *Bhakti* movement condemned ritualism and formalism, which were devoid of real religious or prophetic spirit in theory and praxis. The medieval *Bhaktas* and the Sikh Gurus made supreme sacrifices and struggled hard to revive and retain the essence of ancient spiritual culture.

The aspirant has to develop inner urge to realize his real self. For this purpose, he needs a mentor to guide him. Spiritual mentor (*guru*) is the symbol of wisdom for mentoring him. The spiritual mentor encourages the traveller to undertake inner journey that leads him to self-discovery. Nevertheless, he himself has to take the journey. This is the central linchpin of the Indian culture

When the aspirant starts his pilgrimage, his vision gets wider and sharper; and gradually the limits of the phenomenal world vanish. Fear of death that lurks in his inner mind withers away. His courage strangulates fear of death that paralyzes mind. "Leap of Faith" awakens him to the life of choice of freedom. He can discharge *nishkama karmas*

The mentor's "wise eyes" inspire to undertake life full of strife. Without suffering and obstacles, life is passivity, which does not motivate to reach out the "Beyond", the real purpose of human life. Precondition of "beginner's mind on inner pilgrimage" is to still and empty our mind of all entices of the world and resolve all conflicts. Stilled mind in meditation awakens to vision of truth. Strong will, power overcomes failures. Failures kindle faith in truth. Only genius and talented man visualize new emerging higher visions. This inward journey cannot be possible without emptying mind of the worldly attachments and strong will to achieve eternal truth. Fortification of will and knowledge are supplementary factors. Failures kindle faith in truth and strong will defeats failures. This is the spirit of dynamic view of Indian life.

Stilled and purified vision of truth of the mystics echoes *cosmic* music ("*anahad-nada*") of eternity. To realize it is fraught with many challenges and obstacles. For achieving this target, natural talent is to be coupled with acquired skill and strenuous steadfast striving (*sadhana*) for autonomous life. The sage realizes it and thousand others can take clue from his life. We can sum up the argument : evergreen stream of life flows with spiralling states of consciousness surging to the eternity. Wisdom lies in flowing with the flowing stream of eternity that is attuned to the cosmic law from within and without.

Man is born imperfect in the world within the narrow walls of egocentric self (*jiva*). If the "I" is to be true to my authentic and unique self, it needs to transcend the illusion of the "me". He is to come out of it and identify himself with "others" and the cosmic Self. In the beginning, he is oblivious of the oceanic consciousness. For voluntarist life, consciousness is to be dominated by will. This is the secret of heroic life and culture.

"Others" become "I", yet also remain the "not-I." It implies distinct and independent nature of "others". When the "I" remains as a distant observer, the "I" sees only the manifest behaviour in the society. Nevertheless, when the "I" identifies itself with its inner self, the "I" becomes fully realized and perfect. From the mundane point of view, it is distancing oneself from others. The "I" identifies myself with others' anxieties, greed, or their whole 'self'. I could not understand myself in forlornness, aloneness, alienation, hope or love.

For perfecting himself, the hero is to struggle in the world. He is to transform his imperfect self (*jiva*) into perfect self (*atman*). Self-transcendence from the limits of the empirical world and distanced involvement in it is the essence of Indian culture. It does not imply actual withdrawal from the worldly responsibilities, but inward detachment from it. One is to grapple with ordeals of the world with disinterested involvement and live life of continuous striving till the claws of death strangulates him.

The conceptual framework of the heroic culture and spiritual values is preserved in the repositories of the sacred Vedic and the Buddhist scriptures. The medieval devotional literature of the *Bhaktas* and the *Gurus* is replete with heroic culture and martial values. They created a new composite and heroic culture and values. Urge for transcending the fear of death is the natural offshoot of it. Transformation implies awakening the self to free will. When man plunges into adventurous life, it gives birth to heroic view of life and culture

Man is an animal and creative being, but he is distinct from the lower species. Culture tames and transforms the beast in him for making it a creative being. He is the only species, which can create the worldview with tools of language. For this purpose, he creates the worldview. He creates his own world of the values and strives to live according to them. He tries to translate these values in use. This is the purpose of human life. His basic objective is to have complete harmony with the Nature and other fellow beings.

My "I" is to be attuned to the very essence of the real self. This is realization of the *"personal identity"* of man and his autonomy. Authentic self mirrors freedom that is the central linchpin of man in the world. The personal identity is not a given fact. It is to be cultivated with meditative continuous striving both from within and without. From within he advances to autonomy of the self and from without he socializes himself in the society. The inward journey of the self terminates when the "I" realizes that I am a drop of water on the crest of the oceanic waves. I am concerned with others not as an observer, but as an active participant and co-traveller in the existential predicaments. They ushered in Cultural Revolution in India and prepared the nation to confront alien incursions. They identified themselves with the subaltern for their emancipation. They formulated egalitarian ideology for the welfare of the subaltern populace. This is existential and concrete view of man of the Medieval *Bhaktas* and the Sikh Gurus. The scholars have not highlighted this aspect.

Culture is the undercurrent of inner life of the collective psyche of the people. It is the secret that is preserved as "ciphers" in the sacred scriptures. Being a lived experience, it can be realized by the intuitive mind. Mystic or the religious celebrity is competent to understand it. Philosophical analysis can crystallize the concepts, which are the undercurrents. From this standpoint, philosophical study of culture is justified. Since no comprehensive work has been done in this field, this chapter may inspire the researchers to go deep into the problem.

The western researchers have done work from their own perspectives. The philosophical understanding of the Indic culture from the Indian perspective is the central problem of this chapter.

Culture, being a lived experience, is very difficult to understand for the "outsiders". It is difficult for them to penetrate into the citadel of others' onto-theology and ethos, and traditions. Similarly, the "outsiders" cannot easily grasp the Indic scriptures and the cultural traditions. In addition, Indian scholars have not given a serious thought to the problem. Ceaseless endeavour is needed for presenting coherent and systematic philosophical picture of the culture. Being "insiders" the Indian thinkers with profound conceptual understanding of the scriptures can do justice to understand them from our cultural perspective.

The Europeans were masters of the world during colonization period. For the last three hundred years, they dominated the world cultures. They introduced education loaded with Western culture and religious ideology. Education is always goal-oriented. There is no neutral education. It is either for domestication or for freedom of man.[1] Education is the key to recuperation of the mystified reality. In the medieval period, Indian culture was "culture of silence" because Indians lacked freedom of expression. In the present research work, I propose to highlight the contribution of the medieval intellectual celebrities and the religious dignitaries who revived Indian culture. They had freedom of expression. They expressed their ideas without any fear. In the medieval period, we were not free to express our native culture.

In the field of conceptual framework of philosophy of culture, Indian scholars have been exegetically explaining it from the perspectives of linguistics (philology, semantics, etymology, semiotics, etc.), sociology, anthropology, sculpture, architecture, etc. These tools are useful for exposing and explaining literal meanings of the texts. From the philosophical standpoint, cultural understanding in the area of the proposed study is irrelevant. We have been explaining Indian culture with traditional linguistic tools. Western scholars, especially the German philologists, have done researches on the sacred scriptures. They claim that they are masters of Sanskrit and are competent to understand the Sanskrit texts. Their works are mostly concerned with preparing dictionaries, mythological indices, concordances, literal translations of the scriptures, etc. Their translations are done from the Christian standpoint. Their coloured explanations of the sacred texts have presented distorted picture of the Indian culture. They did not have in-depth understanding of the Indian ethos, traditions, conventions and customs. They provided improvised material. Philosophical perspective escaped their studies. Thus, our objective conceptual understanding of the Indian culture is lagging far behind. We are still living in the medieval ages. Our understanding of Indian culture is that of ropedancers. We have been interpreting Indian culture from the Western perspective. The lenses of Eurocentric methodology shadow our interpretations. It is unfortunate that Indian religious discourses continue limping along Hindu *ashramas,* siddha or yogi *mathas,* sikh *gurdwaras,* muslim mosques, *shivadwaras,* jaina *mandirs,* and *buddhist pagodas/stupas.*

Eurocentric methodology and hermeneutical contribution of the Jews to the Christian sacred scriptures is significant. Being 'outsiders', the Westerners cannot do full justice to our cultural heritage. The native Indians have been experiencing it since times immemorial. They breathe in cultural fragrance of the Indian soil day and night. Western interpretations of our texts are overshadowed with their conscious or unconscious cultural prejudices. It is very difficult to interpret culture of "others" because they are alien. Nevertheless, there is no harm in using Eurocentric methodology. But it should be modified which should fit in with the indigenous culture of the land.

Since sixth century Christian era, influence of foreign languages (Arabic, Persian, English, etc.) cannot be denied. In addition to it, we have been aping the Westerners for the last three hundred years. The prevailing knowledge of the English knowing Indian elite is of the post-colonized impact. It is unfortunate that we have not come out of their domination though they have trivialized our culture, religion, and philosophy. They claim that they are experts to interpret Indian culture. We could not dispense with English language. It is said that language is the "house of culture". All ideas and concepts are preserved in the sacred repertoires. The Westerners have studied them from their limited perspectives. Max Muller, Monier-Monier Williams, Ernest Trumpp, B. Walker, H.H. Wilson and many others have presented lopsided and distorted picture of Indian thought and culture.

Precondition of interpreting others' culture is the sound grasp of Indian culture with critical and creative mind. One is to put aside one's prejudices and appreciate other's perspective. They are to abide by the objective rules of hermeneutics and logic. Lavish repeated quoting from the texts does not reveal creativity. Innovation of new ideas is the outcome of creative mind. The lenses of Eurocentric methodology have shadowed the interpretation of Indian culture. My endeavour is to interpret the Indian culture from the standpoint of Indian cultural milieu.

In earlier studies of Indian culture, emphasis was on historical and philological approaches/methods. Now there is a shift on the coeval Philosophical hermeneutics of social sciences and culture. In the modern times, emphasis is on interdisciplinary symbiotic method of studying culture, religion and other social disciplines. It includes historical, sociological, psychological, philological and exegetical tools and techniques. Nevertheless, history provides improvised data of persons, dates and places, but these are interpreted for working out philosophy of culture. Similarly, philological method takes us to the roots and semantics of the words. Many words traveled from Greece after Alexander's incursion in 320 B.C.E. When the Arabs and the Persians came to India, after the seventh and the eighth centuries, many words travelled from Arabia and Persia. They changed their phones and meanings to adjust to the new cultural milieu of India. Their core meanings were wrapped in new languages. These will provide raw materials on which the world picture of our culture can be built.

It is hoped that our scholars will develop distinct tools for presenting Indian culture. They are to abide by objective rules of language. Lavish quoting from the texts does not show creativity.

It requires creative and critical mind. I hope this study will stimulate the minds of the elite of India and abroad. If this shift sets in new trend of critical and analytical understanding of Indian culture and values it shall be at par with the Western cultural and civilizational advances. It will strengthen our faith, which anchors on sandy ground of irrational beliefs and traditions.

It may be pointed out here that the Indians did not have a sense of historical time. When the Arabs and the Turks came to India, the Indians developed sense of time. In Sikhism, Guru Nanak, the founder of Sikh faith showed practical sense of time, which other Gurus continued. Guru Gobind Singh's creation of the *Khalsa Panth* is the outcome of it.

It is difficult to tease out veridical information from scatted manuscripts that can be treated as benchmark for articulating the Indian culture. We are standing on a volatile point. If the materials available are philosophically interpreted, our perspective of Indian culture will be changed.

The material is scattered in different manuscripts, books, journals and traditions. The material on the ancient and the medieval periods pertaining to social, religious, political, and other areas is not available in compact form. It is because no critical and systematic research has been done. The materials are available in scanty form. Most of the works in the Muslim period available are written from the Qur'anic and the Semitic (Islamic) standpoints. The Indian researchers are seemingly oblivious of the Semitic philosophical framework of the Semitic scriptures and the traditions.

No systematic relevant material is available on philosophical perspective. The works of Muslim scholars have Islamic bias and the Indian scholars suffer from their religious myopia. Their works are lopsided because they lack holistic perspective of the medieval era. If an Indian scholar writes, his perspective shall be either Vedantic or Buddhistic because both were dominating religious traditions of India. The Sikh scholar may be swayed in either the Vedic or the non-Vedic stream. If you want to present a holistic medieval world-view, a balanced and rational viewpoint will be an objective perspective. A comprehensive picture shall emerge if the Indic and the Semitic perspectives are taken together. From this point of view, the original works on the medieval religions, history, culture and philosophy are being perused for articulating coherent Indian culture and values. .

This chapter is dyed in the vision of secrets of dynamic view of life and the heroic Indian culture. It will inspire the readers for brooding and culling subtle meanings of the 'cipher' of Indian culture and the values that are life breath of our philosophical heritage scattered over the ages in the sacred literature and the religious and folk traditions. Indian culture inspires man for evincing strong will-power to come out of the muzzling conditions that were prevalent in the medieval India. One who has inherent "strong desire" can go beyond to reach out his original source for regaining freedom and bliss.

The earlier researchers have not emphasized this aspect. The Sikh movement is the revival of "cultural identity", which culminated in the creation of the *khalsa*. The *Khalsa* ideology is representative of the militant social structure that reaffirms the heroic culture of India. Hence, one of the most significant contributions of the Gurus was to develop heroic culture of India. This is the philosophy of voluntarism, which the *Gita* propounded. The Gurus carried it forward. In the modern time, Mahatma Gandhi was the advocate of it.

Culture spirals round human life. Its nature and purpose is to mirror inner human life. Culture is a living and dynamic phenomenon that accompanies man from womb to tomb. It is not a sheer concept, but a lived experience of inmost forms that are potential and actualized. The former are hidden forms, which come to the surface. The creative celebrities cull the hidden culture-forms. The world cultures oscillate between the two aspects. Progress of human history is from potential to actualization of culture-forms through chequered historical epochs. Thus, culture is its inner possibilities. Man hopes that one day he shall be successful in knowing the "Beyond". It is continuous progression from chaos to unity, and from ignorance to knowledge. We are trying to transcend our *finitude* for becoming one with the Numinous. It is existential approach to culture. The temporal and the eternal are clubbed together in theory and practice.

Culture is a system of the pattern and modes of aspirations and expressions of values, institutionalization of life in society. It is an attitude and mode of dealing with objective reality and subjective personality. Three points are noteworthy in understanding perspectives on culture. First, culture is human creation. Second, it provides 'objective reality' and 'subjective interpretation' while churning the ideals, values, ideology, and so forth. Third, it represents interpersonal relationships for harmony and justice. It endeavours for adjustment that emanates from spontaneity and freedom of action. One can formulate new value system for bettering the existent social order. Here revival of Indian culture means restoration of freedom and self-dignity of man. This determines cultural identity of India.

If we go deep into the meaning of the term "culture," we will find that it is concerned with mind or consciousness. Culture is a principle of interlacing society into a unity. It brings connectivity between hearts and minds of the people in multi-cultured composite society of India. It is not primarily concerned with external progression of civilization. It is concerned with progression of the inner self (*atman*).

Now the philosophical questions arise: is culture divine creation? What is the spirit of the culture? What is the concept of spirituality? Is Indian culture spiritual or non-spiritual? What is uniqueness of spiritual Indian Culture? What is the distinct cultural identity of India? Can it be motivated and learned? It means that '*atman*' (consciousness) is representative of Indian "culture". If we go into etymologies of the term "culture" in Latin ("*cultura*") and German ("*kultur*"), (Arabic—*tahjib*), we find that both emphasize on cultivation of mind. Culture in Sanskrit language is '*sanskriti*', which means cultivation of mind. It is said that "*atma ce sanskrite*" (consciousness is culture). The term '*atma*' stands for consciousness. Consciousness guides all human activities. At the initial stage, beastly desires dominate the sensuous self. These are refined by spiritual discipline

Culture (*sanskriti*) is cultivation of mind for fashioning its beastly, barbarian and uncivilized nature. It can be extended to society. Therefore, culture is a way of life of the people including their attitude towards other people and the world. Attitude implies values, beliefs, arts, aesthetic sense of sensibility, vision of social ideals, or values, etc. Cultural patterns of life are acquired in the society. These are mirrored through values, beliefs, and religious ways of living.

Suppression of culture does not mean annihilation of values, but the disappearance of certain means of expressing values. Expressions may change but the values once created become lasting. Once they are created in time, they transcend time. No culture dies. Thus, values are eternal and are for the ages to come. In this sense culture, which deals with network of values, is eternal and its spirit in the form of ideas and ideals hovers over heads of the people.

Culture is like an epic, which represents spirit of human life in a particular country. No one will be there to observe the progress of a "culture as an epic". Epic is a written prophecy. One can foresee one's death (ideology) in the future as an inevitable phenomenon, but no one is definite about its exact form. Thus, culture is to live in the blending of past, present and future into the 'eternal present'.

Man creates culture. It is not a divine creation. It is always in flux or 'becoming'. Spengler and Goethe are of the view that every culture passes through the epochs of history of the individual man. Ancient Vedic and the medieval periods are the blossoming phases of the Indian culture. Old cultures become a heap of rubbles and finally a heap of ashes, but spirit hovers over the ashes. History of cultures of the world reveals that cultures recycle in the progressive process of history. New cultures are rebuilt on the debris of old cultures.

The concept of progress may be linear or cyclic. It is primarily based on the cyclic view of time and the concept of time is a "universal flux". Disappearance of a culture does not imply annihilation of values, but temporary cessation of expression of means of expressing the values. The values are eternal but their expressions go on changing. The world cultural history oscillates between progress and retrogression, but it continues forever. It is a lived existential experience, which needs cultivation of mind. It is evinced spiritual discipline. Reason and insight both put together can discern continuity between eternity and temporality. It is only the mystic or the genius that lives in the 'eternal present' and discerns its continuity. The genius brings out spirit of culture-forms in new forms and puts them to use in history. This is how the human history retrogresses and progresses in different epochs. This is not a straight and linear prophetic path, but a zigzagged circuitous journey of the global cultures.

4. Heroic Nature of Indian Culture

Heracleitus (d. *c.* 480 BCE) avers, "War [conflict] is the father of all things". This strife is the stuff of dynamic life. If life is an eternal conflict of head and heart, then the central problem of human life is to wriggle out of the tension of suffering and pleasure. Then the self will be attuned to the eternal bliss of the spiritual self (soul/*atma*). Perhaps, the Buddha was the first thinker who made earnest endeavour in this direction. He tried to overcome the phantom of death and the perennial strings of sufferings. He started his quest to find out permanent solution of the tragic sense of life, but ended his journey in *nirvana* that goes beyond the empirical world. It should recycle after climbing to the apex of self-transcendence. The realized person should be always active in society for eradication of suffering humanity. The Bhaktas and the Gurus created this heroic dimension of Indian culture.

In the transitional period from ancient to medieval epochs emphasis has been laid on cognition and will (*samkalpa*) was relegated to the subordinate position. Fortified will power paralyzes fear of death. Courage muzzles fear of death. Acquiring of courage and transcending the fear of death is the strenuous inward pilgrimage to the 'Beyond'. The purposeful self-transcending process, continuously expanding vision, spirally ascends to Eternity. It paves way of new culture. Persistence and strong will lead to emancipation and autonomy of the self for discharging *nishkama karma* (categorical imperative). This chapter lays emphasis on heroic aspect of culture, which has roots in the tribal primitive traditions of the land. Heroic values are the necessary outcome of the heroic culture. It anchors on dynamic view of life, which advocates continuous striving for perfecting man in the world and discharging his worldly responsibilities.

An endeavour will be made to portray development of our culture through the vicissitudes of ancient and medieval epochs. In the medieval ages, Indian culture digressed to life-and-world-negation, dismal and pessimistic view of life. The medieval Bhaktas reaffirmed the status of the world and restored the historical action (*karma*). During medieval period, the Bhaktas and the Gurus developed historical sense of time. It added new dimension to the Indian culture. It rejuvenated voluntarism in Indian tradition. The heroic culture revisited with greater vigour and revolt. The Bhaktas bitterly castigated the existent social order that marginalized the subaltern folk. They steeled will of the subaltern marginalized populace so that they could confront boldly tyranny and rebel against inhuman atrocities. It was a movement of voluntarist culture. There was a powerful resurgence in cultural revival in India. The medieval Bhaktas emerged as a powerful counterforce. Thus, odysseys of the central theme will represent microscopic philosophical analysis of the concept of the Indian culture along with multidimensional aspects of social affirmation and restoration of historicity of human action that led to healthy ideology.

"To do, think and aspire is to be". The sage embraces the primordial one and becomes model for others. The Buddha rightly said "*atma dipo bhava*". It means that thousand candles can be lit from a single candle. This is the altruistic ideal of the world's living religions and cultures.

Our ancient sages refined the barbaric culture. The purpose of human life is to control the body for the sake of higher values which man creates for living a life of bliss (*anand*). When man controls his bodily person and lives life of human values, he is living real human life. Thus, the Sikh movement emphasizes on active resistance to evil and struggle in life. It fortified will of the Indians. It leads to heroic life in the world. The Gurus steeled will of the humiliated masses. They prepared martial heroes who were ever ready to stake their lives for the supreme sacrifice for the sake of higher values. They developed steadfast faith in the *Akalpurakh*.

REFERENCE

1. *cf.* Paulo Freire, *Cultural Action for Freedom,* Australia, Penguin Books, 1974, p. 9.

Chapter – 24

Rajneesh and his Eco-Concerns: First Attempt at constructing his Environmental Philosophy

Shiva Nath Prasad

The present day thinkers, philosophers, scientists are too much obsessed with tasks of ecology, environment and eco-concerns. Everyday, many things are said and written on ecology and we have today in existence ecological ethics, eco-chemistry, eco-bio-chemistry, eco-feminism, eco-economics and so many things. In philosophy, there is now a special branch called "Applied Ethics", which covers all such topics as bio-chemistry, bio-technology, bio-informatics, eco-economics, bio-ethics, environmental ethics, and so many allied topics. Though the word "applied ethics", which covers all the above topics has been newly-coined, it is not a fact that environmental concerns were alien to man's mental concerns in the past. Nature is something which is a perennial subject of concern and no one can remain away from it. Every living thing lives in the midst of nature, finds life and sustenance from nature, and dies in the lap of nature alone. How can any one remain cut off from his own life's concerns, his own existence, his own being. A human being is a "being" and in 'being' lies his pure 'existence', and in this fact of his being, he is separated from thing. Human being is a subject, a pure Becoming, all the existentialists speak. Nietzsche's hypothesis of "consciousness of consciousness" is the one metaphysical notion behind every aspect of his philosophizing: Becoming (does warden) Being or existence, which is also a pure Becoming does not allow us for a second to be 'objective', to get outside our experience and to arrive at things and events and Nietzsche says (in his Posthumous works) "The object is only a kind of effect from a subject upon a subject. . . . a mode of the subject." We find a deep hermeneutic utterance of Nietzsche in the expression "There are no facts, only interpretations", as against positivist's standpoint, that "there are only facts". Rajneesh's writings are fond of existentialist leanings, as also his writings are full of hermeneutic readings in which fields, no research has yet been made. I wish to write on such of Rajneesh's contentions, but from the vast store of his discourses, lectures, which have been compiled in book form, it is very difficult to find anything easily and such attempt would be something like searching an ant in the city, but if proper attention is given, one can find enough scope of writing substantially. Rajneesh's writings are very enormous, he has said so much, that it may be said safely that he has spoken on all subjects under the sun; and environment philosophy is one among them. He has given his own interpretation, his own method which is quite inimitable and singular.

Like a true existentialist, he abhors anything abstract. Like the existentialist, he says that the word 'humanity' is an abstract word and it has no meaning. One cannot catch hold of anything called "humanity", it is an abstract term and what is abstract cannot satisfy "being", or existence. Like the word "humanity", there is the abstract word "friendship", this is also not meaningful in the eye of Rajneesh, because, 'friendship' is far detached from human concerns, as being a term cut off from human existence. Instead of the word "friendship", he prefers the word "friendliness" for nature, or for environment. When Rajneesh speaks of environmentalism or environment or his environmental concerns, he refers or prefers to an attitude of "friendliness" with nature or environment. For him, nature or environment is a "friend, philosopher and guide", forming a trinity, unlike the trinity of *Brahma*, *Visnu* and *Mahesh* or the trinity of Christianity, God, the father; God, the Holy Ghost; and God, the begotten son". Rajneesh has not only bitterly criticized the Hindu trinity or the Christian trinity, he like the true existentialist, Kierkegaard, condemns the idea of Christianity, which again is an abstract term, like the terms 'humanity' or 'friendship', he prefers to becoming a Christian rather than adopt Christianity. Christianity or Hinduism is a cult, and he has distinguished the word "cult" from the word 'religion'. It is this cultism what has robbed religion of its heart, alienated religion from being human individual, individual with his own distinct individuality, but leaves him only as a 'personality' and personality is something glued upon man, it is something imposed, while 'individuality' is one which is acquired by man out of his own efforts, it is his own innermost love, his life, his own existence, original being, his own acquisition, which can neither be robbed, separated or detached from his own being. True religion requires one to be individual and not 'personality'. All the religions reformers have been stamping impression on the innocent child and he becomes so much obsessed that fails to be in true sense 'individuality'. He is forced to imitate in the name of conscience and according to Rajneesh "conscience is coffin of consciousness", "imitation is cremation" of being, "faith is the suicide of intelligence". The words like Belief, Faith, or Trust are misnomer.

With the growing hold of science, an attitude of "dominionship" has come into existence so far nature, ecology or environment, and this "dominionship" has made people to adopt an inimical, lifeless approach towards nature. The history of science is history of man's attempt to overthrow nature, to tame nature, to tear off the veil of nature. But such attitude has created indifference, dissympathy, disharmony, while the fact is that it is impossible to live and find sustenance for life without nature, ecology and environment, since can anyone live without water, air, fire, and if one is a slave to nature, to ecology and environment, why keep such an attitude of antagonism, distrust? If there is distrust from one side, it is quite possible that the other also starts distrust, starts to react, or retaliate, so the best way is to have the relationship of "friendliness" with nature, adopt or keep or maintain a relation of harmony, an attitude of "give and take", rather than slap and dash, discard and distrust, mistrust or ill-trust or ill-treat.

Out of the huge literature of Rajneesh available on all subject under the sun," I wish to refer to one autobiographical instance from Rajneesh which speaks for his deep instinctual love for nature and natural surroundings. Rajneesh himself refers to this instance out of his most outstanding frankness. He states that after graduation he was admitted to Benaras Hindu University to work under one of the most outstanding scholar Sri Raj Bali Pandey. Benaras Hindu University is seat of Hindu learning of the ages and the university has been made in the manner of Oxford or Cambridge University. When Prof Raj Bali Pandey came to know about Rajneesh joining the university to work under him, he was immensely pleased and assured him to give all possible help to him. Raj Bali was then Head of Department of History. Only some small and petty discussions with Prof. Pandey and Rajneesh too much distracted from him (Prof. Pandey) and he was quite disillusioned.

Rajneesh told Dr. Pandey that he has no grudge against the university itself, but he will not be living here because of him (Dr. Pandey) and he left the university in twenty four hours. Dr. Pandey tried his best to persuade but he (Rajneesh) did not care. He said that in Jabalpur there are more trees, more natural surroundings and Saugar is far more beautiful than either Benaras or Jabalpur. In Saugar the trees are very dense, there is a big lake, the plan is very beautiful, so he later shifted to Saugar University. The main cause of Rajneesh's disagreement with Dr. Raj Bali Pandely was due to Dr. Pandey's views on nature, trees, fresh air etc. which all combined, is termed "environment". In course of discussion between Dr. Pandey, and Rajneesh, Dr. Pandey had once said that "I hate the trees because trees are enemies of man. If just for five years if you stop cutting them, they will run out of the whole city and destroy all houses". This version was the main point of difference between the two, while Dr. Pandey was hating trees and their out-growth, Rajneesh had a typical affinity and love for the big trees as well as the natural surroundings, the beautiful scenery, sweet morning and evening, because, the sunrise and sunset colouring of the horizon in gorgeous costumes and colours and that myriad ways of nature's expressions, the environment overwhelmed him with unknown joys. Rajneesh told in return that you (Dr. Pandey) you are so much offended by the trees and I love the trees, the big trees, the shady ancient trees. Even if it is a fact that sometimes trees have to be cut for constructing houses and cities, but this does not mean that all the trees should be destroyed to construct houses and destroy the whole greenery. He said, Benaras is "barren, no trees at all, the whole university is just buildings and buildings, beautiful hostels, but no trees at all". "In Benaras without trees", "I am feeling dry", without greenery your eyes will lose lustre, so I cannot live in Benaras, though it is undeniably true that there are good professors, good library, it has all good facilities, hostels, etc., but "I prefer some huge, big ancient trees and he wandered all over India to find a university which has better environment of greenery and he found Saugar far better than Jabalpur, is un imaginably a beautiful small city, the city is on the one side of lake; on the other side, there is a range of hills; and on the hills is the university — all around, huge trees. Benaras is crowded and so buzzing with ten thousand students in the university, Saugar is a small place and he remained there. Rajneesh has poured his heart expressing his genuine sentiments of love for the environment and he blatantly says that "man has completely destroyed the environment." And this is his historic comment of his deep eco-philosophy.

It is an speciality of Rajneesh, that whatever he speaks, that springs forth from the farthest depth of the soil of his heart and in his views and visions, there is irresitible frankness, outstanding clarity, irreconcilable accuracy and unfathomable sincerity and glaring transparency of a mirror. He has said on one occasion that the deeper the roots of the trees, the higher are their twigs and branches, to support the load of the trees, the root has to go deep down. So, we have to take his thoughts deeply. When he says that "Man has destroyed the environment", he has ample grounds to support his contention and his grounds and facts supporting his views and more scientific, more dispassionate but also mingled with his deep emotion and love for the environment. He speaks on environment more like a scientist-turned environmentalist, a bio-chemist turned environmentalist, a geologist, an ethicist, a social activist, he speaks of eco-wisdom as an eco-scientist. He adduces his arguments which touches the heart and soul both simultaneously.

He says, that man is behaving with nature and environment, as if, nature is a big enemy of man. But can human being live even for a single moment without the bountiful pourings of nature in the form of oxygen, to take nature in a more pragmatic, more scientific ways. Who can deny that the trees take nitrogen and leave oxygen, and oxygen is the food, far more an ēlan vital for all lives to exist and continue to live in the universe? If all the trees of the world die out, the living beings would also die of suffocation, and no store of oxygen, no amount of oxygen howsoever big, produced by thousand and lakhs of oxygen companies can cope with the requirement of oxygen needed by the living beings, as such the perils of nature is really a death-knell for the entire human race? So should nature be destroyed to conquer nature, to plunder nature, to rob nature? That enterprise would be quite foolish one. Rajneesh says that we should at once stop the attitude of destroying or subduing nature and adopt instead an attitude of balance, an attitude of give-and-take, in the spirit of trusteeship, rather than attitude of dominionship. Nature works on the principle of 'balance', giving oxygen for living beings and nitrogen for the trees "when you breathe in, you take oxygen; the oxygen is absorbed by your blood system and carbon dioxide is thrown out". Nature works on the principle of good "friendship" says Rajneesh, "they (trees, plants, etc.) live on carbon dioxide and you live on oxygen. Neither they have to destroy the civilization, nor do you have to destroy them, you should live in co-existence; that is the only way to live"— Rajneesh, says "what a friendship"! Nature works in harmony, in which not a single aspect of nature is totally divorced from the other, they work in unity, harmony, while all the limbs are important for the body, but no one limb is useful but all combined works and forms the unity called the body. Can eyes in isolation work, ears cannot work, nose cannot work, lips or tongue cannot work, unless all these are made a part of the body? The whole body cannot stand without the spinal chord, though only spinal chord or a particular limb cannot function as a body. The importance of limbs or bone lies in the constitution of the whole body, otherwise the limbs in isolation are useless. Similarly, there is unity in nature. The words used for the whole of the world are uni-verse, not "pluri-verse" not "multi-verse" to use the expression of William James' coinage or cosmos. The words universe, cosmos entail unity in diversity, i.e., though there are objects of the world of nature, but all the things of the world taken in combined and composite form is called uni-verse, cosmos. Universe and cosmos speak for unity, without unity the world cannot exist. In the religious literature of India, there is a dictum "*yatha pindey tatha brahmande*", that means that what is in human body, or what is in the principle of the body, the same principle is applied to *Brahmanda* or cosmos or universe. While human being is a miniature world, the *Brahmanda* is the biggest, the biggest world, a cosmos. So multiple things of the world cannot be alienated from the unity that combines to make a world. And all have to work in unity, to serve the best interests of the other, nature serving the best interest of human beings, and the human being serving in the interests of the nature, environment. This principle of "give-and-take" or as Rajneesh says, "friendliness" should guide man in his behaviour with nature. The most important fact to be marked here is that Rajneesh sees the world with "friendliness" attitude with environment, not the word "friendship", since the word "friendliness" is more near, heart-to-heart, more human approach, more concrete and subjectivity attitude than 'friendship' which means cold, distant, abstract relationship. Rajneesh speaks to adopt human approach towards nature rather than to adopt a cold, unsympathetic, inhumane approach, taking nature as brand enemy of man. The fact that nature or environment does not discriminate between one or the other, or nature does not favour one or the other is also a great truism. When sweet scented breeze containing the fragrance of flowers blows, it touches the trees, plants, living beings, and gives equally to all; we find the impartiality of nature and environment which ought to be kept always in mind. The whole world today speak for justice and nothing is more impartial judge than nature and environment. Rajneesh believes in the impartial way of environment, which entails not good to one or bad to the other, it does not work on "unequal justice" or partisan attitude.

I have referred to the take-and-give way of nature, so far oxygen and nitrogen. Man thinks himself to be wise enough, potent enough to manufacture such items of destruction as atom bomb, hydrogen bomb which can destroy the world within the winking of an eye, that has anyone of the scientist thought even once, even for a fraction of a such moment, that if nature at once stops its oxygen and nitrogen over for a few moments, all the atom bombs would be kept in stock, all living things would die a complete death. Has the scientist made any such item which can suffice to cope with the requirement of the entire world of things with requisite oxygen and nitrogen? Really, according to Rajneesh, man is more a pigmy before nature/environment, a 'minikin' a word from Jonathan Swift who wrote his famous book *Gulliver's Travels* which is called a tale for 'six and sixties", that it is useful for six year's innocent child it is a nursery tale; and for a man of sixty years, who has grown by age it is an experience, an exploration.

Rajneesh asks, man has made atom bombs, hydrogen bombs and other items of mass destruction, but can they really destroy a particular stone or rock? No, not at all. The scientific developments have shown that things change in forms, but cannot be destroyed at all. The principle of Conservation of Energy is the watchword of the scientist. Forms change but are not destroyed. Even the smallest particles called atom, on splitting and splitting and further splitting turns into electrical energy, but not really destroyed. So nature and environment are invincible, undestroyable, and even the thought of altogether destroying anything in nature is a boastful claim of human mind.

It has been said and repeatedly said that man is the crown of God's creation, that God created man in his own image, so man is no less powerful than God, in some respects, at least. Man is also boastful of his knowledge and power, but Rajneesh says that it is man's vain boast that he is most learned and most powerful creature in the world. Man is, he says, most ignorant and powerless creature, even compared to animals. Man's knowledge, Rajneesh says is limited, and "even small things make you aware of your ignorance". For example, he says, can you fight successfully with animals, the animals are mean creations of God compared to man? Can you fight with lions, tigers? You cannot, you can kill a tiger or lion in ambush, but no one can have a duel fight with a lion or tiger. They will tear human being in a moment. No one can think of fighting. Can you fight a dog? You cannot. Can you fight with flies? You cannot. If flies attack man, he cannot do anything. Elephant is a big animal, but if an ant goes into its trunk, the big elephant irrespective of its size and strength suffocates. What is it? Can anyone reply? Rajneesh States that there are plants in South Africa which drags birds and animals or man towards the trunk and without using any of the syringe or any sucking instrument, sucks the entire blood of the creatures and leaves the body to fall down dead. Rajneesh says, what a surgery, "Very perfect surgery", while even in small scratches in human body, blood starts coming out but here the trees suck the entire blood and not a drop of blood drops out and the entire blood is squeezed and man or animals or anything falls dead. What a beautiful surgery of nature? Has any scientist found out such method of surgery without a drop of blood, without anaesthesia, without local injection, without pinprick? Nature's surgery, the trees of south Africa know such surgery without a syringe or anaesthesia. Are man really powerful? Not in the eyes of Sri Rajneesh. Further Rajneesh says that there are trees which can crush man, even elephants or any other animal, and if any man comes near such trees, near the trunk of the trees, the branches all bind together and crush them to death. Can human being, man, crush any elephant? Where is his strength?

Aristotle boasts of the superiority of man, not the animals, that man is rational, animals are not, while man has got a brain, a reasoning brain but the animals have not. But Rajneesh says that trees, plants, etc., also have brain though quite unlike the brain of human beings, whose brain lies in the head, though the brain of these are not like the human. Plants do not have a separate head like human beings but undeniably, says Rajneesh, they have brain. If they had no brain, how could trees fear, or become happy? Thousands of years before, twenty five centuries ago, Buddha and Mahabir said, "don't hurt the trees", people laughed at them, how can the trees be "hurt", are they any living thing like man to feel of being 'hurt'? Buddha and Mahabir knew the art of silence, the science of silence and silently sitting under the tree, they felt the language of the tree, their sentiments of being hurt or rejoiced, Buddha suddenly felt that the tree is not dead, that is thriving with life. "But these were their personal experiences. They could say it, but they could not prove it", and it was left to Sir Jagdish Chandra Bose, who devoted his whole life to finding scientifically whether Buddha and Mahabir were right or wrong. He was awarded Nobel Prize for proving that the trees are endowed with life. "More researches went into it. Just to live is not enough". Soon it was found that they have a different kind of brain system, *but they do have one,* brain not like human brain, *not* the "same brain", it is quite possible to have different kinds of brain says Rajneesh and asks "if there can be many kinds of bodies, why cannot be that there can be many kinds of brain? This is a stupid human idea that your brain is the only kind of brain, soon it was found that they have a certain kind of brain system, and things went on. Just a few years ago, it was found that trees not only have certain way of knowing which we call brain, they have a heart too. Certainly it does not beat like our human heart, they have their own kind of heart. Rajneesh points out that if it is given to the surgeons of the trees (their surgeons) like us, they will also examine our heart and say that human beings have no heart, no brain, because they will be looking for their type of brain, their type of heart".

Trees feel emotions, sentiments. For example, when the gardener approaches the tree for watering the trees, plants, the trees feel happy. Their happiness can be measured on the graph like the cardiogram. When the trees are cut, they feel hurt. When a song is sung or music is played, the trees feel happy. If a man passes by the trees with axe with an intention to cut the trees, i.e., to select and cut, certain sentiments arise in them of fear or anguish. If the tree is cut, the trees shake in fear and the other trees around start going berserk. They feel disturbed because their fellows, friends, neighbour's limbs were being cut. All such feelings and emotions can be seen in graph form, in the form of harmony; when they are rejoicing, the graphs show rhythmic, when in fear, anguish, the graph shows zig-zag marks, the marks of disharmony. All these instances shows that the trees, etc., are all a part of environment, they are also endowed with life, endowed feelings and emotions like the human beings. So why should man keep an enemy-attitude rather than be 'friendly' and keep a feeling of fellow being. So Rajneesh is not in favour of taking environment as enemy but friends. Friendliness lies in maintaining an attitude of reciprocity, a reciprocal giving and taking whenever needed. According to Rajneesh, "friendliness" means being open-hearted, being in "nakedness", coming in true colours, as he is, without any adorning, without superficialities, without coverings of artificialities, without any feeling of hiding, because only in hidings, friendliness goes. According to Francis Bacon and a host of other great writers, poets, a "friend in need is friend indeed", this requires reciprocity, helping in the hour of need, this means timely help. The same type of attitude should be kept with environment.

Karl Marx's famous dictum is "Proletariat of the world unite, you have nothing to lose but your chains and you have the whole world to gain", Rajneesh humorously asks only to change the word "trees" in place of 'Proletariat', and then what would remain as the dictum, "trees of the world unite, you have nothing to lose but your chains and you have the whole world". What does Rajneesh mean, if all the trees unite, the result would be that they will lose the hold of cruel mankind, who have always been trying to destroy the trees, the entire environment, not only when it is essential to outdo but when there is no need even for their destruction. If the trees/environment are rid of man, nature has nothing to lose but to attain freedom to grow, here in they will gain freedom to adopt their own patterns of life without any let or hindrance cruel from human beings.

Rajneesh goes on step further. He says, "my idea is not outlandish; sometimes they (trees) can go crazy, because all these things (plants/trees) are needed to go crazy. They have them; and man has done so much harm to them that it is time they should go crazy. And he goes on harming them. These must be a limit and it is not far away. . . ." If all the trees go crazy then what man can do? Man's all efforts to save his life, his existence would become impossible. Rajneesh says that it is good, if the trees go crazy and start harming man as they have been harmed, by way of reaction, retaliation, the poor man, the boastful man, the boast of his vanity would vanish in a single moment. When the scientists go crazy, the atom bombs are exploded to destroy an enemy country, the enemy country is destroyed, the scientist who are responsible for all these remain alive, but when the trees would go crazy, not only a cruel person who harms them are destroyed, the innocents also will be destroyed, the lovers of nature/environment would also be destroyed, the wise man, the scientist all will be destroyed without discrimination of country, creed or caste. Man has to think many times, what to adopt, being enemy to environment or be friendly to environment.

Birds are small things in the eyes of man. Rajneesh cites that there is certain kind of bird in Indonesia. Once these birds went crazy and these birds attacked only the eyes of several men and force out the eyes of men and by the time tried to rid from such birds, the several hundreds of people lost their eyes. Rajneesh also cites, that once it happened in Africa, that a certain birds started attacking man and by the time proper safeguard could be managed, several persons lost their lives. A certain kind of bird called vulture, they are very dangerous. If a man is left alone at a solitary place and a crowd of vulture see that man, within no time, they will snatch all the flesh of the man and eat them leaving only the skeleton of the man, only the bones would be left. Can a man fight with these vultures or African birds or the Indonesian birds as cited by Rajneesh above? Whither is this powerful man! Where is his cunningness or wisdom?

Today everyone, whether he is a scientist, a biologist, bio-chemist, a philosopher, a novelist or an ordinary man, he is worried about environment pollution and every man now thinks of saving the environment. One of the main pollutant and most recalcitrant pollutant, but very commonly used is the poly-bags. The poly-packs are used by everyman in course of purchasing any item of daily use, the vegetables, oils, cereals, flower, etc., etc., and they throw those poly-bags outside. With air, the poly-packs goes from one place to another, it chokes the drainage system creating foul air, it contaminates water sometimes, the cows or buffaloes, etc., chew these poly-packs floating outside containing remains of vegetables, left out food articles, etc. These poly-packs goes into the stomach of these animals and create stomach cancer in them and the animals die due to man's negligence, uselessly. So the Government has also banned their use but because it is very cheaper compared to the bottles, which the animals cannot chew and swallow, but the government's ban is not becoming effective. The peculiar quality of this poly-packs is that even if it is kept below the earth and remain covered for several years, they are not decomposed or destroyed. Rajneesh has spoken about the poly-packs in the context of the creations of God. He speaks about God in very satirical vein in the context of one of the most important pollutant, "the Poly-bags". Rajneesh's expressions are very hyperbolic.

In India, it is said that life is temporary, short-lived, it consists of as if of four days. Two days roll in, in desiring and the rest two days in waiting. Waiting for what? Waiting for an eternal world, eternal paradise, eternal happiness. So the religious people, the priests say that one should not care for the small life of the world but always try to get eternal heaven or paradise where there are eternal pleasures. It has also been said that in the heaven or paradise, there are *apsaras* who always remain young, never become old. To think of anything as eternally existing is quite unnatural, opines Rajneesh because everything of the world is guided by the law of nature. The law of nature is eternal 'becoming', nothing is static, only things like plastic or plastic things can be eternal, life cannot be unchanging or static. The world consists of things and 'beings', the things are guided by their own rules, while the 'being' is guided by natural rules of change and becoming. If the *apsaras* are said to be eternally existing, eternally young, they cannot be living *being* or being but only *'thing', plastic thing*. In this context he has used the word 'plastic'.

Rajneesh is an existentialist in true sense of the term. If one tries to find existential elements in him, he will find so much materials, since so much he has spoken on it that if they are collected in one place that will form a very big corpus, a very big book. In this direction, I have devoted a chapter in my book on Charvaka/Lokayata (which is in the process of printing) and further attempts are being made by me to write on Rajneesh's Existential Approaches. There is a glaring difference between existentialism of the existentialist thinkers like Sartre, Kierkegaard, Jaspers, Heideggar, etc. and Rajneesh. Existentialism as known to the above mentioned names are opposed to scientism, naturalism and rationalism as such, but Rajneesh is a genuine naturalist in the truest sense of the word. The word 'plastic' used by Rajneesh comes in the background of deep-rooted naturalism. Rajneesh says that there is nothing wrong in life being momentary, because what happens from moment to moment is more exciting, more ecstatic. Static life is dull and monotonous, hence like rotten water of pond, it is stinking, giving foul smell and nobody relishes to breathe foul air, nature itself does not like, since the water of the stream or river is always moving, giving fresh flow, fresh ripples, fresh waves. Hence, static life is like plastic flower which has no freshness, which have no life, which is not possessed of the qualities of 'being', but it is a thing. Rajneesh is not in favour of having plastic flowers or plastic ladies, the *apsaras* of the paradise. That is Tom foolery. Everything permanent is death. It is only the being or existence which is lively, it is only 'being' that is bubbling and vibrating with the pulsations of life. Anything plastic can not be that. Flowers of nature blossoms one moment, and dies a natural death. Death is not the end of all. Death is only a continuation of existence. It is like adding on one wave of the ocean and giving place to another wave for the second moment. It is this change, this law of change which is at the back of all natural laws. Existences flows from moment to moment, it is found in the here and now, it is not enough in the past, existence cannot think of the past, being cannot be caught in past or future tense, it is always in the present. The flower blossoms in the morning, it is full of beauty, fragrance and life, it can not live for ever and the beauty of the flower, or nature lies in this. So there can not be a permanent flower. Rajneesh favours existence and wants to follow existence, which is a continuity. A child comes in the womb, is born, grows to youth, becomes old, does he know how everyday he has been changing? Can he feel such thing daily, that he is growing. This is a natural process. All natural objects follows this rules. So Rajneesh comes to the conclusion that "If you like to remain permanent, but then you need a *plastic flower*, a real flower would not do. A real flower has to be momentary. To be real, it has to be momentary; only *plastic* things can be permanent. *Plastic* is a new discovery. It was not known to Buddha, Mahavir, Mohammed, Jesus, but I can say to you that paradise must be made of *plastic*. If there is a paradise, it cannot be anything but *plastic*, because *plastic* has the quality of not *dying, it is deathless*." Permanency is negative of existence, hence Rajneesh is not in favour of permanent life in heaven, permanent joy in heaven or *swarga* or paradise. Unless the entire heaven or paradise is a plastic show, then how it can be permanent, even that may not be so.

There is another way if interpreting in the disfavour of *plastic*, which is a newer discovery. It has been said that God created the world as temporary. God created man, in his own image, as crown of the whole creation. While God created everything of this world as temporary, except perhaps heaven wherein all things are permanent, but in fact, contrary to this, Rajneesh says that God is a man-made something, God is a great fiction created by priests, etc., to dupe the masses. Plastic has been created by man and these plastic things are undying and undecaying. Even if it remains under the earth for a long time, it does not decay. Very humorously and sarcastically Rajneesh says that God created everything, but he was not knowing what plastic is, he had no power to create such a thing as plastic which is undecaying. Is God really all-knowing, all-powerful, i.e, omniscient and omnipotent and was not knowing about a chemical which is undying, the chemical from which plastic things are made. Why did God not create any chemical in the earth which could decompose plastic things, the poly-packs which are troubling the mind of the environmentalists and scientists. Rajneesh says, "If God has made this world, he certainly is all-knowing. At least one thing he did not know that plastic was going to happen one day. He has not made anything in nature, any chemicals, which can dissolve plastic, so plastic goes on accumulating. Soon it will have accumulated so much that it will destroy the fertility of the earth, it will poison the waters. Nothing can destroy it, it will destroy everything." What a fun, God creates transitory things and man creates plastic which is quite permanent.

Further Rajneesh said, in this context, "Now scientists are worried— particularly the environmentalists are very worried— because plastic is so cheap that you go on disposing of it. Glass was not so cheap, you were saving the bottle or returing the bottles and getting your deposit back. Plastic is so cheap that everything made of plastic is disposable, use it once and dispose of it. (We have disposable syringe, which is once used and thrown away) But you do not know where it is going. It is getting collected in the ocean, in the river beds, in the lakes under the earth, and there is no way in nature to dissolve it because nature is not prepared, was not made to absorb plastic."

We know from the books of history, there was one *sat-yuga*, during which period, *tapa* or *tapas* was the main duty of man for his own spiritual upliftment. Then there was the *Treta-yuga, dwapar yuga* during which man has to do the rituals prescribed in the *Vedas*, and the present *yuga* is *kali-yuga* whereby it is said in the *dharma sastra* that reciting of god's name is the only most beneficial thing for man which can lead one to salvation. The way in which plastic use has developed, plastic cover-file, plastic chairs, plastic tables, plastic watches, plastic bucket, plastic bottles and so many innumerable things that an Indian *yugas* now will have to be sub-divided, and add 'Plastic-*yuga*' within *Kali-yuga*. One has to wait for an *avatar* of God, or a messenger of God, or the son of God to come on earth and remove the havocs created by the evil-doers, to kill the evil-doers and bring in a reign of righteousness, and to bring justice in the world. But who is going to be punished? If God was not knowing about *"Plastic"* who God created the world, either he would have to make a research, when He takes an *avatar*, and if it was not up to the power of God to create such thing as plastic thing, the poly-packs, how is it that it was created by God. If Rajneesh was alive he would have questioned God, if God happened to descend on earth, Rajneesh would have asked God, where you failed, your created thing man, has succeeded, do you not realise that man created you, not you created man. The "image theory of God", i.e., man created in the image of God is as fictitious as the fictitious idea of God Himself. We live in fiction and die in fiction. But who should be punished for the plastic. If according to Rajneesh God is pure fiction, the paradise or hell is also fictions, a big lie, the whole idea being implanted in the mind of man by the priests from the very beginning to vitiate man, to create a fear psychosis.

Rajneesh says that the so-called religions, Pseudo-religions are one of the main basis of environmental crimes, which in turn, after a long gap came to bring in its fore a new science called ecology. Rajneesh calls environmentalism or ecology a "new movement in Europe", which believes in the inter-relationship of organisms with their environment. According to ecologists, man is the cause of his own degradation, fall, his own sufferings, who has destroyed the things of nature. It is man's folly to think that the birds that sings in the remote jungles, in natural surroundings, are not part of man, if man causes the birds not to sing, by destroying forest, etc., then we will not remain in peace and our joys, ecstasy, which were coming from the sweet music of the birds would not come in our lives in future. Nature's songs are sources of our ear's thrill, the full being's joys, the throbbing of hearts. When the birds sing joyfully, we are full with joys, when the birds sing pensively, their pensive song consoles us, that birds are not only great fellow-sufferer or fellow sharer. Man is a small creature, who spends all his life in a corner of his own. He does not know the vast world. He cannot roam or fly like birds from one place to another, from one country to another, from one hill top to other remote hill tops, from one forest to another forest, thousands of miles away. He is quite unaware of the clouds that glide in the skies, he does not see the flowers blossoming in the trees, nor does he hear the song of birds in the spring. Once it happened in England that due to some fault of atomic energy research experiments, a catastrophe occurred which caused the death of a great member of singing birds of England forever and their sweet songs of that species have never been heard. The question is, if the singing birds, who sing in the remote corner of forest can affect the life of persons living away from forest? Definitely it makes a difference in the life of human beings. The bird, or for that matter any bird, any creature, any species is not separate from the other. "Everything is joined and inter-related. If a star becomes extinct, it affects the earth, even if it be millions of light years. If the moon is no more, there will be enormous changes on earth. There will be no longer waves in the oceans; the menstrual cycle of women would become erratic. It would not move in the cycle of 28 days, as it does now. Then everything will change. A slight difference— and everything changes", says Rajneesh. This means that all ecology/environment and the whole world of living beings, all form an organism and nothing can be totally segregated from the other and the whole of organism, will lead to ecological balance. Nothing of nature, nothing in nature is useless, they have their own utility, their ways of life, and each life acts and interacts with other lives and so an organic life of nature, the nature's cycle runs in its own way, without any hindrance to any other. This is the so-called ecological balance.

The moment this balance is blocked, impeded or stopped, nature reacts and consequent damage starts. Man should realise this, before it is too late. Already, there has been neglect on this account, let this be stopped once for all, all at once, in the interest of the greater part of humanity at large.

Rajneesh has tried to explain the fact that everything in nature is invincible, undestroyable, useful, essential by quoting a story of LaoTzu. One day LaoTzu asked his disciple to pluck a few leaves from a tree. The disciple mislead of taking a few leaves broke a full branch and was going to the Master. The Master saw this and stopped the disciple and said, "Don't you know, you fool that if any part of this tree is destroyed, you too become less to that extent? When this tree stood before us, full and green, we too in a manner, were also full and green. Today, its wound has caused a scar within us also. We are not apart, we are one". This is the wise words of LaoTzu who had a sympathy for ecology. In spite of this, even with full knowledge, we have cut off so many trees! We have destroyed forests after forest for our own selfish ends. We have cut trees in huge number, indiscriminately taking them to be our foes "Man was afraid of the wild life they harboured and so destroyed them and built townships. He did not realise that all the rains that poured on his land, all the breezes that blew and cooled the land cannot be without the jungles! If we cut down the jungles, our towns will no longer exist. Now all over Europe, there is a stir against cutting of trees. While LaoTzu said it 2,500 years before that the tree is very much a part of our existence, cut a single branch, we too are lessened somewhat, perhaps in the reciprocal dimension. It is like removing a part of painting from the main and the work will not remain the same. Work a single stroke of brush can change the whole picture. A slight digression changes the total form and hence, all the following connections. The trees that stood between hut and the space outside is hewn down. Now the sky and the hut stand bare and naked. We cut down the trees, unscrupulously in order to clear a good place for man's dwelling. We have also completely destroyed many species of animals".

LaoTzu says, "Let things be as they are". Accept them as companions. Do not segregate the opposite. That which seems hostile and unfriendly, let even that be where it is, for the patterns of nature is deep and profound and full of mystery. Everything is joined within you do not know what problems you create when you set apart a single thing in nature.

Now the science of ecology have began to realise and how difficult it is to tell in how many ways we are inter-connected. For example, if we cut down trees, indiscriminately out of our greed, then the life-elements that trees gather for us will no longer exist. The trees absorb the rays of the sun and make them fit to be absorbed by our bodies. The direct rays of the sun cannot be converted into a fit form of consumption for our bodies. The plants draw the elements from the soil and turn them into food for us. Little do we realise that if trees as plants had not been there to produce the vegetables we eat, they would be under the soil a mass of earth. It is the soil below that turns into the food that is capable of bag digested by our system.

All the twenty four hours of the day, we take oxygen and throw out carbon dioxide. The trees take in the carbon dioxide and take out oxygen. If the trees of the world are destroyed, how will we escape the poison of carbon dioxide, that we ourselves produce? Then the quantity of oxygen will grow less and less everyday. Ultimately, all life will come to a stop, for the trees that give us life giving oxygen are no more.

When LaoTzu lived, there was no knowledge of oxygen, LaoTzu was not knowing but was realising that all things are inter-connected, there is one integrated existence, if there is even a slightest change in the order of things, we have to feel an equal change within our own selves. The whole existence is one, integrated existence, not even death is separated from it, illness is not separated and LaoTzu says, "If there is the attitude of friendship, of companionship, between the various parts of existence, if there is the feeling of oneness with each other, instead of over-*powering each other*, a wonderful music is created in life. "This very music LaoTzu calls Tao, that very music is religion, that very music is rita. It is now becoming increasingly clear that as the understanding of ecology expands, our understanding of Lao Tzu will become more profound. The more we begin to understand the unity within diversity, the less we shall be in a hurry to change the order of things." LaoTzu was against any kind of change. He used to say "Accept life as it is. Accept the opposite also, for there is a secret to it. Embrace death, when it comes. It too has its secrets. Do not fight with life, yield to it. Fall at the feet of existence and surrender. Do not enter into any struggle with it".

Rajneesh says about the menace if oil thrown into the seas through the factory's waste-matter, or from ships. In sixty years, such waste would form a layer in the seas and then we will need no more fear, for more world wars to finish us, because the life-elements formed by the sea water with the help of the sun, will no longer be formed owing to the layer of oil.

Rajneesh says that we are now using detergent more than soaps. The soaps were not as harmful as the detergents. Soaps get absorbed in the soil within fifteen days, while detergents take 150 years to be reabsorbed in the elements. So it will remain in soil for 150 years and it will begin to turn into poison within the first 15 years. This means that it will stay in the soil for 135 years, as a poison. The scientist proclaim that at the rate these detergents are being used in the world today, whatever grows on the soil will become poisonous within 50 years. Then we will not be drinking water, but poison. Then the vegetables we eat will be poisonous. But this understanding we do not have now, we use detergents because soaps cost more. It seems right now, we are being thrifty but remember, whatever we do, is interrelated. The slightest modification causes a great deal of difference.

Rajneesh holds that the religion, and the *Bible* in particular, is responsible for all ills against ecology and environment. He quotes the book of *Genesis*, "Be fruitful and multiply, and replenish the earth and *subdue* it; and have *dominion* over the fish of the sea and over the forest of the air and over living things that move up on the earth."

Dominion theory

In the above version of *Genesis*, two words are worth emphasizing, and these two words are *subdue* and *dominion*. The intent of the word 'subdue', is to suppress, to subjugate, to overpower by superior force, to bring into mention subjection. The word '*dominion*' means, the power or right of governing and controlling, governing or controlling a territory of considerable size in which a single rulership holds sway, sovereignty, control, realm, domain, historically self-governing territory of the British commonwealth. The word subdue also means to *subjugate*, or *tame, tone down,* etc. These two words speak for themselves the intensity of the meaning. The two words mean "*forceful control*" instead *wilful control*. These words are indicative of bestiality like forceful animal's way of controlling anything. Further, the word of the *Genesis* "the fowl of the air", this indicates not the territory in terms of land, but the territory of the air. Thus the three words combined, mean subjugation of everything in landterritory, air territory. The word 'fowl' means birds. Thus according to *Genesis*, control of birds, beasts, etc., forcefully has been guaranteed and allowed. This has given to man a great sanction to control anything and everything, not only controlling things humanly, but also allowed to deal inhumanly too. And with sanction and power of the *Bible* has made man not only inhuman towards birds, beasts forests, etc., but to entire domain of nature also. Thus forceful control has been religiously allowed. *Genesis* speaks of having dominion over the fish of the sea, and over fowl of the air, over every living thing that moved upon the earth. "This is a man-oriented vision of existence", says Rajneesh and feels that "this sort of attitude is bound to create catastrophes in nature, it is bound to destroy the ecological balance, it is bound to give man the strange idea of the ego". And when the ego swells, one goes on doing wrong things right and left, he can ride rough-shod on anything and anyone. *Genesis presents* a man-centred view" a view coming from the authentic *Bible*, what the *Bible* says can be nothing but what is justified not in the eyes of an ordinary being, but the God Himself. What else can be the security of such an egoist one. The *Bible* says, "God created man in his own image and man believed it. Just look at your face in the mirror: is it God's face in the mirror? The truth, says Rajneesh feels that "Christianity has been befooling humanity. It is not that God made men in his own image. And all the scriptures of *all religions* have given man a strange licentiousness over nature, over animals and birds. That has culminated in destroying many species of animals and birds. It has destroyed millions of trees for no reason. "When India became independent it had thirty three million hectares of trees now it is only eleven million hectares."

Rajneesh feels that the main cause of our suffering is that one have been destroying trees continuously due to which balance which the law of existence has been disturbed. Due to felling of trees, oxygen required for men is diminishing. Trees are like our brothers and sisters, each need the other for life's successful growth. The quantity or ratio in which trees are destroyed, in the same ratio the oxygen content in the air is also diminishing. We are living only a fragmentary life. We do not breathe fully. In our lungs we have six thousand sacs which have to be filled, but we breathe shallowly, only two thousand sacs are filled, and four thousand sacs remain stagnant, filled with dead carbon dioxide which is the cause of millions of diseases. It reduces life-span, it weakens our body, it weakens our spirit, it destroys our intelligence. We are living at the minimum, just the *Genesis* says for keeping dominion over nature.

During the British Raj, lions which are rare species of India were killed indiscriminately in hunting and decorating their drawing rooms. The whole species is on verge of extinction. Due to this, the Government of India had to change its national animal from lion to tiger, because lions are disappearing and once lions die, they are not replaced. This is about the British, who had ruled India.

The Hindus, our own countrymen have not done less to destroy such rare and beautiful species. The Hindu monks sit on lion's skin, and lions have to be killed for the monks. What is the plea behind sitting on lions skin. It is thought by sitting on lion's skin, one can be celibate, but asks Rajneesh, how many monks are celibate, what is the scientific proof behind one maintaining celibacy. The lions do not remain celibate, how can the monks be celibates? Rajneesh says, "I don't find a single monk who is celibate and I have known thousands of monks, Hindus; Jainas. . . ." So Rajneesh concludes that "religions seems to give a certain stupidity to people who were born intelligent."

Rajneesh says that the religions have done much to destroy nature's balance, and sciences have done further more damage to nature and environment. Science is beneficial. Life is not only matter, it is also suffused with something tremendously transcendental. When the transcendental element is missed, then science becomes or turns into technology, becomes purely mechanical, and becomes a means to exploit nature, to manipulate nature. The very beginning of science has been the idea; how to conquer nature. And this is foolish idea, according to Rajneesh.

The beautiful thing of science and technology says Rajneesh is that it "creates problems just to solve them. And the problem can be solved when it has been created; then it becomes a challenge. Now the greatest challenge before technology is how to maintain the balance of nature, how to maintain ecological harmony. It was never before, it is a new problem".

Rajneesh says that, "science is an act of rape. It is an assault on nature — as if nature were some kind of an enemy, as if it has to be conquered, defeated". That is why, science believes in cutting things into pieces. Analysis, destruction, it believes in dissection. If a flower, beautiful flower is given to a scientist, he will take it to the laboratory, cut it, dissect it, press it, he may keep the elements contained in a bottle. In this process the flower is gone, but can the scientist who has squeezed the watery element of the flower which he has kept in the bottle, again make that beautiful flower with such sweet fragrance. In the process of dissection etc., not only the flower has gone, its body has gone, its soul has also been destroyed.

There is a craze of science and technology in the world today, which started as a wave from the west. Science and technology made men crazy. Man feels more powerful with science and technology. There is a truism that science has given many things, but they are at the cost of nature. It has destroyed nature's balance in its pride for all knowing and all powerful. But the power of man has not only made man powerful, it has also weakened man too much, such that he would not require to use atom bombs manufactured by the scientists, he would not require his bombs to be used in the Third World War. It may be impossible that even before the scientists, the egoists of the nations think of using the bomb, they would either commit suicide or they will die out of suffocation for want to oxygen or for over pollution of air, by nitrogen or by poisonous water or some other gas, Rajneesh would advise to stop all such atrocities on nature or nature will destroy you within seconds. Thus we find that Rajneesh is a great champion of natural life; he is a great supporter of "balance in nature", and stands for environment protection and is dead against any one who indulges in harming the natural ecological balance. He stands for saving the Earth and Environment so that man can live a long and peaceful life.

Index